KANT'S THEORY
OF SELF-CONSCIOUSNESS

Kant's Theory of Self-Consciousness

C. THOMAS POWELL

CLARENDON PRESS · OXFORD
1990

Oxford University Press, Walton Street, Oxford OX2 6DP
Oxford New York Toronto
Delhi Bombay Calcutta Madras Karachi
Petaling Jaya Singapore Hong Kong Tokyo
Nairobi Dar es Salaam Cape Town
Melbourne Auckland
and associated companies in
Berlin Ibadan

Oxford is a trade mark of Oxford University Press

Published in the United States
by Oxford University Press, New York

British Library Cataloguing in Publication Data
Powell, C. Thomas
Kant's theory of self-consciousness.
1. Man. Self-consciousness
I. Title
126
ISBN 0–19–824448–7

Library of Congress Cataloging in Publication Data
Powell, C. Thomas. 1954–
Kant's theory of self-consciousness / C. Thomas Powell.
Includes bibliographical references.
1. Kant, Immanuel, 1724–1804—Contributions in philosophy of self.
2. Self (Philosophy)   3. Kant, Immanuel, 1724–1804—Contributions in
philosophy of mind.   4. Philosophy of mind.   I. Title.
B2799.S37P685 1990   126'.092—dc20   90–30170
ISBN 0–19–824448–7

Typeset by Joshua Associates Limited, Oxford
Printed in Great Britain by
Biddles Ltd, Guildford and King's Lynn

For my father and mother

Preface

M O R E than is usual, perhaps, this book owes its existence to the help of a great many people. Realizing that anything said here in thanks will be completely inadequate, I will still try. In writing this book—which began as a dissertation written at the University of North Carolina and at Magdalen College, Oxford—I have had the benefit of advice and provocative conversation from a wealth of first-rate scholars and philosophers. Jay Rosenberg was a paragon of dissertation advisers, skilfully offering just exactly the right amount of supervision. But I owe Jay a good deal more than that: he has the remarkable gift of being able to make Kant *live*, of making the study of Kant an exciting and contemporary project. Put simply, without Jay this work would not have been written—at least not by me. I am delighted to be able to thank Ralph C. S. Walker and Sir Peter Strawson, whose supervision of my research while in Oxford was enriching, challenging, and invaluable; my work—and, for that matter, the study of Kant in its broadest sense—would have been poorer without their scholarship. I have also benefited from discussing Kant with Karl Ameriks, Catherine Elgin, David Falk, Sir Stuart Hampshire, Douglas Long, William Lycan, Jonathan Malino, Gerald Postema, Richard Smyth, Rick Varcoe, and others whose contributions are no less valued for their not being explicitly acknowledged here. Any infelicities in what follows are made all the more egregious by the wealth of philosophical scholarship of which I am the grateful beneficiary.

It is important that I also thank: Angela Blackburn, for her paradigmatic editorial encouragement; a reader at Oxford University Press, who was anonymous, insightful, and extraordinarily helpful; the Fellows, Tutors, and students of Magdalen College, for taking in their first Visiting Student in Philosophy, for making him welcome, and for welcoming him back; the Graduate School of the University of North Carolina, whose Off-Campus Dissertation Research Fellowship helped make it possible for me to undertake my research at Magdalen College, Oxford; Claire Miller, for her sage counsel; Sam Schuman and Anne Ponder, Deans of Guilford College, for their support and encouragement, and for providing so positive an environment for completing this project, which was finished with the help of a Guilford College Faculty Research Grant; and the typists, Lucy Powell and myself.

The last four sections of Chapter 3 first appeared in *Philosophy and Phenomenological Research* (1985) under the title 'Kant, Elanguescence, and Degrees of Reality', while Chapter 5 represents a reworking and development of my article 'Kant's Fourth Paralogism', which also appeared in *Philosophy and Phenomenological Research* (1988). In both instances, permission to include this material here is gratefully acknowledged.

Some debts cannot conceivably be repaid, and must only be acknowledged. Among these are my debt to my wife, Lucy Allen Powell, who stuck it out through, in her words, 'the beginning, middle, and end of this awful process'; my debt to Kit Wellman, who proof-read the manuscript, checked sources, insisted that I explain myself clearly, and whom I will always be proud to have been able to call my student; my debt to my parents, Charles and Eleanor Powell, for their support and encouragement; and my debt to Carolyn Gardulski Hartz, Brad Goodman, and Jonathan Malino, who have always reminded me, at critical moments, why I devote my time to such arcane and impractical matters: κοινά τά τῶν φιλῶν.

C.T.P.
1989

Überdem war ein großes Werk gekauft und, welches noch schlimmer ist, gelesen worden, und diese Mühe sollte nicht verloren sein. Daraus entstand nun die gegenwärtige Abhandlung, welche, wie man sich schmeichelt, den Leser nach der Beschaffenheit der Sache völlig befriedigen soll, indem er das Vornehmste nicht verstehen, das andere nicht glauben, das übrige aber belachen wird.

Kant, *Träume eines Geistersehers*, Preface

Contents

Introduction   1

1. The Self and the Transcendental Deduction   11

2. The Subjects of the First Paralogism   65

3. The Self as Simple: The Second Paralogism   91

4. Kant on Self-Identity: The Third Paralogism   130

5. Kant and the Mind–Body Problem: The Fourth
   Paralogism   174

6. Kant and the First Person   207

Notes   237

Bibliography   253

Index   259

Introduction

H o w are we to give a cogent account of the self? That is, what can be known about what Kant, in a tellingly cautious phrase, calls 'this I or he or it (the thing) which thinks'? It is certainly true that the self as experiencing subject[1] has presented a recurring problem for philosophers. Descartes's *cogito*, Hume's 'bundle' theory, Kant's Paralogisms, and, for that matter, contemporary theories of indexical self-reference all derive from consideration of questions about '(the thing) which thinks'. In order to draw out this problem properly, and to determine how *Kant* answers these questions, it will be useful to examine, albeit somewhat cursorily, some of the ways in which this problem has been addressed leading up to Kant's own investigation. It hardly needs saying that this will be a cursory sketch, rather than a detailed portrait: but even a sketch can capture revealing features of its subject.

It is a commonplace that Descartes discovered, in his attempt to determine the limits of absolute certainty by employing a thorough-going scepticism, that the one thing he could not doubt was his own existence as a thinking thing (*res cogitans*). Though everything that is encountered in the world may be the result of deception by a *genie malaign*, still, according to Descartes, 'whilst I thus wished to think all things false, it was absolutely essential that the "I" who thought this should be somewhat'.[2] Even if the deception of the senses is ubiquitous, and all experiential encounters false, there still must exist something which *is* deceived, which *has* these encounters. To transpose the point into a more contemporary mode, Descartes's insight is a reflection of the logical grammar of talk about experiences: deceptive or not, experiences are *had*, and if these experiences are had, they are had by something. For Descartes, this something (or 'somewhat') is the 'I', the subject which encounters the world. But the key is this: in so far as it merely encounters the world, the 'I' is not itself encounterable; the 'I' of the 'I think' *has* thoughts, it cannot itself be *had*. And if it cannot be encountered, it rather obviously cannot be encountered falsely. The source of Descartes's certainty, then, lies in the unencounterability of the self in experience. It is this unencounterability that is a necessary condition of the possibility of the *cogito*, preserving the self from the hyperbolic doubt which plagues all experience. Given the datum that the self is immune to the kind of doubts which may be appropriate to the contents of experience, then, Descartes purports to derive a number of *a priori* truths about the self, asserting its substantiality, simplicity, and unity.

Leibniz as well accepts the non-experiential awareness of the 'I' of the 'I think'. At times he seems to argue for this on strictly Cartesian grounds, as when he says that 'to say *I am thinking* is already to say *I am*'.[3] But rather than this being a matter of accepting a necessarily true proposition, as for Descartes, Leibniz argues that the existence of the 'I' is rather 'a proposition of fact, founded in an immediate experience'.[4] In other words, the 'I' is encounterable directly by the mind, and not through either sensation or reflection *a priori*. In a pointed bit of aphorism revision, Leibniz suggests that 'Nihil est in intellectu, quod non fuerit in sensu, excipe: nisi ipse intellectus',[5] roughly, 'Nothing is in the understanding that was not [first] in the senses, *except the understanding* (or the 'I') *itself.*' The 'I', then, is in a sense immediately accessible to itself. None the less, the nature of this existing self can be known only through what Leibniz calls 'Reflective Acts'. These reflections correspond to Descartes's *a priori* reasoning, and are the source of our knowledge that the self is simple, substantial, etc.[6] To this extent, Leibniz's view of the self is clearly Cartesian. But a new note is struck as well, for Leibniz also points out that 'It is not enough in order to understand what the me is that I am sensible of a subject which thinks, I must also conceive distinctly of all that which distinguishes me from other possible spirits and of this latter I have only a confused experience.'[7] In effect, Leibniz is recognizing that there are three kinds of self-knowledge: (1) immediate awareness of the pre-reflective 'I', (2) reflective knowledge of the simple and substantial subject of thoughts, and (3) knowledge of myself gathered from observing my experiential encounters. And the recognition of the last of these leads Leibniz to make an extraordinarily significant point. He says that when we consider the constitution of the mind, 'there is nothing besides perceptions and their changes to be found in the simple substance'.[8] Indeed, says Leibniz, though by reflection we can posit certain

Cartesian qualities of the mind (or monad), if over a given time minds have no distinct perceptions, then they are 'Monads which are wholly bare'.[9] Brevity (and, perhaps, diffidence) precludes a discussion of Leibniz's views of unconscious processes, and of how this fits into the question of 'wholly bare monads', but this kind of consideration of the 'bare' mind will be used with telling effect, as we shall see, by Hume. Leibniz, then, has injected a new element into discussion of the self, namely, the relation of the 'I' to the encounters of which it is the encountering subject.

Actually, however, this element is not wholly novel with Leibniz. Spinoza presents a similar point in his account of the nature of the mind. For Spinoza, the mind is not created substance but is rather a mode of God's cognition. Mind and body are for Spinoza two modes of one thing, the one viewed as thinking, the other as extended (not unlike Strawson's person to whom are attributed both M-predicates and P-predicates). The mind, says Spinoza, is actually the mental expression of the body's states, so that 'The object of the idea constituting the human mind is the body.'[10] Knowledge is in the first place a matter of the mental characterization of bodily modifications (= sense perceptions), yielding 'confused experiences'; only in terms of 'reflexive' knowledge (*ratio*) can 'adequate ideas' be formulated which capture formal essences that are clearly and distinctly conceived. Yet this reflection is not clearly *a priori* but involves the development of 'common notions' out of an awareness of bodily modifications. And in both cases knowledge of the 'I' arises out of awareness of the encounters of which the 'I' is subject: Spinoza says that 'The mind does not know itself, except in so far as it perceives the ideas of the modifications of the body.'[11] Thus does Spinoza anticipate the point made by Leibniz, that in a certain sense the 'I' is knowable only in so far as it has perceptions and thoughts—it is encounterable only through its encounters. Like that of Leibniz, Spinoza's account of the self is grounded in *a priori* reasoning; also like Leibniz, however, he recognizes that there is a vacuity in the concept of the self considered apart from its role as mere experiencing subject.

Thus the concept of the self has shifted from Descartes's purported *a priori* characterization to the views of Spinoza and Leibniz, who present an *a priori* account of the self but who also underscore the self's unencounterability in experience except as the bare experiencing subject. It is left, then, to Berkeley and Hume to draw out the consequences of this unencounterability, given the rejection of the rationalist, *a priori* account. Berkeley, in his *Principles of Human Knowledge*, says that since ideas are inherently passive they cannot represent (at least not adequately) the agent which has these ideas.[12] He says that

> there can be no *idea* formed of a soul or spirit . . . Such is the nature of Spirit, or that which acts, that it cannot be of itself perceived, but only by the effects which it produceth.[13]

Clearly echoing the insights of Leibniz and Spinoza, Berkeley denies any clear conception of the self apart from its experiences. He concludes, then, that 'we have some *notion* of soul, spirit, and the operations of the mind . . . (as a) simple, undivided . . . being',[14] but leaves open the question of the character of this notion. In any case, it is neither *a priori* nor an idea derived from experiential encounters, which raises the question of whether or not Berkeley can maintain it to be anything at all. And, in a sense, this question is asked by Hume: does Berkeley's 'notion' in fact have any ontological counterpart?

Against the Cartesian tradition, Hume argues that the self is not only not encounterable in the world, it is not encounterable by introspection either.[15] In effect, Hume accepts Berkeley's position that we can have no idea of the self, but he then pushes the position to its likely empiricist conclusion, and questions whether the self exists at all. He says that

> For my part, when I enter most intimately into what I call *myself*, I always stumble on some perception or other . . . I never catch *myself* at any time without a perception, and never can observe anything but the perception . . . were all my perceptions removed by death, and could I neither think, nor feel, nor see, nor love, nor hate . . . I should be entirely annihilated, nor do I conceive what is further requisite to make me a perfect non-entity.[16]

Hume, then, is taking up, and in a sense approving, Spinoza's point regarding the mind's knowing itself through its perceptions—but at the same time he rejects the claim that any sort of positive *a priori* truths about the self can be deduced. And in terms of empirically discovered truths, Hume argues that experience of the self yields nothing more than 'a bundle or collection of different perceptions, which succeed each other with an inconceivable rapidity'.[17] The purported 'unity' ascribed to the self by Descartes, in other words, is for Hume merely the 'virtual unity' of a sequence of impressions and ideas: the self, then, is a *construction* of ontologically more basic entities. It is not a continuant substance but merely a sequence of impressions; it is not simple but (at any given time) a complex bundle of impressions. So there is for Hume neither a synchronically nor a diachronically unitary self: thus it is not encounterable, because it does not, properly speaking, exist at all.

Attendant on all these positions is the recognition of a most curious fact: the 'I' of the 'I think' is, in Ryle's perspicuous expression, systematically elusive:

> the more the child [who asks 'Who am I?'] tries to put his finger on what 'I' stands for, the less does he succeed in doing so. He can catch only its coat-tails; it itself is always and obdurately a pace ahead of its coat-tails. Like the shadow of one's own head, it will not wait to be jumped on. And yet it is never very far ahead; indeed, sometimes it seems not to be ahead of the pursuer at all. It evades capture by lodging itself inside the very muscles of the pursuer. It is too near even to be within arm's reach.[18]

It is thereby the source of a curious tension, in that it is the *object* of no perception but at the same time—and speaking carelessly—it is the *subject* of all perceptions. Given that the self is never encountered but is in some sense always present at each experiential encounter, it is not entirely surprising that the attempt to give a cogent account of the self has generated the range of views which, demonstrably, it has. To speak slightly fatuously, the self can, in a way, be profitably compared to Christopher Robin's place on the stairs: it isn't really anywhere—it's somewhere else instead.[19] But where is it? To speak more philosophically, I am aware of myself as an entity which has my thoughts, but in what way am I so aware? And what is the 'I' of which I am so aware?

Now we can begin to see the milieu entered by Kant in the Paralogisms of Pure Reason, where he examines the nature of the self and the problem of apperceptive consciousness as inherited from the 'rational psychologists'. Kant's account begins—but certainly does not end—with the clear recognition, after Hume, of the unobservable character of the 'I', pointing out that the representation of the 'I' is not an intuition (B408). Given this recognition, Kant develops an account of the self which confronts not merely Descartes but Leibniz and Hume as well. And Kant is not merely engaging in local squabbles over minor points: as he realized, the elusiveness of the 'I' of the 'I think' has import not only for epistemology but for our view of persons, and thus for our moral philosophy as well. I will explore the consequences of Kant's view of the self in some detail. But for now, the significant point to be made is that the value of Kant's treatment of the self lies not only in the wealth of his philosophical insights about self-knowledge proper (of which the Paralogisms can claim not a few) but also in the awareness he had of the relevance of this problem for widely disparate areas of philosophy. One of the claims I propose to argue for here is that Kant at least implicitly recognizes the curious tension generated by the elusive character of the experiencing, or epistemic, self, and uses this recognition to adjudicate the claims of conflicting theories of the nature of the self. In doing so, he makes a number of substantive contributions to our own understanding of the character (and limits) of self-knowledge.

Again, Kant's primary goal in the Paralogisms is the dismantling of claims made by the 'rational psychologists' (Descartes and Leibniz are exemplars) about the nature of the self. Kant's motive in refuting these claims is clear: since the representation of the 'I' is not an intuition, and since the only source of experience according to Kant is intuitions 'thought through the understanding' (A19/B33), nothing can be known about the 'I' that is not analytic—and yet the rational psychologists purport to make substantive claims *a priori* about the self independent of experience. Given the Critical Philosophy as set out in the Transcendental Analytic, Kant obviously cannot countenance this sort of non-empirical knowledge claim, and so he attacks the rationalists' demonstrations as fallacious or 'paralogistic'. Using the key insight that nothing about how a thing is in itself follows from anything known about how it is represented, Kant sets out an array of diverse arguments intended to show that the rationalists' arguments are both fallacious and incapable—even if charitably interpreted—of serving the purposes for which they are intended. Though this effort is tactically negative, it can be shown that a positive theory of the self emerges in the Paralogisms as well, and I plan to show it: this positive theory is in fact presented in the Transcendental Deduction of the Categories, but a good deal of textual spadework will be required to see what this positive theory includes. Working on the methodological assumption that Kant's attacks on the rational psychologists' theory of the self can best be understood given an understanding of his own positive theory, I will begin with an extensive consideration of how, in the Transcendental Deduction, Kant develops his theory of the (necessary) representation of the epistemic self.

A brief overview of this positive theory may be helpful here, before I plunge full tilt into what P. F. Strawson rightly calls the 'jungle' that is the Transcendental Deduction. In the Deduction, Kant argues that the necessity of the representation of the 'I' as unitary can be demonstrated by showing that 'there must be a condition which precedes all experience, and which makes experience itself possible' (A107). Experience, says Kant, requires the capacity to 'synthetically bring into being a determinate combination of the given manifold' (B138), to unify representations and relate them in a determinate way to an object. But, Kant says, 'all unification of representations demands unity of consciousness in the synthesis of them' (B137). In other words, for my representations to be taken up into a synthesis which will yield intelligible experience, they must be brought together *as mine*: unless each of a succession of representations can be thought to belong to one and the same subject, there is no ground for their relation to one another at all. It is, then, one consequence of the Transcendental Deduction—specifically that part known as the Subjective Deduction—that the possibility of the synthesis of a manifold (in experience) requires that the manifold be synthesized as thoughts of a unitary subject. This point, as will be seen in the Paralogisms proper, is crucial for understanding the nature and logical function of the 'I' of the 'I think'. I will argue that the nature of the 'I' precisely *is* its logical function: that this is the source of what Kant calls the 'transcendental illusion' of rational psychology will be demonstrated in detail. In effect, Kant accepts the Cartesian 'I', but only as a *form of representation* that is necessary given the actual character of our experience: it is necessary that we conceive ourselves to be simple, substantial, and unitary if we are to order our cognitions as we do—if, in fact, we are to be cognitive beings of the kind we are. But for Kant the actual character of the 'I' apart from its mode of representation is completely inaccessible to us. What we find, on examining the Transcendental Deduction and the Paralogisms, is that Kant recognizes, as he often does, that his predecessors have presented an antinomy which is itself illuminating. Given Descartes's view of the self as simple, substantial, and unitary, and Hume's view that the self which experiences is no more than the set *of* those experiences, Kant argues that we cannot know the 'I' to be substantial—which goes a long way towards explaining the persuasiveness of Hume's minimalist theory of the self. At the same time, the 'I' does exist, but as a necessary form of representation, a logical operator within the domain of our cognitions, which is represented as simple and unitary substance—thus the source of Descartes's introspective conclusions. Kant, then, accounts for the Descartes–Hume antinomy via a sophisticated analysis of how the self is presented to us, and of what must be the case with regard to this representation given the actual form of our experience.

In the process of explicating this antinomy of the self, Kant does a good deal more than merely (though certainly *that* is not the right word) dismantle the science of rational psychology and partially defuse Hume's attack against claims of the possibility of knowledge of the continuous self. He also, in the Transcendental Deduction, presents a sophisticated phenomenology of mental states and their interrelationships, shows the epistemic connectedness of the unitary self and the objective world, and explores the logical form of judgments. In the Paralogisms, he suggests—thoroughly obliquely—a possible common foundation for the epistemic self and the self as moral agent, considers the possibility of (and necessity for belief in) personal immortality, and deals with the mind–body problem in a way which has suggested an incipient functionalism to more than one commentator.[20] All of these developments will be touched on here, and not inappropriately: as Kant recognized, these are not unrelated aspects of the problematic of self-awareness. In terms of formal structure, this study will be divided into three parts. First, I will present salient aspects of Kant's positive theory of the self as it is presented in the Transcendental Deduction. Second, I will give a detailed exegesis and discussion of each of the Paralogisms in turn. Third, I will transpose this study into a somewhat more contemporary mode, and will suggest certain philosophical morals to be drawn from the story which Kant has rather cryptically been telling.

One way of understanding Kant's theory is to see what positions it is intended to correct or supplant, and that is certainly part of what I will try to show. An extension of this approach is to see where other commentators have gone awry, and this is the predominant strategy used here: there have been many plausible readings of Kant which are clearly presented, persuasively argued, and lead to intolerable muddles because they are plausibly, clearly, and persuasively mistaken. Murder will out, and a misreading of one part of the *Critique* will often give itself away when applied elsewhere—if only to the next paragraph. Kant is by no means perfectly consistent, but one claim that I hope to substantiate is that Kant is a good deal more consistent than many of his commentators take him to be, and if a textual reading leads to inconsistencies or incoherence, it is a fairly safe bet that the reading is, in fact, a misreading. This is an important maxim, especially given the fact that Kant's Paralogisms are often taken to be a patchwork, a misconcatenation which Kant forces on himself by his tactically misguided reliance on the Table of Categories and by his insistence that the arguments of rational psychology be read as syllogisms. Certainly the categorial assertions in the Paralogisms should be taken *cum grano salis*. But I intend to show that a number of confusions about the Paralogisms are explicable only if their syllogistic form is taken seriously. If the *substantive* presupposition of this study is that the Paralogisms are only understandable given an understanding of Kant's positive theory of the self, then the reigning *methodological* presupposition is that the Paralogisms themselves are considerably more consistent, and contain considerably less architectonic garnish, than other commentators have faithfully assumed.

To borrow a Nietzschean metaphor from Jay Rosenberg, one way of cutting up the pie of philosophical methodology is to say that there are two ways of doing that kind of philosophy which involves writing about philosophers. Apollonian philosophy is done with an eye towards precision of form, placing much emphasis on historical accuracy and valuing a certain fastidious approach to texts. Dionysian philosophy is more creative, speculative, and strides over textual minutiae with seven-league boots. As will become rather quickly apparent, this study falls not quite squarely in the Apollonian tradition. Not *quite* squarely, because, as the comments above about Kant's interlocutors should suggest, I am convinced that, in addition to looking closely at the text to be explicated, the philosophical scholar can best engage his text by making *it* engage— with certain caveats—contemporary philosophical issues. Despite its Copernican revolutions and linguistic turns, philosophy does address perennial problems, and one of the tasks of philosophical scholarship is to make the relevant connections clear. The trick, of course, is creative anachronism combined with a sense of historical context—a regulative if not a constitutive idea in this study. And it should be obvious that both ways of doing philosophical scholarship are necessary. To misquote Kant: 'Apollonian philosophy without a

1

The Self and the Transcendental Deduction

Can we know the self to exist across time? And if we can, is it such that we can know it to exist as a unitary entity, in some sense unchanging and persistent? Hume, again, is taken to have denied forcefully that we can have any such experience of a unitary self. Strictly speaking, though, Hume finesses the question, denying merely that *he* has such experience: he concedes that others—presumably Descartes is lurking here—may, but he says that

If any one upon serious and unprejudic'd reflexion, thinks he has a different notion of *himself*, I must confess I can reason no longer with him. All I can allow him is, that he may be in the right as well as I, and that we are essentially different in this particular. He may, perhaps, perceive something simple and continu'd, which he calls *himself*; tho' I am certain there is no such principle in me.[1]

Rather than engage Hume's dispute with Descartes directly, we will do well to ask a prior, more Kantian, and probably more productive question: what *must* be true of the self, or how must we conceive it, given the nature of our experience? Though Kant pursues various projects in the Transcendental Deduction, at least part of what he is doing there is attempting an answer to this question. And Kant's more explicit discussion in the Paralogisms of the self and self-knowledge draws so heavily on the cryptic and difficult account in the Transcendental Deduction that the Paralogisms are almost incoherent when detached from the Deduction. It is to the Transcendental Deduction, then, that we need to turn.[2]

THE SUBJECTIVE DEDUCTION: KITCHER'S SYNTHESIS

It has been argued, I think rightly, by Patricia Kitcher that the task of Kant's Subjective Deduction is to show what properties a self must necessarily have, and—importantly—that Kant is obliged to undertake this task as a response to his recognition of the import of Hume's account of the self. This is an interpretation which is borne out by a good deal of recent scholarship regarding Kant's awareness of Hume's arguments.[3] Kitcher also argues that Kant agrees with Hume about the impossibility of introspection's yielding up direct awareness of a perduring self; as we shall see later, this too has ample textual support in the *Critique*, both explicit and implicit. What I wish to focus on, and criticize with an eye towards ultimately making clear Kant's own position, is Kitcher's interpretation of an argument against Hume which Kant purportedly presents in the Subjective Deduction. Kitcher suggests that Hume, by denying any 'real or necessary connection among mental states' is in fact denying 'any relation of existential dependence among mental states' and thus is denying our being able to know that the self, presumably 'an interdependent system of mental states', exists.[4] She goes on to say that:

Kant successfully meets Hume's challenge by showing that we cannot attribute mental states (judgments or intuitions) at all unless we acknowledge a relation of existential dependence among them. The linchpin of Kant's argument is the claim that we cannot attribute any *content* to judgments as intuitions unless we regard those states as part of an interdependent system of states. When Kant talks about the relation of 'synthesis' among mental states, at least part of what he means is that mental states occurring at different times depend on each other for their contents (and so for their existence as mental states).[5]

And, says Kitcher, this interpretation suggests a reading of Kant's extraordinarily cryptic expression, 'the transcendental unity of apperception'. She says that 'one thesis Kant marks by the phrase "transcendental unity of apperception" is the thesis that a necessary condition of the possibility of ... judgmental experience is that mental states occurring at different times are ... part of an informationally interdependent system of states.'[6] In considering Kitcher's reading of Kant's Subjective Deduction and her understanding of the notion of the transcendental unity of apperception, two main questions need to be borne in mind: (1) does the argument Kitcher attributes to Kant actually defeat Hume's scepticism regarding the perduring self, and (2) is Kitcher's argument Kant's argument, and if so, is it all of Kant's argument?

Kitcher's exposition of Kant's putative argument is sophisticated and needs to be set out in some detail if we are to see what is true here. As pointed out above, Kitcher argues that Kant is impelled to establish existential connections among mental states as a response to Hume's scepticism. Indeed, if Kant intends to defend, in the Second Analogy, the applicability of the idea of causal dependence, he must first establish 'the legitimacy of talking about the mental states of one person', which presupposes 'the legitimacy of the idea of existential connection', which is one of the things that Hume denies in his attack on causal dependence.[7] To break this 'Humean circle', then, Kant—on Kitcher's reading—argues (not surprisingly) in the Subjective Deduction that the existence of existential connections among mental states 'is a necessary condition of the possibility of experience'.[8] If part of the very ground of any possible experience is the actual existential connection between at least some mental states, then Hume will be faced with the choice of either rejecting the possibility of experience *tout court* or accepting the existence of at least some real connection between at least some mental states. The former option would be prima facie absurd; the latter is precluded by its potential consequences for his scepticism regarding both causal dependence and self-identity. So by arguing for the real connection of mental states, Kant can, according to Kitcher, at least *begin* his argument for causal dependence in the Second Analogy, since by establishing the transcendental necessity of such mental connection he has established 'the legitimacy of talking about the mental states of one person'. Actually, of course, by establishing the transcendental necessity of such connections Kant has only established the *possibility* that it is legitimate to talk about the states of one person: such connections are a *necessary* condition of such talk, but Kitcher does not show them to be *sufficient*. In any case, to establish this possibility Kant forces a retrenchment by Hume, who denies even the possibility of real connection, and thereby asserts the impossibility of talking about one person's mental states.

Kant, says Kitcher, provides us with an example of a relation of representations, which is such that its representations can be demonstrated to be (necessarily) existentially dependent. The relation Kitcher suggests is the relation of *synthesis*, to which she says Kant 'continually adverts'.[9] As an 'explicit definition' of synthesis, she suggests Kant's comment at A77/B103, that 'By *synthesis*, in its most general sense, I understand the act of putting different representations together, and of grasping what is manifold in them in one [act of] knowledge.' What Kant is saying, according to Kitcher, is that two different mental states, which occur at different times, 'cannot literally be put together'. It follows that the content of a third mental state, dependent on the contents of the first two, is itself more than a mere duplication of the first two.[10] Kitcher then gives what she calls the 'sense' of Kant's 'synthesis':[11]

$$\text{Mental state } M_1 \text{ and mental state } M_2 \text{ are synthesized} = \begin{array}{l}\text{There is some mental state} \\ M_3 \text{ such that, } ceteris\ paribus, \\ \text{the content of } M_3, \text{ and so } M_3 \\ \text{itself, would not exist or} \\ \text{would be different had } M_1 \\ \text{and } M_2 \text{ not existed or had} \\ \text{[they had] different contents.}\end{array}$$

More generally, any two mental states stand in a relation of synthesis if they are synthesized, or if one is the synthetic product of the other.

There is, however, a problem with this definition of synthesis, if it is to be used to demonstrate the legitimacy of talking about one person's mental states. As Kitcher points out, by this definition 'If Harry screams "Smoke!", the content of my mental state will be dependent on the content of the state of Harry's that precipitated his scream.'[12] In other words, my mental state and Harry's will stand in a relation of synthesis, and given this definition of synthesis, Kant has put forward no sortal proviso which could limit relations of synthesis to just my, or any one person's, states. Kitcher dismisses this problem, however, by (1) suggesting that a 'dummy sortal' like 'the right kind of causal connection among the contents of mental states' can be offered as 'a promissory note [that] can be redeemed',[13] and (2) pointing out that for Kant's purpose of refuting Hume, all that is required is the demonstration that *some* mental states are existentially dependent. About Kitcher's first dismissal I will say more later. With regard to the second, what I take her to be saying is that Hume is arguing for the *impossibility* of the self's identity on the basis of the lack of any real connection among mental states, and that all Kant need show is that self-identity is a *possibility* by showing that at least *some* mental states are in a state of contentual causal connection, which is a 'real' connection. That Kant's definition of 'synthesis' does not restrict these connections to one person's mental states does not matter in this context, according to Kitcher, since

Kant has only to establish real connection among two or more
mental states of any kind. That Kant probably thought himself to
be establishing more than this, says Kitcher, does not alter the fact
that he need not accomplish more than this to ward off Hume's
attack.

Kitcher proceeds to distinguish 'Kant's two senses of "synthesis"':
'Synthesis' (upper-case 'S') in her analysis designates 'the precise
relation of contentual causal connection that holds among the
mental states of one's mind', 'synthesis' (lower-case 's') designates
'the generic relation', while 'synthesis*' designates the undis-
ambiguated usage.[14] Given these terminological distinctions,
Kitcher points out that Kant's main focus is on 'transcendental
synthesis*', which, though sometimes viewed as a faculty of
imposition, is normally for Kant an epistemological term: 'to posit a
transcendental synthesis* is to claim that a relation of synthesis*
among mental states can be known to exist in a special way, viz., by
revealing it as a necessary condition for the possibility of experience'.[15] So the 'endorsement of a transcendental synthesis* can be
understood as support for the claim that a synthesis* among mental
states can be shown to be a necessary condition for the possibility of
Experience' ('Experience' with an upper-case 'E' designating Kant's
notion of experience as always involving the judgment that one is in
fact having experience).[16]

Underscoring the relevance of transcendental synthesis*, Kitcher
suggests that this term is equated by Kant with the transcendental
unity of apperception (e.g., when Kant says at B135 that 'I am
conscious to myself *a priori* of a necessary synthesis of representations—to be entitled the original synthetic unity of apperception').
And here Kitcher makes an important point: if by 'transcendental
unity of apperception' Kant means the claim that there is a necessary
relation of synthesis* among representations, then 'the transcendental unity of apperception can function only as a conclusion of the
Deduction'.[17] It is plausible, then, that the transcendental unity of
apperception, spelt out as the claim that the relation of Synthesis
among mental states is a necessary condition of Experience, is the
conclusion argued for in the Subjective Deduction. This conclusion,
if true, is striking for two reasons. First, it ascribes to the Subjective
Deduction and to Kant's theory of synthesis a goal which lifts each
above its traditional characterization as 'armchair psychology'.
Second, as Kitcher admits, it presents a reading of apperception

which is 'severed' from the categories and thus from the objective side of the Deduction.

How, then, does the argument for transcendental synthesis* (= the transcendental unity of apperception) go? After disposing of three 'hopeless' arguments which Kant offers,[18] Kitcher suggests that 'the best argument' can be drawn as follows:

(1) If I could not acknowledge a relation of Synthesis among the things I describe as 'my mental states', then I could not recognize them as representational. (A116)

(2) Something that is not representational is impossible as a mental state. (A116)

(3) Therefore Experience, i.e., any judgment about my own mental states, is possible only if I ascribe that mental state to an 'I think', i.e., only if I can acknowledge a relation of Synthesis between it and other mental states. (A116, B131–2)

(4) Assuming that I can acknowledge a relation of Synthesis among mental states only if it is there, the relation of Synthesis among mental states is a necessary condition of the possibility of Experience.[19]

There are, says Kitcher, two problems with this argument. The first is that we don't know precisely what Synthesis means, and so 'Given that Kant cannot even define the relation of Synthesis, it is hard to see how he could offer any support for the crucial initial premise.'[20] Thus the most we can get from this argument is that it is in fact an argument for a *generic* transcendental synthesis, with the synthesis not restricted by sortal proviso to the mental states of one person. Second, given a number of recent criticisms of transcendental arguments, Kant cannot show that mental states in fact stand in a relation of synthesis, but rather merely 'that we can have Experience, i.e., we can make judgments about our own mental states, only if we have and employ the concept of a relation of synthesis among mental states'.[21] Considering these criticisms, the argument can be salvaged as follows:

(1′) If I could not acknowledge a relation of synthesis among the things I describe as 'my mental states', then I could not regard them as representational.

(2′) If I could not record (*sic*) a state as representational, then I could not regard it as a mental state.

(3′) Therefore Experience, i.e., any judgment about my own mental states, is possible only if I can recognize a relation of synthesis between that mental state and others.[22]

As Kitcher points out, (2´) is uncontroversial, and (3´) is entailed by (1´) and (2´), but it is not immediately obvious why (1´) is true. This is clearly right, and Kitcher offers a detailed account of why Kant considers (1´) to be true, relying on the interpretation of Kant as a functionalist of sorts, and on an insightful discussion of representational systems.[23] The question at hand is: if we grant Kant (1´), and thus grant the argument entire, where does Kant's refutation of Hume now stand? Kitcher suggests that, even though Kant cannot show that mental states *do* stand in a necessary relation of synthesis, he has, so to speak, 'raised the ante' for Hume, by showing that 'Hume's proposal to abjure talk of real relations among mental states while continuing to attribute impressions and ideas is incoherent'.[24] In other words, Hume cannot judge that he has an idea, that he is experiencing, unless he admits that the idea he is having stands in a real relation of contentual causal dependence to other mental states. In effect, Hume's denial of such 'real connection' among mental states revokes his licence to talk about mental states *at all*. If Kitcher's suggestion is right, this is a far from negligible result to achieve on the basis of what Rorty, for example, would call a 'fallible parasitism argument'.[25] Has Kant (as read by Kitcher) painted Hume into this particular transcendental corner?

Before considering this question, I will briefly summarize Kitcher's development of Kant's argument in the Subjective Deduction. Given that Kant's strategy is to refute Hume's scepticism regarding the existence of a perduring self, and given that this scepticism asserts the impossibility of such a self on the basis of denying the existence of any real (= existential) connection between mental states, Kant tries to establish that a person's mental states do in fact stand in a relation of synthesis, such that they are contentually causally connected. Kant's strategy for establishing this claim is to show that it is necessary for experience that this relation of Synthesis exist between these mental states. This necessary Synthesis Kant refers to as a transcendental Synthesis = the transcendental unity of apperception, the necessity of which is a conclusion of the Deduction. However, Kant cannot establish that one person's mental states stand in this necessary relation of synthesis, since he has not specified the relevant causal connections in a way which rules out the

causal connections between one person's mental states and those of
other persons. Therefore, all Kant can prove is that, for experience
to be possible, at least *some* mental states must be so connected. But
this is adequate to refute Hume's claim that no existential connections obtain between mental states at all. Kant's conclusion is
further circumscribed by the qualification that transcendental arguments can only show that some *concepts* are parasitical on other
concepts, so that Kant cannot establish the *actual* connection of
mental states themselves, but only that it is a necessary condition of
making judgments about mental states that we consider these states
to be contentually causally connected. But this is devastating against
Hume in that it forces him (on pain of inconsistency) either to admit
the existence of real connection among mental states or to admit the
incoherence of talk about experience at all. And this, according to
Kitcher, is Kant's strategy.

THE SUBJECTIVE DEDUCTION: A DOSE OF HUMEAN SCEPTICISM

Is this, then, Kant's strategy against Hume? A rather oblique but
effective way to see that it is not is to see how Hume might respond to
such a strategy. First of all, it should be noted that premiss (3´) of the
final version of the argument involves the use of a first-person
possessive: Experience is defined as 'any judgment about *my own*
mental states' (my emphasis). And it is easy to imagine Kant's
Humean opponent bridling at this usage. Kitcher has made an
explicit distinction between synthesis, a generic relation of mental
states, and Synthesis, that relation which defines precisely *my own*
mental states. Further, she has pointed out that Kant has no
adequate definition (in fact, no definition at all) of Synthesis; in other
words, Kant cannot specify, on the basis of contentual causal
connection, just which mental states belong to whom. Thus the
argument (1´)–(3´) is 'an argument about the generic relation of synthesis'. Since Kant cannot even provide a characterization of a specific individual's mental states in terms of that synthesis for which he is
arguing, it glaringly begs the question to assume in the course of that
argument that talk about one person's mental states is legitimate.
Given this objection, (3´) could at most state that 'Experience, i.e.,
any judgment about mental states, is possible only if relations of

synthesis can be recognized between that mental state and others' (the use of 'I' also being omitted for the sake of coherence).

But, Kitcher could respond, there is really no weight being pulled by the expression 'my own mental states' in $(3')$, because this is merely an abbreviated reference to what is explicitly called, in premiss $(1')$, 'the things *I describe as* "my mental states"' (my emphasis). In other words, Kitcher can say that of course we each have some common-sense notion of what are 'our own ideas', and so we can talk in terms of our own ideas, as long as we realize that we are not assuming that we can also specify the precise relation of Synthesis which (theoretically) obtains among these ideas. Indeed, Hume himself adopts what could charitably be described as a 'theory-neutral' usage with regard to the attribution of mental states to persons: though he argues against the idea of an 'I' which exists as a continuing subject of experience, he still refers to what happens 'when I enter into myself'. Given the notion of a common-sense, theory-neutral characterization of 'the things I describe as "my mental states"', we can use this notion to produce 'a (generic) set of mental states' for the purposes of the argument at hand—and such a generic set of mental states is all we need for purposes of the present argument. Would this not be an admissible designation of a set of mental states, since it does not imply that any given set *is* specifiable in terms of Synthesis as actually being '*my own* mental states'?

This does, in fact, seem plausible. Kitcher's argument, lacking any sortal proviso for my mental states that does not itself implicitly assume the attribution of mental states to one person, cannot rely on the assumption that my mental states can be defined in terms of Synthesis. But there is no obvious reason to think that it need so depend: as Kitcher says, 'if Kant can argue that we are justified in imputing this general type of relation to a set of mental states, he will have countered Hume's general objection'.[26] In other words, all Kant has to do is show that for some set of mental states, these states must stand in a relation of synthesis. Given the qualification that those references to 'my mental states' and to myself in the argument *do not* imply an ability to give an account of these expressions in terms of contentual causal connection, there is no compelling reason not to deploy our common-sense usage to select a suitably generic set of mental states about which to argue. Given that 'all Kant needs' is some mental states to consider, there is nothing wrong with his picking those 'which I describe as my own'.

None the less, the point should be pressed a bit further. We can easily imagine a slightly more careful advocate for Hume, one who has rounded the linguistic turn, raising this objection: though Hume himself speaks of 'my thoughts', 'my perceptions', and so on, this must be regarded as a mere *façon de parler*, given his scepticism about the existence of a continuing experiencing subject. If Hume were more linguistically cautious, he would not speak of 'I' or '*my* thoughts' so readily, since the use of these expressions may well imply a continuant Hume as experiencing subject. In any case, it is prima facie inconsistent on the one hand to deny the existence of a continuant self, and on the other hand to use without fail terms which, given our linguistic conventions, indicate the existence of just such a self. And regularly to attribute mental states to an ostensible *something* (designated by 'I') is to use just such terms. Let us suppose, then, that this linguistic Hume has argued convincingly that our common usage of such pronomial expressions is not theory-neutral, and that therefore Kant's argument, which is after all designed to establish the possibility of legitimately attributing mental states to one person, itself assumes the possibility of doing so—indeed, that by its use of pronomials it implicitly sanctions these attributions as legitimate.

To avoid this kind of objection, the argument (1´)–(3´) needs one further revision, namely, one that avoids use of those expressions which imply the legitimacy of attributing mental states to a continuant self:

(1´´) If a relation of synthesis could not be acknowledged among mental states, then they could not be regarded as representational.

(2´´) If a state could not be regarded as representational, then it could not be regarded as a mental state.

(3´´) Therefore Experience, i.e., any judgment about mental states, is possible only if a relation of synthesis can be recognized between that state and others.

Does this revision adequately meet the Humean objection with regard to implied reference to a continuant self? There is at least one immediate problem that presents itself, namely, that Kant does not equate 'Experience' with 'any judgment about mental states', if 'Experience' is taken in Kitcher's sense as 'acknowledgement of *one's own* mental states'.[27] But this might be cleaned up as follows:

(3‴) Therefore no judgment about any mental state is possible unless a relation of synthesis can be recognized between that state and others.

(4′) Experience requires judgments about one's own mental states.

(5) Therefore Experience is possible only if a relation of synthesis can be recognized between (some unspecified) mental states.

Premiss (4′), of course, asserts less than Kant is prepared to assert, but avoids the first-person usage implicit in (3″). This revision, then, should salvage the point of Kitcher's argument—that 'the denial of real connection among mental states' entails the illegitimacy of 'all reference to mental life'[28]—and it seems to fend off the charge of begging the question by implicitly assuming the legitimacy of attribution of mental states to a continuant self.

But in fact this revision of the argument only buries the implicit question-begging assumption a bit deeper. Consider the use of 'Experience' in premisses (4′) and (5). It is true that 'Experience' as presented here does not refer to '*my* own mental states'; none the less, it does imply the attribution of mental states to *someone*. In effect, the first person has been expelled from the definition of 'Experience' and has been replaced by the third person. But the point is that we have only substituted one person for another, and so the use of experience in this argument implies 'the legitimacy of talking about the mental states of one person'—and *this* is precisely what Hume is denying, and what Kant must establish to be true. The point is that any reference to Experience, where Experience implies someone's awareness of mental states as his own, implicitly assumes the legitimacy of attributing mental states to a person; in other words, the possessives and personal pronouns which our linguistic Hume has demanded be removed from the argument are implicit in the very notion of Experience itself. And once it is seen that Experience has only been presumptuously admitted into the argument, representations and mental states begin to exhibit a questionable status as well. And if mental states cannot be admitted into the argument for transcendental synthesis, then synthesis itself is ruled out of order, being a relation without relata. And without a notion of synthesis that can justifiably be deployed, this argument cannot get off the ground. This strategy against Hume, however carefully constructed and however revised, fails by begging the question under discussion.

Before abandoning Kant to the Humean sceptic, though, the implications of the sceptic's position should be considered in more detail. It is worth noting that if a relation of Synthesis could be specified for precisely those mental states which are mine, and could be specified solely in terms of 'contentual causal connections of the right kind', then the objection of our linguistic Hume would be satisfied, and the argument would go through. Without going into a full-dress retranslation of Kitcher's argument for Synthesis, it will suffice to say that each reference to 'my own mental states' would be replaced by the definition which serves to specify precisely these mental states in terms of causal connection. Similarly, references to 'Experience' and *my* acknowledging something to be the case could ostensibly be replaced by expressions which mark these mental states as particular subsets of that set which contains all and only my mental states. By having available a terminology which would, depending only on a description of causal connection, be 'person-neutral', the argument could be presented without use of those possessives and pronomials which may leave open the charge of begging the question. And, significantly, it is also reasonable to assume that it would be a more or less superfluous argument: by being able to specify the 'right kind' of causal connection among mental states so as to describe—impersonally—the mental states of a given person would in all probability yield a criterion of personal identity that would at least present some kind of continuant 'self' to oppose Hume's 'bundle of perceptions'. But such a definition is not presented by Kant, and all Kitcher offers in this regard is the aforementioned 'promissory note', which she believes to be redeemable. So (1) we are left with an argument for synthesis rather than Synthesis, and (2) if personal possessives are disallowed, we are in fact left without even that.

Neither (1) nor (2) should, however, be surprising. The linguistic Hume presented above is a remarkably implausible sceptic, to be sure, since it is quite difficult to imagine anyone rejecting all talk of self-conscious experience and all use of pronomial expressions. And it is worth noting that this is the real, if not the intended, force of Kitcher's argument against Hume. The idea of ruling 'Experience' out of discussion seems wilfully perverse, since it is a truism that experience requires a subject. Why, then, even consider such a far-fetched interlocutor? Precisely because of this: truisms are not necessarily trivial. It may be a truism that experience requires a subject, but it is not trivial that this is true. That it is impossible to talk about experience without at least implicitly talking about possession of experience by subjects—or, more precisely, by subjects *who experience*—reflects the logical grammar of experience-talk: words like 'thought', 'sensation', and 'representation' are verbal nouns.[29] These are nominalized forms of words which denote actions, such as 'think', 'sense', and 'represent'. And the key, of course, is that actions require an agent ('I think', 'she senses', 'the mind represents'). A subjectless experience is precisely as nonsensical as an agentless action, and for precisely the same reason. When Hume says that 'what we call a *mind* is nothing but a heap or collection of different perceptions', he has reified 'perception', taken it not as a mere verbal noun but as a noun denoting an object. Thus he can say that he 'stumbles' upon thoughts and perceptions without at the same time stumbling upon *himself*. The problem is that 'perception' and 'thought' are nouns derived from such verbal expressions as 'I think' or 'you perceive', and that when they are reified as if they refer to objects and are considered apart from questions of their (necessary) subject, they yield incoherent notions. Interestingly, Hume's meta-phorical use of 'stumble' in a cognitive context makes especially pointed the reification of verbal nouns, and sharpens the point to be made regarding the nature of mental states: that mental states are by their very nature *had* by an experiencing subject, and this subject is an irreducible aspect of experience. The moral is that failing to acknowledge this aspect of experience leads to philosophical muddles—and it is worth noting here that the very expression 'mental *state*' has a great deal of hypostatic muddle-potential.

This moral is clearly missed by Hume; I believe that it is also missed by Kitcher, as can be seen from an examination of her suggestion that it is possible to define a relation of Synthesis. This definition would be a specification of 'The right kind of causal connection among the contents of mental states',[30] where, as was pointed out, we (pre-theoretically) assume 'the right kind' to be that as yet unknown connection which precisely includes all of one given person's mental states and no others. To find a way of picking out one person's mental states by such a specification requires that something be true of all of that person's mental states, for example, that they all stand in relation R to one another. Further, this relation R must be such that while each member of this (person's) set of mental states is in relation R, this is not true of any other mental state (such as, for example, Harry's scream). So the causal connection theorist wants to say something like

$$x\text{'s mental states} = \frac{\text{that set of mental states which}}{\text{are in relation R to one another}}$$

where relation R is *generally* understood as 'being part of a system of representations'. And this relation can only be specified in terms of some 'right kind' of causal connection which defines the system of representations = person x's mental states. The problem, of course, is how to specify this general understanding for the particular case of x's mental states, without importing a possessive that refers even obliquely to x—which would certainly not count as *any* kind of causal connection among the contents of mental states. In other words, how is it possible, with regard to mental states, to *pick out which ones* you are talking about without indicating *whose* mental states they are? Defining relation R as 'being part of that system of representation which is such that each member of the system is predicated of (x under some redescription) as is no other representation' looks rather suspiciously analytic. In other words, my mental states are distinguished, *qua* members of a (presumably) unique set of mental states, simply by their being *my* mental states. There is no reason to posit any other criterion of membership in this set, unless one aspires to eliminate the experiencing subject from the notion of the experiences themselves, which we have seen to be an incoherent project. Finally, if 'the right kind of causal connection' = 'my kind of causal connection' (and there are no other plausible candidates), then the operative criterion for personal identity (whatever it may be) seems to be operating at one remove from criteria of causal connection.

In his discussion of 'no-ownership' theories of the self, Strawson has made a similar point, which is applicable to the causal-connection theorist. The 'no-ownership' theorist argues that experiences are in fact only 'owned' in the sense that they are causally dependent on, and thereby contingently 'owned' by, a body. This causal dependence is contrasted with the theory (or cluster of theories) within which experiences are said to be owned or had by 'an Ego, whose sole function is to provide an owner for experiences'. This latter type of ownership is non-contingent and thereby, according to the no-ownership theorist, senseless, since ownership is transferable. But, says Strawson, the no-ownership theory

is not coherent, in that one who holds it is forced to make use of that sense of possession of which he denies the existence ... When he tries to state the contingent fact [of causal dependence] ... he has to state it in some such form as 'All my experiences are had by (i.e. uniquely dependent on the state of) body B'. For any attempt to eliminate the 'my', or any expression with a similar possessive force, would yield something that was not a contingent fact at all ... He must mean to be speaking of some class of experiences of the members of which it is in fact contingently true that they are all dependent on body B. The defining characteristic of this class is in fact that they are 'my experience' ... where the idea of possession ... is the one he calls into question.[31]

Clearly Kitcher's causal-connection theory is to a certain extent a no-ownership theory, in so far as it suggests that the totality of a person's mental states can be defined in terms of a system of (presumably contingent) causal dependencies. It seems unlikely that Kitcher would go so far as to suggest that experiences are not had by an owner of some sort. But by focusing on mental states as causal relata and not as entities by necessity belonging to a subject she has obscured the irreducibly definitive role of the subject in describing experience. The no-ownership theorist and the causal connection theorist are both faced with the daunting challenge of finding a way of precisely characterizing that set of experiences which are mine without referring to me as the experiencing subject. In fairness, Kitcher does suggest that 'this epistemological criterion of personal identity is inadequate as it stands'.[32] But this seems to refer more to our present need to provide a 'dummy sortal' in our definition of Synthesis than to any implicit inadequacy in the project. And so the success of Kitcher's argument must be qualified by saying that this entire line of argument, focusing on a 'system of mental states', in effect does not get us any further than Hume's 'bundle of perceptions', since both approaches to experience obscure the irreducible role the subject plays in experience.[33] It is this last point which must provide the insight needed to refute Hume's denial of a continuant self; it is a point which I want to suggest is made by Kant, and which is used by Kant to construct just such a refutation.

To see how Kant actually does this, however, we must briefly consider whether or not Kitcher's argument is in fact Kant's refutation of Hume. If it is Kant's, then Kant's Subjective Deduction has a remarkably defensive quality, for though he may have forced Hume to admit 'real' connections between mental states, he has not made any further advance towards actually establishing the necessary existence of a continuant self. In fact, except for pointing out the necessary connectedness of experience, he has conceded the game, for the system of causally dependent mental states gives us no more reason to posit a continuing self than does Hume's bundle. Moreover, Kitcher's own point that her version of Kant produces an account of apperception 'severed' from the Categories militates against this reading. Though Kant himself says in the Preface to the first edition that the Subjective Deduction is 'not essential' to his purposes, he does not say it is unimportant or unrelated. Indeed, if the Subjective Deduction 'seeks to investigate the pure understanding itself, its possibility, and the cognitive faculties upon which it rests' (Axvi–xvii), then the cost of severing the two deductions will be to detach completely Kant's theory of self-consciousness from his theory of objective experience. This detachment may be too high a price to pay, especially given a number of remarks by Kant which indicate that the two theories are actually more closely related than his own comments in the Preface would indicate.[34] An alternative reading of Kant's Subjective Deduction should be considered: one in which Kant explicitly recognizes the irreducibility of the experiencing subject. If this reading brings out a more effective rebuttal of Hume's argument, then so much the better.

Though Kitcher concentrates on Kant's arguments at A116–18 as the core of the Subjective Deduction, Kant in fact makes many of his most crucial points (and with more substantial argumentation) in what he calls four 'preparatory' passages between A99 and A114, where he attempts to present at least a sketch of the relation between the synthesis of representations and the necessary representation of a continuant self. Kant begins this project by somewhat cryptically pointing out that representations 'must all be ordered, connected, and brought into relation' in time (A99). He elaborates by saying that 'Every intuition contains in itself a manifold which can be represented as a manifold only in so far as the mind distinguishes the time in the sequence of one impression upon another.' And, Kant says, this requirement is 'quite fundamental' to what follows (A99). Kant is making an extremely significant point against Hume, specifically, against Hume's notion of a *sequence*, which is taken by Hume to be merely a succession of impressions. To the extent that slogans can capture acute philosophical points, Kant's objection to Hume here is well expressed by the slogan 'A sequence of representations is not the representation of a sequence.' In other words, that I perceive each of a succession of images does not in itself give me the representation of the succession itself: this representation cannot be the result of the mere addition of images. Kant makes this point in more detail in the Elucidation, where he says that

I can indeed say that my representations follow one another; but this is only to say that we are conscious of them as in a time-sequence, that is, in conformity with the form of inner sense. (A37/B54n.)

Furthermore, time is not 'an objective determination inherent in things', and it cannot therefore be a product of the simple reception of appearances. The representation of a sequence, then, is an 'act' undertaken by the mind when it takes up a sequence of representations, an act in which the manifold of representations is 'run through, and held together' (A99).

Implicit in this brief account is the key to Kant's notion of synthesis: our senses can present us only with myriad unrelated bits of data, and these bits of data must be combined, reproduced, and 'held together' by the mind as occurring in time and space. Roughly, what Kant is saying is that we don't get the ordering of our experience from the world but rather from the understanding (that these are in an important way correlative remains to be shown—and is shown by Kant, partly in the Objective Deduction). It should also be noted that 'synthesis' for Kant operates at various levels of mental complexity: apprehensions must be synthesized in intuition, appearances in the imagination, and intuitions into object-concepts. This taxonomy of the mental needs some sorting out; for now, though, what is important to recognize is that for the course of our experience to be orderly and coherent, it must be synthesized, 'run through and held together'. Furthermore, any synthesis of intuitions must be accomplished 'in accordance with a fixed rule' (A100, A105). Clearly, a great deal too much can be read into Kant's use of 'rule': what it means *at least* is that experience must be 'represented as in thoroughgoing and orderly connection'; that intuitions are thought under concepts (A110) and representations in general thought as occurring in a unitary space and time are but two cases of experiential 'synthesis'.

Indeed, experience itself would be impossible if individual representations were not such that they could be reproduced in memory, synthesized in thought under object-concepts, or synthesized in some other way or ways. As Kant says, 'If each representation were completely foreign to every other, standing apart in isolation, no such thing as knowledge would ever arise. For knowledge is a whole in which representations stand compared and connected' (A97). The case of *reproduction* Kant seems to find clearest for the exposition of this point.[35] One example will suffice here, that of reproduction as required for mental counting:

> If we were not conscious that what we think is the same as what we thought a moment before, all reproduction in the series of representations would be useless . . . If, in counting, I forget that the units, which now hover before me, have been added to one another in succession, I should never know that a total is being produced through this successive addition . . . and so would remain ignorant of the number . . . (A103)

What Kant is saying is that if I am to add a sequence of numbers, whatever their internal relation, in my head, then I must be able to see each separate addition as part of the entire operation. If I could not view the successive additions *as* successive and as part of a connected whole, then I would not know to perform them sequentially, or even know when or how I had reached the sum, were I to do so at all. Actually, Kant can make his point even more strongly: if I am incapable of *holding* a thought for more than a moment, I could not relate it to another thought at all, since it would not be present in thought to relate. Thus I could not perform even the initial addition in the series, since by the time the second number was present in thought the first would already be gone. In this light we can see the significance of Kant's point that the word 'concept' itself should suggest this kind of reproductive synthesis. 'Concept' is a translation of *Begriff*, which is etymologically related to the verb 'to grasp'—thus to have conceptual experience, it is essential that we be able to grasp, to hold on to, separate and momentary experiences, and to unite them via various mental syntheses in an orderly fashion. If we could not do this, then 'The manifold of the representation would never . . . form a whole, since it would lack that unity which only consciousness can impart to it' (A103). Unless representations can be grouped and related *over time*, experience would be 'a mere flux of appearances' that would have no relation to one another that I could discern. Kant, then, has made his first important claim in the Subjective Deduction: that for experience to be possible at all it must be organized and unified in time by the mind, for this order cannot be derived from the 'mere play of appearances' considered as a succession of representations.

This leads directly to Kant's second claim: that for my representations to be taken up into a synthesis which will yield intelligible experience, they must be brought together *as mine*. In other words, unless each of a succession of representations can be thought to belong to one and the same subject, there is no ground for their relation to one another at all. To cite another of Kant's arguments for reproductive synthesis:

> When I seek to draw a line in thought . . . obviously the various manifold representations that are involved must be apprehended by me in thought one after the other. But if I were always to drop out of thought the preceding representations (the first parts of the line . . .) , and did not reproduce them while advancing to those that follow, a complete representation would never be obtained . . . (A102)

But so to reproduce representations over time requires a continuing consciousness, an experiencing subject to which all experiences can be attributed. To see why this is true, it is useful to look ahead briefly to the Second Paralogism. There, Kant says that the subject of consciousness must be in some way unitary, if thought is to be coherent:

> For suppose it be the composite that thinks: then every part of it would be a part of the thought, and only all of them taken together would contain the whole thought. But this cannot consistently be maintained. For representations (for instance the single words of a verse), distributed among different beings, never make up a whole thought (a verse), and it is therefore impossible that a thought should inhere in what is essentially composite. (A352)

In other words, if a complex thought (requiring synthesis) is to be possible at all, it must be possible for all its parts to be had by the same subject, as opposed to a collection or succession of different subjects.[36] Again, for me to be conscious of my drawing a line in thought, I must remain present throughout as the subject who has each of the representations which, when synthesized, constitute this drawing. And so the very possibility of experience itself depends on its being characterizable as experience had by this kind of unitary subject. Kant says that

There can be in us no modes of knowledge, no connection or unity ... without that unity of consciousness which precedes all data of intuitions, and by relation to which representation of objects is alone possible. This pure original unchangeable consciousness I shall name *transcendental apperception*. (A107)

Transcendental apperception, then, refers to the necessary unitary experiencing *subject*, which makes possible the necessary synthesis of experiential contents.

This transcendental apperception, which Kant calls 'the bare representation "I"' (A117n.) is usefully contrasted by Kant with *empirical* self-consciousness: 'No fixed and abiding self can present itself in this flux of inner appearances ... What has *necessarily* to be represented as numerically identical cannot be thought as such through empirical data' (A107). All experience is had through empirical self-consciousness, but empirical self-consciousness with its various synthetic functions requires the 'bare' representation of a unitary and continuant subject as the unitary experiencing— 'logical'—subject which has all these empirical representations. It has been suggested by Walsh that the contrast between transcendental and empirical apperception can be understood in that 'Insofar as the unity of apperception operates in my consciousness I think as a rational being and not as a particular individual.'[37] This is an accurate contrast, as far as it goes, except that it is not clear why, given that the transcendental unity of apperception grounds all our experience, Walsh wants to circumscribe its role to that of 'rational' thought (unless 'rational being' is a wry derivation from 'logical subject'). On the present reading, it is somewhat more accurate to say that in so far as the unity of consciousness operates in my consciousness I am the unitary experiencing subject of all my experiences; in so far as empirical self-consciousness operates in my consciousness I am a particular, experiencing, individual. What Kant is getting at is this: given that experience requires a subject, and that experience is not simple and must be synthesized to be intelligible (to be experience rather than a chaotic onslaught of disorderly appearances), then it follows that experience must be ordered by a unitary subject who persists through, and is thereby the ground of, the synthesis of experience.

It may be useful to set out a brief outline of the relation between synthesis and the experiencing subject.[38] The most primitive form of apperception (more a proto-apperception) which is relevant here is Hume's 'bundle of perceptions'. Letting M = mental state, this becomes

(1) '(M_1 and M_2)'

where the self is aware of itself only as a sequence of impressions. But given the qualification that there must be a subject for any experience, this becomes

(2) 'I think M_1 and I think M_2'

But, says Kant, given the synthetic nature of experience, it is clear that my experiences require a unitary subject to which they all belong for them to be experienced at all. And he gives us a convenient clue to the propositional form expressed by this insight when he says in the Paralogisms that 'we demand the absolute unity of the subject of a thought, only because otherwise we could not say, "I think" (the manifold in one representation)' (A354, brackets, significantly, Kant's). This unity of apperception, then, is expressed by

(3) 'I think (M_1 and M_2)'

and is what Kant in the second edition refers to as the *synthetic* unity of apperception: it is the unity of consciousness which is the ground of, is necessary for, synthesis of experience (B133-4). Finally, given that M_1 and M_2 must be thought by the same 'I' (the 'I' of the synthetic unity), we can conclude that the 'I' which accompanies each of these experiences is identical through time. This is the *analytic* unity of apperception (B133-4):

(4) 'The "I" that thinks M_1 = The "I" that thinks M_2'

And Kant asserts in both editions that the analytic unity of apperception depends on the synthetic unity of apperception. Though this is more obscure in the first edition, it is still reasonably clear: 'the mind could never think its . . . identity *a priori*, if it did not have before its eyes the identity of its act, whereby it subordinates all synthesis of apprehension ... to a transcendental unity ...' (A108). As Rosenberg puts it, Kant's point is that it is possible to infer (4) from (2) only if

> a certain *presupposition* is satisfied, on the condition that it is also *possible* to 'unite the manifold of given representations in *one consciousness*'—that is, possible to have the (meta)-thought:
>
> ... I think (X+Y),
>
> a thought in which the represent*eds* X and Y are first brought into relation to *one another* (caught up in a 'synthesis') and in which the resulting unity X + Y (the 'synthesized manifold') is ascribed to 'one consciousness' in the sense of being thought within the scope of a *single* 'I think'.[39]

And this, broadly speaking, is how Kant argues for the identity of a continuant self as necessary experiencing subject.

For now, though, what else can be said about Kitcher's reading, given this alternative interpretation? First of all, though Kant's text gives no evidence that 'existential dependence' or 'contentual causal connection' is what is meant by 'synthesis', still—and up to a point— these are not inappropriate notions to use to describe the results of Kant's synthetic functions. But this is to say no more, I suspect, than that a person's mental states are related in complicated ways. None the less, this is worth saying, and Kitcher does draw our attention to the kind of strategy Kant presses against Hume: that experience, if it is to *be* experience, must be systematic and orderly. Kitcher has forcefully argued—with Kant—for the necessity of a thoroughgoing interdependence of mental states: and this is surely a far from negligible result. What Kitcher misses—along with Hume—is that this order depends on, but *does not constitute*, the existence of a unitary logical *subject* of experiences. In other words, and to paraphrase an earlier point, we must not mistake a system of representations for the representation of a system. Thus any equation of the transcendental unity of apperception with transcen- dental synthesis is too quick: Kant, in the Subjective Deduction, first argues the necessity of synthesis of mental states if experience is to be possible, and then argues that the representation of a unitary subject is necessary for synthesis to be possible. Neglect of the role of the subject in experience leads, understandably and almost inevit- ably, to a conflation of Kant's two arguments. And this conflation in turn obscures the crucial role of the experiencing subject in this part of the Transcendental Deduction.

For the account of the Subjective Deduction which has emerged here to be conclusive, a great many loose ends need to be tied up—and to do so properly would go well beyond my present purposes. These purposes do require, however, that some attention be devoted to the relation between empirical and transcendental apperception, and to the relation between Kant's theory of synthesis and that aspect of the Transcendental Deduction from which it is usually considered separate—specifically, the Objective Deduction. In order to develop the dexterity needed to tie up at least *these* loose ends, it will be useful to consider first—and in some detail—one relatively recent entry into the problematic posed by Kant in the Transcendental Deduction: Strawson's 'Objectivity Argument'.

THE OBJECTIVE DEDUCTION: STRAWSON, SELF, AND OBJECTIVITY

The goal of Strawson's argument is not particularly controversial, at least as a reading of Kant's own intent in the Transcendental Deduction: 'to *establish* that experience necessarily involves knowledge of *objects*'.[40] Yet the *argument* which purports to establish this conclusion has come under fire in much of the recent literature on the Deduction.[41] That the argument which Rorty has dubbed 'Strawson's Objectivity Argument' has spurred so much controversy and close analysis creates some presumption that either Strawson's argument is unsound (but in a philosophically useful way) or he is misreading Kant. I want to suggest that Strawson's argument (1) is sound, or can be made to be, (2) is not—properly construed—a misreading of Kant, and (3) is a useful starting-point for understanding at least part of what Kant is doing in the Transcendental Deduction. I will start by presenting, with some comments, what I take to be a fairly standard reading of Strawson's argument.

The argument begins with the assertion of the 'conceptualizability of experience, i.e. the applicability of general concepts to the particular contents of experience'. This conceptualizability is reflected in Kant's 'fundamental duality' of intuition and concept.[42] It is worth noting briefly just what this 'fundamental duality' is. As Sellars has pointed out,

It is often taken for granted that Kant was clear about the distinction between conceptual and nonconceptual mental states or representings. 'Empirical intuitions' are interpreted as nonconceptual and construed, on the above lines, as the epistemically more important members of the sensation family.[43]

As Sellars points out, intuitions traditionally have been taken to fall on the sensory side of Kant's sensory–intellectual dichotomy, though they are normally acknowledged to have *some* sort of privileged status, usually as some kind of unspecifiedly pregnant sensations. And it is not always clear from Kant's own usage that this is wrong. But such a reading ignores the fact that Kant does distinguish intuitions (*Anschauungen*) from sensations (*Empfindungen*). At B44 Kant says that 'the sensations of colours, sounds, and heat . . . are mere sensations and not intuitions'.[44] He also makes it quite clear that intuitions are *conceptual* entities, as opposed to sensations, which relate 'solely to the subject as the modifications of its state' (A320).[45] But what kind of conceptual entities are intuitions? Sellars again:

Actually the pattern of Kant's thought stands out far more clearly if we interpret him as clear about the difference between *general* conceptual representings (sortal and attributive), on the one hand, and, on the other, *intuition* as a special class of *nongeneral* conceptual representings . . . 'Intuitive' representings would consist of those conceptual representings of individuals (roughly, individual concepts) which have the form illustrated by

    this-line

as contrasted with

    the line I drew yesterday

which is an individual concept having the form of a definite description.[46]

In other words, an intuition is a singular thought, a representation of a *this*. But as Kant is well aware, we do not perceive bare particulars: the logical form of 'This is an avocado' is not 'This thing is an avocado', but rather 'This-avocado'. That is to say, our singular representations are not bare representations of a 'this', but are representations of a 'this-such', an Aristotelian $\tau\acute{o}\delta\epsilon\ \tau\acute{\iota}$.[47] And in so far as an intuition is a representation of a 'this-such', it is conceptual: it involves bringing experience under concepts. And it was Kant's genius to recognize, however obliquely, that all experience, to *be* experience, must be brought under concepts. But another important consequence follows from Kant's awareness of this fact about singular representations: if the logical form of an intuition is that of a 'this-such', then, even though the intuition is not itself a judgment, it does embody the form of a subject-predicate judgment: an intuition represents something ('this') as being of a certain kind ('such')—as falling under a certain concept. When I have a singular thought of the form 'this-book', I think of a thing *as* a thing which falls under the concept *book*. So for Kant the categorial forms of judgments are present in intuitions, as well as in judgments proper.

To return, then, to this recapitulation of Strawson's argument: from the datum that experience is brought under concepts it follows that there is a distinction in all experiences between the item that is experienced and the *recognition* of the item (presumably its recognition as being of a kind, as falling under a concept). This 'recognitional component can be present only because of the possibility of acknowledging the experience as one's own'.[48] In other words, to be able to recognize a datum as a datum of a certain kind, I must be able to recognize the datum as mine, to self-ascribe the experiencing of the datum. To be able to do this implies that I can distinguish a '"subjective component within a judgment of experience" (to distinguish between "It seems to me that *p*" and "*p*")'.[49] And, importantly, in this being–seeming distinction we have the grounds of the objectivity thesis itself.

What, though, are Strawson's reasons for asserting these implications of the conceptualizability of experience? It may be useful to set out what seems to be Strawson's own argument in more detail:

(1) I recognize items in my experience as items of certain kinds.

implies that

(2) Experience must include both a recognitional component and a content that is recognized as of a certain kind.

implies that

(3) It is possible to self-ascribe my experiences = to judge that an experience is mine.

implies that

(4) I can distinguish in my experience a subjective component = an awareness that my experience *is* an experience.

implies that

> (5) I have a distinction between something's *being* the case and *seeming to me* to be the case.

implies that

> (6) I have the concept of something's being different from the way it appears to me, that is, the concept of something whose *esse* is not *percipi*.

> (7) The concept of something whose *esse* is not *percipi* is the concept of a physical object.

therefore

> (8) If I can recognize items in my experience as objects of certain kinds, then I must have the concept of a physical object.

And (8) is, of course, the objectivity thesis itself, derived from the fact that experience is conceptual. If experience were not conceptual—if we were not discursive creatures—another argument would be needed. But Kant, for one, suggests that we cannot imagine what such 'experience' would be like (A 1 1 1). It should be noted that Strawson's critics have often misread the actual formal structure of Strawson's argument. As an example, Stevenson presents this argument in five steps, corresponding roughly to my (1), (2), (3), (5), and (8)—this terseness renders the latter part of Strawson's argument glib and unintelligible, which it is not, and leads Stevenson to say that 'Strawson appears to assume that [the distinction of a subjective component in experience] implies his objectivity thesis.'[50] In fact, a minor effort (steps 5–7) shows one way of justifying, and not merely assuming, this implication. But even the most accurate reading of the structure does not remove all, or even the more interesting, objections to this argument. Two of these objections must now be considered.

THE OBJECTIVE DEDUCTION: RECOGNITION, JUDGING, AND CORRIGIBILITY

First, is it true that the existence of a recognitional component in experience implies the possibility of self-ascription of experiences?

Mackie argues that it is not clear why this implication holds, suggesting that 'if there were ... creatures who had successive experiences but were incapable of self-consciousness', then Strawson would be right in saying that we 'add nothing but a form of words' to our concept of these successive experiences by saying that they 'belong to a single consciousness'; none the less, says Mackie, we *could* have a concept of such creatures.[51] And Stevenson suggests that there may well be such creatures: 'we can surely imagine a creature (perhaps an infant or a chimpanzee) who can linguistically evince a recognition of various kinds of perceptible states of affairs, but who shows no sign whatsoever of self-ascription of experiences'.[52] And so, to continue Stevenson's transposition of the objection into linguistic mode, 'it is not at all obvious why the making of a judgment must imply the possibility of self-conscious awareness'.[53] It at least seems quite possible for an experiencing subject to operate with a distinction between item recognized and recognitional component, while not actually ascribing any of his experiences to an experiencing subject (himself).

Recalling comments made earlier, however, may lead us to reject this possibility. It was pointed out that the concept of experience implies the concept of an experiencing *subject*, in that it is incoherent to suppose that experience can be considered apart from (at least the implicit) assumption of a subject who *has* the experience. And the same seems to be true of judgments. If experiential nouns such as 'thought', 'sensation', or 'intuition' are merely *verbal* nouns implying an action ('thinking', 'sensing', 'intuiting') and hence an agent, then similarly it could be argued that 'judgment' is also a verbal noun, implying a judging and therefore a judge. This certainly seems to be right, and is the key to why it is strongly counter-intuitive to suppose that three people, each uttering one of the words in the judgment 'snow is white', have in fact made a judgment.[54] If this is the case, then, can we not refute Stevenson's claim that 'it is not at all obvious why the making of a judgment must imply the possibility of self-conscious awareness' by simply pointing out that for any creature capable of making judgments, his judging implies the notion of himself as a judge?

It is important to see that in fact this does not discredit the possibility suggested by Stevenson and Mackie, and for this reason: that one can do something does not in itself imply that one has a grasp of the necessary (conceptual) structure of what one does, and that one's not having a grasp of this structure does not in itself imply a deficiency or flaw in one's ability to do what one does (albeit in ignorance). In this regard, it is worth noting Plato's account of knowledge as requiring an αἰτίας λογισμῷ: one can have 'true opinion' of the way to Larisa if one can get there from Athens, but to have *knowledge* of the way to Larisa one must be able to give an account of how one goes. But what is easy to overlook is this: though the man who can go to Larisa but cannot tell others how to do the same is admittedly deficient in *something*, he is not deficient in being able to *go to Larisa*.[55] Similarly, that one has the ability to make a judgment does not in itself imply that one is fully aware of the necessary implications of judging. It has not been established that making a judgment implies knowing that the logic of 'judgment' implies a judge. And, of course, it is always possible that I can deploy a concept without recognizing *its* full implication; that I do so regularly is very likely indeed. It is easy enough to imagine, for example, a person whose untutored reasoning-ability includes a proficiency with a primitive rule of inference, such as *modus tollens*, but does not include a proficiency with any number of rules of inference derivable from the primitive rule (in this case, perhaps, transposition). Stevenson is not denying that making a judgment does imply the existence of a judge. Rather, he is claiming that one can make a judgment without being conscious of this particular feature of the logic of judging. Of course, it would be absurd to claim that a creature could (*a*) make perceptual judgments, and (*b*) be aware of the fact that judging requires a judge, and (*c*) be aware that its perceptual judgments *are* judgments, without (*d*) actually ascribing its own judgments to itself as a judge. But all Stevenson and Mackie are arguing is that the mere fact of being able to make perceptual judgments does not imply the knowledge that judging requires a judge. So the fact that one can make perceptual judgments does not clearly eliminate the possibility that one could do so without ever ascribing them to oneself. To see whether or not this possibility is itself coherent, however, it will be helpful to look at a second objection to Strawson's argument.

This second objection, directed against the inference of a seems–is distinction from the possibility of the self-ascription of experiences, is expressed by Stevenson. He indicates that this inference is effected by an implicit notion of judgments as necessarily corrigible, and trades on an ambiguity in the idea of corrigibility.[56] Roughly, according to Stevenson, by making a perceptual judgment = '*p*', one admits the possibility of '*p*' and of 'not-*p*', but not necessarily the possibility of 'apparently-*p*'. Stevenson points out that our non-self-ascribing infant or chimpanzee makes judgments that (1) make use of the conceptual distinction between '*p*' and 'not-*p*', and (2) are corrigible in that they tend to agree with our own judgments. But their judgments need not make use of the *third* conceptual notion implicit in *our* notion of corrigibility—that of 'apparently-*p*'. Stevenson says that 'Explicit talk of "seeming that" or "appearing that" involves an extra conceptual dimension which does not follow from judgment-making alone.'[57] So it is argued that Strawson's statement that 'it is possible to self-ascribe experiences' implies the making of perceptual judgments, which implies corrigibility, but that there are two senses of corrigibility, and the one that is needed to get from perceptual judgments to a seems–is distinction is richer than that which is actually implied by the making of perceptual judgments.

This objection, however persuasive initially, offers too parsimonious an account of judgment. If we consider the minimum apparatus necessary for the making of perceptual judgments, we begin with the ability to distinguish between the concepts '*p*' and 'not-*p*'. The ability to make this distinction is necessary for any judging to take place: to judge is to judge that some state of affairs *is the case* rather than *is not the case*, and thus it is essential that the judge be aware that there is more than one possible state of affairs. Another way of putting this is to say that something else may have been the case *rather than* '*p*'. So judging at least requires the actively deployed concept of one thing's being the case rather than another, and, importantly, of one thing's being the case *to the exclusion* of something else's being the case: minimally, this exclusion is of 'not-*p*' when one is judging that '*p*', and vice versa, since if one did not have this distinction there would be no sense in the notion of judging at all. Does the practice of judging—again, as opposed to the concept of judgment—require anything further?

Let us consider the case of a creature, along the lines of the one posited by Mackie, who makes perceptual judgments on the basis of awareness of just this implication of judgment, that is, one who can make judgments of the form '*p*' and 'not-*p*', and can know that he is so judging, but who uses no judgments of the form 'apparently-*p*'. We know that his experience is conceptualized and that he recognizes perceptual items as being of certain *kinds*, falling under certain concepts: 'this green patch', 'this sharp pain', etc. Similarly, one supposes, he can recognize certain concepts as themselves falling under certain other concepts, for example, 'this *colour* green'. And by stipulation he does not have any object-concepts, and hence no experience *as of* objects. Nor does he employ a seems–is distinction. Since his judgments in part concern perceptions which tend to be momentary, it is not clear that he 're-encounters' the same perceptions which he had earlier: to say that he did would belie the way perceptions, as opposed to objects, individuate. He does, however, have memories of past events, at least in so far as he must be able to reapply those concepts he has applied before; if he has no concepts which remain the same over time, it is absurd to say that his experience is conceptual, and if he does use the same concepts over time, it is clear that, barring some inexplicably innate faculty, he has memories, at least of past concepts. Having stipulated the conceptual apparatus of our imaginary creature, then, let us see what judging must be like for him.

The notion of taking various perceptions to be of the same kind implies the availability of a kind-concept to the taker at each taking. Consider two exemplary concepts of this type—'pink' and 'colour', such that the first is what we could call a 'first-order' concept = one that is applied to perceptions, while the second is, in at least one usage by our creature, a 'second-order' concept = one that is applied to other concepts, that is, to first-order concepts. Now suppose that our creature makes the judgment at t1 that 'Pink is a colour.' This seems unproblematic, since both 'pink' and 'colour' are reasonable concepts for him to have, and the judgment asserts that a given first-order concept falls under a given second-order concept. Now suppose that our creature at t2 judges that 'It is not the case that pink is a colour.' This too seems an unproblematic judgment, though a false one, and for the same reasons that the first was not problematic. The problem arises when we try to determine the *relation* between the two judgments *for the judge*. If he recalls his t1-judgment at the time he makes his judgment at t2, then he is confronted with a decision: he can make both judgments (the conjunction of the two), or he can reject one of them, or he can reject both of them. If he makes both judgments, that is, says that 'Pink is a colour and it is not the case that pink is a colour', then he has affirmed a contradiction—which would be remarkable, given that he has the ability to distinguish something's being the case from its not being the case, which implies his being aware that something cannot both be the case and not be the case at the same time. And the same, obviously, is true of his rejecting both judgments. So for this creature's story to remain coherent, he must reject one of the two judgments. Which does he choose to reject?

The answer, of course, is that he can't choose at all. This is not because he has no *criteria* on the basis of which to choose, but because of something antecedent to the whole question of criteria: he does not have the concept of rejecting a judgment that has been made—an actual judgment—*at all*. By virtue of judging something to be the case, of course, he tacitly judges that something else—its denial—is not the case. But what he lacks is the concept of a *mistaken judgment*: once a judgment is made, it is made, and there is nothing else that can be said about it. And the key point is this: if he lacks the concept of a mistaken judgment, he lacks the notion of a judgment's being corrigible in the first place. And if he does not view his judgments as corrigible, he does not view them *as judgments at all*. Implicit in the concept of judging is the idea of a judgment's being corrigible, that is, that the judge may be mistaken in his judgments, and so the ability to be aware that one is judging implies having the concept of a mistaken judgment. That judging is inherently corrigible is accepted by Stevenson, who suggests that this creature's judgments are corrigible in so far as 'his linguistic responses tend to agree with ours (in situations where we have an equally good view of the states of affairs in question)',[58] but this obscures the most important aspect of saying that a judgment is corrigible, namely, that in saying so one is saying that the judgment *can be corrected*. In effect, it is inherent in the nature of judging that judgments can be rejected upon evidence of their being mistaken. That the creature's judgments can be seen to be mistaken by 'our' linguistic community is not relevant to the question of whether or not they can be seen to be mistaken by *him*. And if he lacks a seems–is distinction which would allow him to regard a judgment as mistaken, then his 'judgments' are not corrigible. Thus they are not judgments at all.

What is essential here is this: to see one's judgments as judgments implies that one sees these judgments as corrigible, as potentially mistaken and subject to correction. And so to be able to deploy the bipolar distinction between judging that 'p' and judging that 'not-p' itself implies having the concept of being mistaken in one's judgments. Similarly, to have the concept of mis-*taking* something to be the case implies having the bipolar distinction as well. And it is worth noting carefully the relationship between corrigibility and the 'seems–is' distinction which underlies the concept 'apparently-p'. A judgment, after all, is an *attempt* to say what is the case: I will judge that 'p' only if I believe 'p' to be the case. And that I view this judgment as such an attempt implies my awareness that it may be a failed attempt, a mis-*taking to be*. How do I describe such a failure, given the nature of judging? Precisely by saying that when I judged that 'p', it *seemed* to be the case that 'p', but *was not* the case. So the concept of corrigibility carries with it an apparatus for explaining failed judgings, and this apparatus *is* the 'seems–is' distinction = the distinction which underlies the concept of 'apparently-p'. The point is that viewing my judgments as judgments is part of a conceptual package-deal that also includes having the concept of corrigibility *and* the 'seems–is' distinction.

By not having a concept of corrigibility, then, our creature cannot reject a judgment as mistaken on the basis of any criteria whatsoever. In fact, the question of criteria cannot even be engaged, because his judgments do not stand in relation to one another: to the extent that he cannot choose between conflicting judgments, he cannot judge his own judgings. And unless there is something which makes it impossible for him to make conflicting judgments, he is bound to confront the dilemma which renders his story incoherent. To say that he need not choose in this case will not do, since his possession of the distinction between 'p' and 'not-p' ensures that he cannot judge a known contradiction to be the case; in effect, his possession of this distinction forces him to choose. In any case, though, we need not worry over how our creature will deal with this dilemma: being an inconsistently described creature, he cannot exist in the first place. Supposedly he is equipped with the bipolar distinction between judging that 'p' and judging that 'not-p', and if he has *this*, it follows that he also has the notion of corrigibility, of having (and possibly correcting) a mistaken judgment. If he has the notion of a mistaken judgment, he also must have the explanatory structure provided by the seems–is distinction—he must be able to judge that 'apparently-p'. But, *contra* Stevenson, he does *not* have the notion of corrigibility, and he was explicitly described as not being able to bring to bear the judgment 'apparently-p'.[59] In a sense, then, Stevenson is right that judging does not require 'a *threefold* distinction between p, not-p, and apparently-p', but this is true only because the *twofold* distinction between the concepts '*p*' and 'not-*p*' itself implies being able to use the concept 'apparently-*p*'. So in a more important sense Stevenson is wrong: if I can make (meta-) judgments to the effect that my judgments *are* judgments, then I do have use of a seems–is distinction as well. Strawson is clearly right, then, that the possibility of self-ascription of experience, in so far as this implies judgment, implies corrigibility, and *that* implies a seems–is distinction in one's conceptual repertoire.

THE OBJECTIVE DEDUCTION: PERCEIVING AND EXPERIENTIAL SELF-ASCRIPTION

Given that we now know that the ability to make judgments at all implies having a seems–is distinction, can we also maintain that judging requires the self-ascription of (at least some) of the judgments made? Before answering too hastily, it is important to note exactly what has—and has not—been established. It was argued above that the *concept* of judgment implies the notions both of a mistaken judgment and of someone doing the judging, and that even though the *ability* to judge does not require having a full-blooded concept of judgment, it does require actually having the concept of a mistaken judgment. None the less, it has not been established that the *ability* to judge requires actually having the notion that judgment requires a judge. To extend the analogy with Plato's case: asserting that a creature could judge without having the concept of a judgment's requiring a judge is like asserting that Meno can go to Larisa without being able to tell Socrates how he does so; asserting that a creature could judge without having the concept of a mistaken judgment is like asserting that Meno can go to Larisa without leaving Athens. The difference lies in the distinction between what is implied by the *concept* of an act and what is implied by the act's *practice*.

Given this qualification, is there any way that self-ascription of experiences can be made out to be necessary for the practice of judging, now that it is clear that the notion of corrigibility and of a seems–is distinction are also necessary aspects of this practice? One way of trying to make good this claim would be to argue that having the concept of a mistaken judgment implies having the concept of judgment's requiring a judge. To view a judgment as mistaken, after all, is not simply to view what the judgment asserts as not being the case: it is to view the judgment as a *failed attempt* at judging what is the case. And being able to view something as an attempt, failed or otherwise, is to view it as an attempt by an agent. Thus the practice of regarding judgments as potentially mistaken is possible only given the ability to apply the concept of a mistake, which is possible only given a working notion of a judge who is mistaken. But this seems to run up against the same objection as did the suggestion that judging implies a judge: that the concept of a mistake implies the concept of someone who makes the mistake does not in itself warrant the assertion that the practice of deciding that a judgment is mistaken requires knowledge of this implication. But there does seem to be a difference between the two cases. When one makes judgments, one says things like 'That is green' or 'Snow is white', such that the judgment itself, in its basic form, need not *point to* the judge. On the other hand, when one asserts that a judgment is mistaken, where 'mistaken' is not taken to mean simply 'not the case' (and as we have seen, it cannot mean only this), then one says things like 'To say that *p* is mistaken' or 'It seemed that *p*, but this was a mistake' or 'It was apparently . . .', all of which fairly explicitly suggest someone's having an experience, making a judgment. Bluntly, one can judge without ever saying 'I judge that . . .', while one cannot judge judgments to be mistaken without bringing the notion of one who commits mistakes very close to the surface indeed. This, of course, does not in any obvious way eliminate the *possibility* of using mistake-talk so guilelessly, but it does suggest its radical implausibility.

Is there any other way of establishing that the possibility of experiential self-ascriptions is implied by the making of perceptual judgments? I think that there is, and that this way is Strawson's own. It is essential to remember what is usually overlooked by critics of the objectivity argument, which is the context of its presentation: the version that most exercises its critics is presented as a refutation of a hypothetical sense-datum theorist. This theorist presupposes that a person's experiences could consist solely of 'essentially disconnected impressions'[60] such as 'a momentary tickling sensation' or a twinge of pain—impressions which are not objective, and which would, as the only constituents of a possible course of experience, refute the thesis of objectivity Kant argues for in the Transcendental Deduction. The sense-datum theorist admits the conceptualizability of experience, but limits his concepts to 'sensory quality concepts'. But this sense-datum experience causes two problems: first, that there seems to be no substance to the idea of a *subject* who has such experiences. Second, 'the hypothesis seems to contain no ground of distinction between the supposed experience of awareness and the particular item which the awareness is awareness of'.[61] Thus the recognitional component in experience, which makes possible the conceptualizability of experience, is threatened with 'absorption into the item recognized'.[62]

This metaphor of 'absorption' has put off, apparently, some critics who should see what it is aiming at: that the problem with tickling sensations is not only that their *esse* is *percipi* but that their *percipi* seems to be merely their *esse*. In other words, in the experience of a twinge there is no object of awareness but merely a way of being aware (in this case, hurting). If all experience requires a 'recognitional component' and an 'item recognized', it is not at all obvious in the case of a twinge what would count as what—in fact, the pain really could be made out to be the recognitional component with as much plausibility as it could be considered to be the item recognized. The point is that sensations of certain kinds defy the fundamental duality of experience which Kant must have to argue successfully for objectivity.

It should be noted, though, that even the sense-datum theorist is unwilling to relinquish the conceptualizability of experience which his tickling sensations put in jeopardy. Similarly, he is unwilling in practice to accept the rejection of the notion of a single consciousness to which his theory seems to commit him. So according to Strawson

the way out is to acknowledge that the recognitional component, necessary to experience, can be present in experience only because of the *possibility* of referring different experiences to one identical subject of them all. Recognition implies the *potential* acknowledgement of the experience ... as being one's own, as sharing with others this relation to the identical self.[63]

The sense-datum theorist admits that experience must include a recognitional component of some sort. Since the nature of the experience precludes such a component in the datum itself, this component must be introduced from elsewhere—and the only 'elsewhere' available is the perceiver himself, who can recognize tickles and twinges *as his*. The virtue of this solution is threefold: (1) it preserves a necessary experiential dichotomy, (2) it reintroduces the role of a single consciousness into experience even of 'essentially disconnected impressions', and (3) by accomplishing (1) and (2)—in which the sense-datum theorist has as much stake as does Kant—it establishes the necessity of the seems–is distinction as an implication of self-ascribing judgments. The key is that even the sense-datum theorist, if he is to hang on to something like the intuition–concept distinction, and to the idea of an experiencing subject who persists throughout the course of experience, must accept as true a premiss which implies the necessity of objectivity, which is precisely what he hopes to deny.

This is the purpose of Strawson's injection of the possibility of self-ascription of experiences into the argument. And the key point here is that if experience is by its nature recognitional, then it must be possible to make a distinction between recognizing and recognized in even the most minimal of experiences. So the deduction of the possibility of experiential self-ascription has two objects: to show that any plausible sense-datum theory (= one which acknowledges conceptualizability) is self-refuting, and to preserve the thesis of conceptualizability from a putative counter-example. Mackie concedes this in part:

I would agree that the recognizing that an experience is of a certain sort, or resembles some remembered earlier experience, must be something other than the experience itself: this recognizing . . . has the experience as its object even where the experience itself has no object. It thus introduces an awareness/object distinction where at first none was allowed. But I cannot see that this has anything to do with the potential *acknowledgement* of the experience as one's own.[64]

Mackie accepts that experience must include a recognitional component, and that certain sensory experiences have no object. But the reason that Mackie sees no need to invoke the possibility of self-ascription here is that, supposedly, these experiences are such that a recognitional component is present, separate from these experiences, which is not in any way a self-ascription of the experiences. But Mackie does not suggest what this recognitional component is, and the only alternative available seems to be that the experience itself is both object of awareness and awareness itself—and it is not terribly clear what it would be to conceive of a tickling sensation taking itself as its object. On the other hand, I can quite easily conceive of self-ascribing, and hence recognizing as an item of experience, such a sensation. Unless there is a third alternative, self-ascription seems the most economical way of preserving a distinction in experience which we are hesitant to abandon. This is the function, then, of the step in Strawson's argument which is said to establish the 'necessary unity of consciousness'.

KANTIAN SELVES AND APPERCEPTION

Is arguing for the 'necessary unity of consciousness' what Strawson is doing in his argument against the sense-datum theorist? At one level, judging from our examination of the argument, it seems that the sense-datum theorist is inclined to *accept* the idea of a single consciousness (and—reluctantly—the idea of self-ascription of experiences). And what, in any case, *is* the 'necessary unity of consciousness'? Obviously there are a number of related terms on the table here, a number that is multiplied by Kant's own usage. As a way of getting at the distinctions between some of the terms Kant uses with regard to the self, I propose to show that Strawson, in arguing for experiential self-ascription, is not, despite the judgment of some of his critics, arguing for 'the necessary unity of consciousness'—at least not in this way.[65]

Stevenson maintains that Strawson argues from the conceptualizability of experience to the 'necessary unity of consciousness', but he rightly says that it is not clear just what is meant by this latter expression. Undertaking an exegesis of Strawson's text, he says the following:

In his original definition ... the unity is just *whatever* is required for the possibility of self-consciousness (and if x is required for y, presumably y implies x) ; he also tells us that unity of consciousness implies the possibility of self-ascription of experiences (which would give us x implies y, and thus logical equivalence). It seems then that we can replace the mysterious thesis of the unity of consciousness by that of the possibility of the self-ascription of experiences.[66]

And the original 'definition' is this: 'that there must be such unity amongst the members of some temporally extended series of experiences as is required for the possibility of self-consciousness, or self-ascription of experiences, on the part of a subject of such experiences'.[67] But Stevenson's demonstration of the equivalence of the necessary unity of consciousness and the possibility of the self-ascription of experiences is, to use a Kantian turn of phrase, paralogistic. As we can see from examining the original definition,

$$\text{necessary unity of consciousness} = \begin{array}{l}\text{the conditions of}\\\text{the possibility of}\\\text{self-ascription of}\\\text{experiences}\end{array}$$

So if it is the case that the necessary unity of consciousness and the possibility of self-ascription of experiences are in fact logically equivalent—as Stevenson says they are—then we should be able to replace the one with the other. Using the above definition, and substituting for the definiens its logical equivalent, we get

$$\begin{array}{l}\text{the possibility of self-ascription}\\\text{of experiences}\end{array} = \begin{array}{l}\textit{the conditions of}\\\text{the possibility of}\\\text{self-ascription of}\\\text{experiences}\end{array}$$

And it is unclear what this could possibly mean, unless it is that this possibility is somehow self-warranting, which would beg the question. So it is reasonable to conclude that the necessary unity of consciousness is the necessary condition (or conditions) of, but is not equivalent to, the possibility of self-ascription of experiences. And, as should be manifest from the context of the argument in question, Strawson is arguing *at this point* for experiential self-ascription. What, then, is the 'necessary unity of consciousness', or in other words, what are the necessary conditions of ascribing experiences to oneself?

There are, I think, two answers to be given here. The first is straightforward, and is supplied by Strawson's argument itself in premiss (5): Strawson says that 'the very minimum' required for such ascriptions is the possession of a seems–is distinction with regard to one's experiential judgments. What is certainly true is that *if* I recognize that making ascriptions is a form of judging, I also must recognize that the practice of ascription is in some way *corrigible*. (And given this recognition, I can also deploy the notion of 'apparently-*p*', yielding Strawson's 'seems–is' distinction as well). It may be objected, of course, that it is inconceivable that I could mistakenly self-ascribe an experience. And that is surely right, if it means that I could not mistakenly think that I am having an experience. But I could ascribe an experience to myself in a mistaken way, or more perspicuously, could misconceive the experience that is incorrigibly my own. Examples abound, but it should suffice to note Austin's case of taking oneself to see a magenta patch when one is in fact seeing a chartreuse patch, because one reverses the meanings of 'magenta' and 'chartreuse'.[68] The point is that ascribing experiences is, again, a matter of ascribing them under a description, and though I cannot be mistaken about my having an experience, I can be quite mistaken about the type of experience I am having. So one of the necessary conditions of self-ascribing experiences is the possession of a notion of corrigibility with regard to one's self-ascriptions.

The second answer is not so straightforward, and is suggested by a remark made by Stevenson:

> after outlining the argument just criticized, Strawson goes on to revise it further, suggesting that what plays the truly fundamental role in Kant's argument is not even the possibility of self-ascription, but something which is a necessary although not perhaps a sufficient condition of that possibility. This is what he mysteriously calls 'transcendental self-consciousness' or 'the necessary reflexiveness of experience' . . .[69]

With the serious qualification that Strawson is not *revising* his argument, since *contra* Stevenson he never equates self-ascription and the necessary unity of consciousness, it is safe to say that this is right. Strawson says explicitly that 'transcendental self-consciousness is not to be *identified* with the possibility of empirical self-ascription . . . but it must be recognized as the basic condition of that possibility'.[70] It seems, then, that two theses emerge from Strawson's account: (1) the necessary unity of consciousness = the necessary conditions of possible self-ascription of experiences, and (2) since the fundamental condition of this possibility is transcendental self-consciousness, it follows that transcendental self-consciousness is the basis of the necessary unity of consciousness. But here Stevenson—understandably—despairs, saying that 'the major problem we are left with is what on earth this transcendental self-consciousness is'. To find out, and thus to do full justice to the objectivity argument, it is necessary, quoting Stevenson, to 'disappear into the mists of Kant's Transcendental Deduction'; it is time to look at some aspects of Kant's own account.

First of all, for Kant there are four principal entities operating in his theory of knowledge which in some way refer to what could, under differing circumstances, be construed to be the self, and if we are to be clear about the various ways Kant thinks one may or may not be conscious of the self, it is essential to be clear about what these entities are. The first is the 'object' of empirical self-consciousness (or empirical apperception), which Kant describes in this way:

Consciousness of self according to the determinations of our state in inner perception is merely empirical, and always changing. No fixed and abiding self can present itself in this flux of inner appearances. Such consciousness is usually named *inner sense*, or *empirical apperception*. (A107)

And 'inner sense' is said to be that 'by means of which the mind intuits itself or its inner state', but which 'yields ... no intuition of the soul itself as an object' (A22/B37). From this, two points about empirical apperception emerge: (1) the mind can be aware of, or intuit, itself in experience but (2) it is not aware of itself as an object. In terms of empirical apperception, one can be conscious of oneself having an experience of such and such a kind, but not have any experiences of *oneself* as an object of experience. It is worth asking whether or not Kant is saying that empirical apperception includes self-ascriptions of intuitions: that is, am I experientially aware not just of 'this such that x' but also, at times, of '*I judge that* "this such that x"'? He does say that empirical apperception yields 'no fixed or abiding self', and so it seems plausible that 'consciousness of the self according to the determinations of our state' means simply *consciousness*: I am conscious of myself in that I am conscious of my experiences, which are in some sense part of myself. Much of what Kant has to say about this is too ambiguous to be of any help. For example, in the Paralogisms he remarks that 'in inner intuition there is nothing permanent, for the "I" is merely the consciousness of my thought' (B413). That he cheerfully alternates between *Bewußtsein* and *Selbstbewußtsein* to mean 'self-consciousness'—as opposed to mere experiential awareness—does little to help resolve these ambiguities. But on this rather penurious interpretation of empirical apperception, when Kant says that

All representations have a necessary relation to a *possible* empirical consciousness. . . . if they did not have this, and if it were altogether impossible to become conscious of them, this would practically amount to an admission of their non-existence. (A117n.)

he is merely underlining an analytic truth: that for experience to be experience it must be such that the experiencing subject is aware of it (where 'being aware of the experience x' = 'is experiencing x'). This seems remarkably trivial, and for it not to be so requires that Kant intend empirical (self)-consciousness to include self-ascriptions of experience. This is further corroborated by the disjunction in Kant's definition of inner sense: 'the mind intuits itself or its inner state' (A22/B37). So empirical apperception implies both experience and some level of conscious awareness of oneself as experiencing (as being part of an activity, and not as an object). A useful way of looking at Kant's empirical apperception, if not pushed too far, is that it includes the range of experience allowed into Hume's 'bundle of perceptions': impressions, ideas, and self-ascriptions (with the proviso that there is no objective self to which these experiences are ascribed).

The second entity Kant refers to which is related to our notion of the self is, simply enough, the man or person. And about persons Kant says little indeed. It is made abundantly clear that, whatever the self of which one is self-conscious may be, Kant does not believe that it is known to be identical with the man. If for no other reason, this is true since (for Kant) the self is not an object of intuition, while the man is such an object. As Kant says in the Antinomies, 'Man is one of the appearances of the sensible world' (A546/B574), something experienced rather than something that—as man—experiences. So in a work that focuses on specifying the conditions of experiencing, rather than on the objects experienced, Kant gives the man roughly the kind of attention he would devote to any other object of intuition, with the result that he practically ignores the man in his account of the self. It is, however, worth noting that Kant leaves room for the possibility that the person (or man) is, at some level, the experiencing subject. He allows that he cannot know 'whether this consciousness of myself would be even possible apart from (my body) . . . and whether, therefore, I could exist merely as thinking being (i.e. without existing in human form)' (B409). Given this consideration, Kant makes one of his brief, rare, and somewhat inconclusive sallies into the mind–body problem (which he calls the problem of 'communion'):

the two kinds of objects thus differ . . . only in so far as one *appears outwardly to the other, and that what, as thing in itself, underlies the appearance of matter, perhaps after all may not be so heterogeneous in character* . . . (B427, emphasis added)

What Kant is leaving outside the bounds of experience, and hence open as a possibility, is in effect Strawson's notion of a person—who has both M-properties and P-properties—as the fundamental character of an experiencing subject. It is less anachronistic, perhaps, to say that Kant is leaving room for a vaguely Spinozistic account of persons, in which mind and body are two *modes* of one thing, the one viewed as thinking, the other as extended.[71] In any case, the main point here is that, for good reasons given the Critical Philosophy, Kant does not take seriously the hypothesis that the self of self-consciousness can be known to be the same as the man: it is a safe guess that ships, houses, and triangles each show up nearly as often in the *Critique* as does man himself.

The third entity we are concerned with is the *noumenal* self, that is, the self as it is in itself and not as it is—or could be—known in experience. To see how this noumenal self operates—or does not operate—in Kant's account, a brief word should be said about Kant's phenomenal–noumenal split. As Allison has pointed out, the 'standard picture' of this dichotomy is that Kant is presenting

a metaphysical theory that affirms the unknowability of the 'real' (things in themselves) and relegates knowledge to the purely subjective realm of representations (appearances). It thus combines a phenomenalist account of what is actually experienced by the mind, and therefore knowable, with the postulation of an additional set of entities which, in terms of the very theory, are unknowable. . . . this postulation is deemed necessary to explain how the mind acquires its representations, or at least the materials for them (their form being 'imposed' by the mind itself . . . Thus, such things must be assumed to exist, even though the theory denies that we have any right to say anything about them (presumably including the claim that they exist).[72]

And there are a number of notorious problems with holding such a 'two-world' view, including its commitment to an excessive subjectivism, its tendency to confuse—as just one example—spatial representation with the representation of space, and its usual corollary, a particularly naïve and problematic phenomenalism. Allison is right, I think, that Kant's own understanding of phenomena and noumena, and the related contrast between the empirical and the transcendental, differs substantially from this interpretation. (Among other things, the mere fact that this account seems to commit Kant to one brand of phenomenalism or another presents us with prima-facie evidence that, whosever view it is, it is certainly not *Kant's*.)[73] Without going into the whole problematic of transcendental idealism at this point, it is important to see, at least briefly, what Kant does mean here. Kant defines phenomena and noumena in this way:

Appearances, so far as they are thought as objects according to the unity of the categories, are called *phenomena*. But if I postulate things which are mere objects of understanding, and which, nevertheless, can be given as such to an intuition, although not to one that is sensible—given therefore *coram intuitu intellectuali*—such things would be entitled *noumena*. (A248–9)

and again, in the second edition,

if we entitle certain objects, as appearances, sensible entities (*phenomena*), then since we thus distinguish the mode in which we intuit them from the nature that belongs to them in themselves, it is implied in this distinction that we place the latter, considered in their own nature, although we do not so intuit them ... in opposition to the former, and that in doing so we entitle them intelligible entities (*noumena*). (B306).

A phenomenon, then, is for Kant an object as it is represented by us, given the nature of, and constraints on, our modes of experience. A noumenon, on the other hand, is, as Allison says, 'the epistemological concept *par excellence*, characterizing an object, of whatever ontological status, considered *qua* correlate of a nonsensible manner of cognition'.[74] As Matthews aptly puts it,

whereas Berkeley was making an *ontological* point about the types of things there are, Kant was making an *epistemological* point about the limits of human knowledge. Limits are set to what we can know by the nature of human experience: in order for a human being to have experience of the world, and hence to have empirical knowledge, his senses must be affected by things, he must see these things as in space and time, and he must be able to describe his experience in terms of certain concepts ...[75]

The concept of the noumenon, then, is the concept of an object considered apart from those ways in which that object could be represented by us; thus, says Kant, it is for us at best 'an unknown something' (A256/B312). Bluntly, and by Kant's own definition, we can have no experience of an object as noumenon, for to do so would require having experience of something in a way distinct from the ways in which we can have experience in the first place. And it is crucial to note that this in no way implies that noumena are peculiar, mysterious, or occult entities: they are objects, conceived as such apart from our possible experience of them. Thus the point, in large measure, of Kant's phenomenon–noumenon dichotomy is as a prescription for a bit of epistemological therapy, a reminder that what we can know and sensibly talk about is importantly constrained by our ways of knowing—and that the view *sub specie aeternitatis* is just not available to us.

What, then, of the self as noumenon, the self as distinct from the way or ways in which it is experienced by us? Of course, Kant's official view has to be that we can know nothing whatsoever about the noumenal self. And for the most part Kant abides by this official view:

> were I to enquire whether *the soul in itself* is of spiritual nature, the question would have no meaning. In employing such a concept I not only abstract from corporeal nature, but from nature in general, that is, from all predicates of any possible experience . . . (a684/b712)

Indeed, the main point of the Paralogisms is to defuse the attempts of rational psychologists to know the nature of the self prior to, or detached from, all experience. Kant says that if these attempts were to succeed, 'it would be a great stumbling-block . . . the one unanswerable objection, to our whole critique' (b409), in that it would demonstrate that the bounds of knowledge go beyond experience. That being said, it must be admitted that Kant appears to do a bit of stumbling himself. He seems at times to see the experiencing subject as 'the tangential point of contact between the field of noumena and the world of appearances'.[76] One example should suffice, startling as it is, coming from the author of the devastating critique of the Paralogisms of Pure Reason:

> Man . . . who knows all the rest of nature solely through the senses, knows himself also through pure apperception . . . He is thus to himself, on the one hand phenomenon, and on the other hand . . . a purely intelligible object. (a546–7/b574–5)

And, of course, a 'purely intelligible object' on Kant's own view is accessible only to God. Kant does not make the rather strikingly heretical inference available to him here, and it is tempting to regard such remarks as unfortunate lapses—but the issue is too important to evade in this way. For the present, however, the official view must suffice: a good deal more will be said later about Kant's views of the noumenal self, when the self, isolated from our experience of it, takes—or tries to take—centre stage, in the Paralogisms.

The fourth entity to which Kant refers which relates to the

intuitive notion of the self is that which he calls the 'I think' or, more memorably, 'this I or he or it (the thing) which thinks' (A346/B404). Kant says 'It must be possible for the "I think" to accompany all my representations; for otherwise something would be represented in me which could not be thought at all' (B131). This appears to be the same statement that Kant makes with regard to representation's being necessarily related to empirical apperception, suggesting that all experiences imply at least the possibility of being self-ascribed. But in fact the role of the 'I think' is not that of empirical self-ascription, if by this is meant such reflexive experiential judgments as 'I hear music' or 'I am in pain'. First of all, the 'I think', according to Kant, 'in all consciousness must be one and the same' (B132), it must be a 'bare representation' (A117n.), and it seems strange to suggest the 'I' of empirical self-ascriptions is not specific in some way to the individual experiencing subject. Further, while Kant indicates that in inner sense 'the mind intuits itself', he says that the 'I think' 'is not itself an experience, but the form of apperception, which belongs to and precedes every experience' (A354). So it is essential to avoid the temptation to conflate the representation 'I think' with the empirical use of 'I' which, Kant implies, is a determination of inner sense, and thus is coloured, or even constituted, by the contingencies of one's experience. Kant actually makes this distinction explicit in Section 16 of the Transcendental Deduction in B: he says that the representation 'I think' is called '*pure apperception*, to distinguish it from empirical apperception, or, again, *original apperception*, because it is that self-consciousness which, while generating the representation "I think" . . . cannot itself be derived from any further representation' (B132). So the 'I think' does not involve any notion of the self which is derived from observation of one's mental states. Clearly, then, Kant's 'I think' which 'must accompany all my representations' is not the 'I' of experiential self-ascription.

What, though, is this 'I'? Consider another comment by Kant in Section 16, that 'The unity of this apperception (= the "I think") I likewise entitle the *transcendental* unity of self-consciousness' (B132). The 'I think' is at the heart of the transcendental unity of apperception, which Strawson says plays the fundamental role in Kant's argument, and which Stevenson professes, with some justice, to be an utter mystery. In what way does the 'I think' function in the unity of apperception? Its function, which should come as no surprise at this point, is to serve as the (necessary) subject of the synthesis of experience. Again, for my representations to be taken up into a synthesis which will yield intelligible experience, they must be brought together *as mine*: they must be thought as belonging to one and the same subject. This is made explicit by Kant in his statement that 'we demand this absolute unity of the subject of a thought, only because otherwise we could not say, "I think" (the manifold in one representation)' (A354). What is extraordinarily significant here is Kant's bracketing of the representation's content after the expression 'I think', suggesting that the 'I think' serves to unite various contents in an experience—and in a course of experiences—by referring them to the same experiencing subject. And as has been shown, there are a number of types of mental synthesis for Kant, ranging from the synthesis of elements in a sentence or arithmetical operations to the synthesis in which images are reproduced, and even to what Kant calls the figurative synthesis, or 'synthetic influence of the understanding upon inner sense' (B154), which allows us to represent to ourselves the intuitions of time and space themselves: given the role of time and space as forms of intuition, there is a sense in which synthesis *prefigures* all experience. Roughly, for Kant synthesis is required whenever the mind has to bring together different contents in a synchronic representation, as well as when the mind must connect different representations diachronically, as in the case of reproduced images in memory. And in all of these cases it is essential that the different contents be synthesized as experienced by a single subject.

It is important that Kant does *not* make the claim that our experiences are experienced by a self which *in itself* is unitary. If we recall the constraints on talk about the noumenal self, it is clear that for him to say this would be to push knowledge beyond the bounds of experience. Rather, he is saying that for experience to be possible it must be *as that of* a single consciousness which brackets all one's experiences together into a unified whole. That there *is* a single unitary *self* underlying this *representation* of a single unitary consciousness is something that cannot be known.[77] Again, this representation is distinguished from that *empirical* representation of oneself that occurs in reflexive experiential ascription. Not only is the 'I' of the 'I think' not determined or characterized by the contingencies of actual experience, but this 'I' must also be present in *all* experiences, rather than just a possible accompaniment to any given experience (which is, presumably, the case with regard to empirical self-ascriptions). If all experiences were not viewed as had by a single consciousness, it would be impossible to 'run through and hold together' one's experiences. The 'I think', then, is for Kant a way of indicating the necessary *mode* of unitary experience—*as had by* a unitary self—rather than a kind of self to which we refer in experiential self-awareness. This should make more clear one of Kant's most curious comments regarding the 'I think':

it must not be forgotten that the bare representation 'I' in relation to all other representations (the collective unity of which it makes possible) is transcendental consciousness. Whether this representation is clear (empirical consciousness) or obscure, or even *whether it ever actually occurs*, does not here concern us. But the possibility of the logical form of all knowledge is necessarily conditioned by relation to this apperception *as a faculty*. (A117n., first emphasis mine)

Kant is saying that whether or not the 'I think' occurs in empirical consciousness is unimportant and belies its actual function, which is not as a representation to be intuited but rather as a mode of experiencing, namely experiencing *as a* single consciousness. Whether or not the experiencing subject is in fact single in this sense, and even whether or not one ever has an experience of oneself as a single consciousness, is not ultimately relevant to Kant's point, which is rather that to have ordered experience, one's experience must be brought together *as if* it were had by such a subject. And this mode of experiencing is a necessary condition not only of unified experience itself, but also of experiential self-ascriptions of the type considered in discussions of the objectivity argument. As Kant says, empirical consciousness is 'grounded in' pure apperception (A115–16).

This, then, is the 'original (or transcendental) self-consciousness', which, 'while it is not equivalent to the possibility of self-ascription of experiences . . . yet . . . does represent the fundamental basis of (this) possibility'.[78] Strawson's distinction between these two kinds of consciousness as the distinction between 'This is how things are experienced *by me* as being' (empirical self-ascription, 'personal' self-consciousness) and 'This is how things are experienced as being' (transcendental self-consciousness) is illuminating in that it points out the lack of a full-blooded *person*-concept in transcendental apperception: as Kant says, the 'I' of the 'I think' may never be thought at all, and the key to its existence is its existence as a *function* of consciousness (or, in Kant's unfortunate usage, as a faculty), that of a logical subject which groups experiential contents. Strawson's distinction also reinforces Kant's own claim that any notion of *personal* self-consciousness is logically parasitical in part on the functional notion of a logical subject of experience.

For Strawson, of course, transcendental self-consciousness is not explicitly a matter of a logical subject *per se* but rather is that aspect of experience which 'provide (s) room for the thought of experience itself'.[79] Charging Kant with the excesses of 'transcendental psychology', he says that

> Of [synthesis] I have so far said nothing. I have treated the Deduction as an *argument*, which proceeds . . . to the conclusion that a certain objectivity and a certain unity are necessary conditions of the possibility of experience. And such an argument it is. But it is also an essay in the imaginary subject of transcendental psychology.[80]

Synthesis, then, is presumably part of transcendental psychology. And certainly Strawson has as his goal the reconstruction of Kant's deduction of objectivity without relying on the notion of synthesis. But what is 'transcendental psychology', and how does Strawson see synthesis as fitting into it? He says that

> Since Kant regards the necessary unity and connectedness as being . . . the product of the mind's operations, he feels himself obliged to give some account of those operations. [This] is obtained by thinking of the necessary unity of experience as produced by our faculties . . . out of impressions . . . themselves unconnected and separate; and this process of producing unity is called by Kant 'synthesis'.[81]

And Strawson goes on to argue that with regard to 'the theory of synthesis' 'we can claim no empirical knowledge of its truth'. But Kant's theory of synthesis is not intended to be *empirically* justified; to see this, we should note two points about what Kant is doing in the Subjective Deduction. The first is that in a sense Kant is not doing transcendental psychology when he describes the various kinds of synthesis. Rather, he is undertaking a very sophisticated pheno- menology, a close analysis of the actual forms of experience, of the ways in which our spatio-temporal manifolds are structured. And the second aspect of Kant's project is this: within the context of this phenomenology he is attempting to show what must be the case for these experiences to be structured as they are (thus a *transcendental* psychology). And again, part of what must be the case, given the phenomenology of our experience, is that our experience be had as that of a unitary subject, or synthesis could not occur at all. As Strawson points out, 'Kant regards the . . . connectedness of experience as being . . . the product of the mind's operations'—but these 'operations' themselves depend on the synthetic unity of apperception. But this (transcendental) investigation of the necessary conditions of having experiences structured as ours are would presumably lead to synthetic *a priori* rather than *empirical* knowledge claims. Of course, Kant's phenomenological account itself must be presumed to make empirical claims, but these are by no means controversial. I suspect that what Strawson does find to be devoid of empirical support are claims about the mysterious 'faculties' or 'operations of the mind' that Kant talks about so freely. Certainly Kant's terminology is not perspicuous. But as Walker has pointed out,

Some people react violently to this talk of faculties. . . . It would be more reasonable to conclude that the faculty terminology is not taken seriously; Kant is succumbing to the temptation to be scientifically fashionable by accommodating Tetens' recent psychological distinctions. Besides which, what more can really be meant by the talk of faculties than that the mind performs these various operations . . . ?[82]

So, even given a good deal of sympathy with Strawson's distrust of Kant's rather mysterious terminology,[83] it must be remembered that if we discount the importance of the synthetic function of the 'I think', it is not clear how experience itself is possible, or what it is *in* experience that provides room for the idea *of* experience.[84] Kant's theory of synthesis, and more particularly his account of the necessity of the synthetic function of the 'I think' of transcendental apperception, is integral not merely to the Subjective Deduction but to the Transcendental Deduction as a whole.

JUDGMENT, SYNTHESIS, AND OBJECTIVITY

If Kant's theory of synthesis (and thus the Subjective Deduction) is not to be dismissed, though, we must consider what relation, if any, there is between this part of the Transcendental Deduction and the objectivity argument (the Objective Deduction)? To see what is true here, it will be necessary to suggest one way that Kant's *own* deduction of objectivity might go. Kant begins, as we have seen, with the conceptualizability of experience, that experience involves the fundamental duality of intuition and concept. But if we are to conceptualize our experience (bring intuitions under concepts), then we must be able to synthesize, 'run through and hold together', our experience, both in terms of mere sensory intakes being ordered (in inner sense) in such a way as will yield determinate intuitions, and in terms of being able to perform the reproduction of intuitions and concepts in the understanding. As Kant says, 'all combination—be we conscious of it or not . . . is an act of the understanding. To this act the general title "synthesis" may be assigned.' This synthesis requires that all representations be thought as had by a 'single consciousness', or else they could not all be brought together in one experience, the result being 'as many-coloured and diverse a self' as is found in the diversity of the (necessarily unrelated) experiences (B134). This bracketing of experience as had by a single consciousness is the function of the 'I think', the 'bare representation' of the transcendental unity of apperception: transcendental because without the attribution of experience to a unitary subject it could not, again, be *experience* at all.

At this point, having established the transcendental unity of apperception, Kant states that 'the possibility of the logical form of all knowledge (has as its necessary condition relation to) this apperception *as a faculty*' (A117n.). What is this logical form which is conditioned by the ever-present 'I think'? We know that 'a concept is always, as regards its form, something universal which serves as a rule' (A106), so that bringing intuitions under concepts is a matter of rule-following. Specifically, however, it is that form of rule-following called *judging*: we judge an intuition to be an instance of such-and-such a concept. As Kant says in the *Prolegomena*'s brief summary of the Transcendental Deduction, 'Thinking . . . is the same as judging, or referring representation to judgments in general.'[85] So conceptual experience is judgmental to the extent that we experience things as being of certain kinds. And this does not merely hold for intuitions subsumed under concepts: intuitions themselves are not for Kant 'bare particulars', not, as Rorty describes them, 'something which we are aware of without being aware of it under any description'.[86] We do not intuit a bare 'this', but rather a 'this blue pen' or 'this loud sound', in which the concept informs the intuition—admittedly to a greater or lesser extent—as it is experienced. For Kant, all our thought is of particular *somethings* experienced *such that* they are thought of as being of *such a kind*. Considering Kant's theory of the synthesis of imagination, Strawson makes this point:

> the thought (or, as Kant might prefer, the concept) is alive in the perception just as it is in the image. The thought of something as an x . . . is alive in the perception of it as an x . . . just as the thought of an x . . . is alive in the having of an image of an x . . . This is what is sometimes now expressed in speaking of the *intentionality* of perception, as of imaging. But the idea is older than *this* application of that terminology, for the idea is in Kant.[87]

Experience is by its very nature intentional, and in so far as it is intentional it is judgmental. This intentionality is underscored by Kant's representation of the transcendental unity of apperception by the judgmental form 'I think'—when in the Paralogisms he refers to the transcendental 'I' as the determining subject of experiences, it is as logical subject of experiential judgment. In this way is 'the logical form of experience' conditioned by the 'I think' as a 'faculty' (or, less contentiously, as a logical function).

If, though, all experience is judgmental, then it must already imply corrigibility. If we are to have conceptual experience, then, this necessitates that we be capable of making judgments. To be capable of making judgments, we must have a working notion of a mistaken judgment (in the case of perceptual judgments, a 'mis-taking'). And this implies that we must have the notion of making mistakes in experience, of taking something to be what it is not, and also a generic explanation of such mistakes = the distinction between being p and apparently being p. Since even our most minimal experiences are for Kant intentional, and thus judgmental, this notion of mistaken judgments must apply throughout the range of experience. But the only way it can do this is if the 'synthetic unity of the manifold of appearances according to rules'—that is, the synthesis of appearances under concepts—is produced by the use of *object-concepts* to structure the appearances (A126–7). Kant says that 'the object is viewed as that which prevents our modes of knowledge from being haphazard or arbitrary' (A104); and it is by the use of object-concepts—concepts of something whose *esse* is distinguished from its *percipi*—that it is possible to provide experience with a seems–is distinction, and thereby makes it possible for us to have conceptualized experience at all. Thus Kant establishes the thesis that experience necessarily involves concepts of objects. And now it is possible to offer a tentative answer to the question, 'What is the necessary unity of consciousness?': it is Kant's way of expressing the insight which suffuses the Transcendental Deduction to the point of making it obscure, namely, that experience requires *two* unities rather than one. For experience to be synthesized as a whole, there must be represented one single consciousness to which all experiences are attributed (= the transcendental unity of apperception). But for experience to be conceptual, it must be experience of a world thought under object-concepts. Kant expresses this, through a mist of transcendental psychologisms, by saying that experience requires

an objective ground . . . which constrains us to regard all appearances as data of the senses that must be associable in themselves and subject to universal rules of a thoroughgoing connection in their reproduction. This objective ground of all association of appearances I entitle their *affinity*. It is nowhere to be found save in the principle of the unity of apperception. (A122)

And to put Kant's 'necessary unity of consciousness' in more contemporary dress, we can turn to Strawson's summary of Kant's general conclusion: 'that any course of experience of which we can form a coherent conception must be, potentially, the experience of a self-conscious subject and, as such, must have such internal, concept-carried connectedness as to constitute it (at least in part) a course of experience of an objective world, conceived of as determining the course of that experience itself'.[88]

It is far from clear that the argument presented here, in which judgment plays a major role, is an exact, much less definitive, reading of Kant's objectivity argument. One observation that should give us pause is that this argument can be read in such a way as to make the transcendental unity of apperception completely otiose in so far as the argument aims at proving the objectivity thesis (which is essentially accomplished by going directly from the notion of the conceptualizability of experience to the intentionality of experience, then to the objectivity implied by the practice of judging). This bypass of transcendental apperception is not necessarily a problem, however. First, Kant does establish the transcendental unity of apperception, in order (plausibly) to refute Hume's attack on the continuant self and to make an important point regarding the necessary conditions of an experience as complex as our own (the necessity, that is, of some functions of synthesis). Second, that transcendental apperception is superfluous to the objectivity argument itself is consonant with Kant's much-cited comment in the Preface to the *Critique* that the Subjective Deduction 'does not form an essential part of [my chief purpose]' in the Transcendental Deduction (Axvii). That the Subjective Deduction is preserved in this account as still being 'of great importance'—which Kant also says in Axvii, and which is usually *not* cited—in demonstrating the other necessary condition of experience, should now be clear. If, given this, Kant can establish the objectivity thesis without direct appeal to transcendental apperception, then his argument is certainly more spare.[89] And it seems clear from this account both that he *would* so establish the objectivity thesis, and that he *can* do so—using a similar strategy to that which Strawson uses in his much-maligned 'Objectivity Argument'.[90]

Before proceeding to a consideration of how Kant's account of the self is applied and developed in the Paralogisms, it may be useful to summarize the results so far obtained: I take Kant at his word regarding the existence of a Subjective and an Objective Deduction. Regarding the Subjective Deduction, I argue that what Kant is really doing there is analysing the relation between the synthesis of representations and the necessary conditions of the representation of the self as a continuant subject. As Kant makes clear, that I am able to perceive each member of a sequence of images does not in itself establish that I can represent the sequence as a sequence of related images: such a representation of a sequence must itself come from something beyond the mere addition of successive images. Hence Kant's first major claim in the Subjective Deduction: for experience to be possible at all it must be brought together and unified in time—in short, it must be synthesized. And Kant's second claim is that, given that experience must be synthesized (or taken up into a synthesis of representations which will be intelligible), it must be brought together as the experience of a continuant subject. Kant's point is that unless a succession of representations can be thought to be representations had by one and the same subject, there is simply no foundation for claiming that they are related in experience at all. It follows that what Kant means by the 'transcendental unity of apperception' is, at least in part, the necessary representation of the experiencing subject as a continuant and unitary subject, and that it it is this subject which makes possible the synthesis of experiential contents; this synthesis is in turn necessary for experience to be intelligible at all. For Kant, the judgment that the self is unitary across time (the analytic unity of apperception) is itself derived from the fact that experience is represented as had by a unitary subject (the synthetic unity of apperception). Here, it is crucial to note the significance of Kant's distinction between the transcendental unity of apperception and *empirical* apperception, which is, in effect, Hume's bundle of perceptions. It is only the latter of which Kant says we can have direct awareness; thus Kant accounts for Hume's denial of a continuant self. But Kant does not give up the game to Hume, and he presses two points against him to devastating effect: that for experience to be experience it must be systematic, and that for experience to be systematic it must be represented to be the experience of a unitary continuant subject.

Kant begins the Objective Deduction by asserting the necessary conceptualizability of experience: for Kant intuitions are conceptual, involve a bringing of experience under concepts, and even the barest intuition (or singular representation of a 'this-such') itself has the logical form of a judgment. He argues that if all experience is conceptual, then it is also judgmental and thus implies corrigibility. But experience can be so structured only if 'the synthesis of appearances under concepts' is structured by the use of object-concepts, concepts of entities whose *esse* and *percipi* are not necessarily identical. It is only given such concepts that corrigibility, and a seems–is distinction, are coherent concepts—and without these concepts, the notion of judgment itself becomes untenable. Thus Kant demonstrates that experience necessarily involves knowledge of objects. And it is worth remembering that (1) he demonstrates *this* necessity independently of, but in parallel with, the necessity of the representation of a unitary experiencing subject, and (2) both necessities are demonstrated by analyses of what is presupposed by our ability to bring together, or synthesize, diverse experiences.

Given this account of the epistemic self as it is presented in the Transcendental Deduction, we can now turn to the Paralogisms themselves.

2

The Subjects of the First Paralogism

I N the Paralogisms of Pure Reason, Kant undertakes a thorough and painstaking critique of several arguments which purport to deduce certain *a priori* truths concerning the actual properties of the self: which traffic, that is, in the illegitimate methods of rational psychology. Kant's historical interlocutors here are rarely obvious, and, with the exception of Moses Mendelssohn in the Second Paralogism in B, never certain. The task of ferreting out these historical interlocutors is further complicated by the fact that, on presumably architectonic grounds, Kant forces each of the main arguments here into the form of a fallacious syllogism, or paralogism, rather than presenting the argument in its author's own formulation. And these arguments are presented not merely as deductive fallacies but as deductive fallacies of a very specific kind, a *sophisma figurae dictionis*, a syllogism which fails because of an ambiguous middle term. Kant is asking us to accept rather a lot here: he not only avoids, for the most part, telling us the sources of the arguments of rational psychology, he also suggests that these arguments all commit the same logical error. In partial justification of this approach, or at least of Kant's lack of textual documentation, it is appropriate to note that most of the arguments Kant deals with in the Paralogisms—or formal variants of these arguments— demonstrably have long and distinguished philosophical histories, and to attribute them to specific philosophers would obscure their more general, and for Kant pernicious, appeal.[1]

What, though, is a paralogism in the first place? In Kant's lectures on logic, compiled from notes and published by Jäsche in 1800, he defines a paralogism in this way:

A syllogism, which is false as to form, though it has the same appearance as a correct deduction, is called a false deduction (*fallacia*). Such a deduction is a paralogism, in so far as one thereby deceives oneself; a sophism, so far as one thereby tries with intent to deceive others.[2]

For Kant, then, a paralogism, generally speaking, is any deductive fallacy which has at least the initial appearance of a valid syllogism and which—interestingly—is not recognized by its author as a fallacy but is presented, without intent to deceive, as a valid deduction.[3] Plausibly, Kant takes the term and its meaning from Aristotle, for whom 'paralogism' seems to refer to any fallacious syllogism, whether constructed with sophistical intent or not.[4] In these lecture-notes, Kant goes on to mention as one example of such a fallacious syllogism the '*sophisma figurae dictionis*, in which the *medius terminus* is given different meanings [in verschiedener Bedeutung genommen wird]'.[5] Aristotle clearly expresses the source of this particular fallacy of ambiguity: 'The error comes about in the case of arguments that depend on homonymy and ambiguity because we are unable to distinguish the various senses (for some terms it is not easy to distinguish, e.g. one, being, and sameness).'[6] As we shall see, it is this inability to distinguish the senses of certain terms—at least the senses certain terms must have, given the Critical Philosophy—that Kant sees as the source of the errors of the rational psychologists. How, then, does Kant apply this aspect of traditional Aristotelian syllogistic to his attack on rational psychology?

THE FORMAL STRUCTURE OF THE PARALOGISMS

Again, the general form of the Paralogisms is that of a syllogism which is fallacious because it has an ambiguous middle term. The major premiss of this syllogism is a categorial proposition, one that Kant regards as both analytically true and conceptually indispensable. The minor premiss is a proposition asserting that the soul itself instantiates whatever property is given in the major premiss as the definition of the categorial concept, and this property itself constitutes the middle term of the syllogism. It is then concluded that the soul falls under the categorial concept defined in the major premiss, since it has that property ascribed, by definition, to the categorial concept in the major premiss. The ambiguity which vitiates this syllogism lies, according to Kant, in the confusion between being an X and being represented as an X. In other words, the Paralogism is supposedly of the form

$$X(\phi X \rightarrow \psi X)$$
$$\phi a$$
$$\psi a$$

But, says Kant, the term 'ϕ' is used differently in the two premisses such that in the minor premiss what is properly asserted is not that *a is ϕ* but rather that *a is necessarily represented as being ϕ*. But this is a different predicate from that used in the major premiss. Designating 'represented as ϕ' by 'ϕ!', we get the following disambiguated syllogism:

$$(X)(\phi X \rightarrow \psi X)$$
$$(\phi!)a$$
$$(\psi!)a$$

which is clearly not valid. Kemp Smith says that in 'the major premiss the middle term is used as referring to real existence, in the minor only as expressive of the unity of consciousness'.[7] In other words (and avoiding any problems raised by 'real existence'), the Paralogism trades on a misconstruction of a claim about how the experiencing subject is necessarily represented (an analytic judgment about the 'I' of the 'I think') into a claim about the properties actually possessed by the subject (and thus a synthetic *a priori* judgment about the nature of the self). It is this misconstruction that vitiates the syllogism, and also is that from which the syllogism derives its appeal for the rational psychologist, whose goal is to derive synthetic *a priori* judgments about the (for Kant, noumenal) self. As we shall see, this form is clearly followed in the first two Paralogisms, and is more or less plausibly that of the third and fourth as well. Kant's best statement of this form is in the second edition:

In the major premiss we speak of a being that can be thought in general . . . But in the minor premiss we speak of it only in so far as it regards itself, as subject, simply in relation to thought and the unity of consciousness . . . Thus the conclusion is arrived at fallaciously, *per sophisma figurae dictionis*. (B411)

It is important to note that on this construction of the Paralogisms, there is a way of reading the premisses such that (*a*) they are both true, and the syllogism is invalid due to having no common middle term, and (*b*) to have a common middle term, one or the other of the premisses must be false, due to its attribution of a property which (once disambiguated) can be seen not to apply to its putative subject. It is also worth noting that Kant finds the conclusion to be true given one of the disambiguated meanings of the middle term, but (obviously) not given the other meaning of the middle term, and—importantly—not as the demonstrated conclusion of a valid syllogism.

As should now be clear, Kant has given us numerous ways to be misled by his text. Some of these misreadings are obstructive to a better understanding of what Kant is getting at, while others are in their own way quite productive, to the extent that, when exposed, they reveal Kant's own often very confusing ambiguous usages. A misreading of this latter sort is given by Bennett in his account of Kant's First Paralogism.[8] I intend to consider Bennett's reading of the First Paralogism, to present (rather unfashionably) a commentary on a commentary, hoping that by understanding the sources of Bennett's errors we will also see what Kant is actually doing in the First Paralogism, and in this way we will understand the basis of Kant's attack on those views of the self which, for Kant, are part and parcel of rational psychology.

Regarding the form of the First Paralogism, Bennett rejects Kant's claim that the formal fallacy of the Paralogisms is that the conclusion is derived *per sophisma figurae dictionis*: 'Although Kant . . . tries to argue that the argument is invalidated by a vitiating ambiguity, that is not his most considered or his best view of the matter.'[9] And given this rejection of Kant's own account of the fallacy, Bennett does not suggest what ambiguity Kant believes is operating in this Paralogism, but goes on to propose an alternative. What is important, Bennett says, is that we don't 'misunderstand and inflate its conclusion in a certain way'. What I take this to mean is that, *contra* Kant, the Paralogism is in fact a valid argument—and ostensibly one with true premises—and that the problem arises from a misconstruction of the content of the conclusion. In effect, then, the ambiguity is shifted from the middle term of the premises to something (as yet undetermined) in the conclusion which leaves the conclusion itself vulnerable to misconstruction. On the basis of this approach, Bennett asks two questions: first, what is the argument itself, and second, in what way would its conclusion be inflated so that it gives aid and comfort to the rational psychologist?

To see the direction of Bennett's analysis, it is useful to look at the First Paralogism in Kant's formal presentation. It is as follows:

That, the representation of which is the *absolute subject* of our judgments and cannot therefore be employed as determination of another thing, is *substance*.
I, as thinking being, am the *absolute subject* of all my possible judgments, and this representation of myself cannot be employed as predicate of any other thing.
Therefore I, as thinking being (soul), am *substance*. (A348)

Bennett finds no immediate difficulty in the first premiss, since it is merely equivalent to Kant's definition of substance at B186, with the addition of the word 'absolute'. It is rather the second premiss which must shed light on the character of the Paralogism; since the first premiss is merely a definition of substance, and the conclusion the assertion that soul is substance, it must be the second premiss which carries the weight of the argument. Bennett points out that this premiss has two clauses, each of which requires interpretation. He begins with the second clause, 'this representation of myself cannot be employed as predicate of any other thing', and says that 'This . . . reminds us that substances *must* be handled substantivally whereas non-substances *need not* be.'[10] As Bennett points out, in the case of non-substances we have a choice of whether or not to refer to them using grammatical substantives: 'the duration of the fight' as opposed to 'how long the men fought'; presumably we do not have the same options when dealing with substances, which must be treated as such. So if my 'representation of myself' must be treated substantivally, then it is a representation of a substance. Since (to get the desired conclusion) the second premiss presumably must link the defining characteristic(s) of a substance with those of my soul, it seems that Bennett's statement that 'substances must be handled substantivally whereas non-substances need not be' is a restatement of the first premiss. The second clause of the second premiss, then, asserts that my representation of myself must be treated substantivally. And, if being necessarily handled substantivally is a sufficient condition of being a substance, then my representation of myself is the representation of a substance.

It should be pointed out that it is not entirely clear exactly what Bennett intends by 'handling something substantivally or adjectivally', or by his claim that substances must be handled substantivally. It seems that he could be making two distinct claims here: (1) that substances, unlike non-substances, simply cannot be referred to by expressions which are not grammatical substantives, or (2) that we are in some way conceptually incapable of representing a substance as an attribute or property of something else. Neither is argued for by Bennett. The first claim, I suspect, is either false or at least vulnerable to the charge of being at best contingently—and somewhat parochially—true, appealing only to the characteristics of certain languages; the second claim, which I believe is the one intended by Bennett, seems to call for a transcendental argument. But we are given no such argument, and this leads us to a related question: why must my representation of myself be substantival? Bennett says that

My concept of myself cannot play an adjectival role, because the difference between the substantival and the adjectival handling of something is a difference between two ways in which I can handle my data. Within the Cartesian basis, any question about how anything is to be handled is a question about how I am to handle it, and so every such question has a substantival 'I' as a kind of substratum or framework.[11]

But it does not follow from the fact that I handle all my data that I cannot have an adjectival way of handling some putative datum which represents me, even though it is granted that this handling of the datum has 'as a kind of substratum or framework' a substantival 'I'. It is not in question that we *don't*, as a matter of course, do this—the question is rather why we *can't* do this. Were we to have an adjectival way of handling a self-datum, then the self would be something which is in fact handled both substantivally and adjectivally—and this, by Bennett's definition of substance, is not impossible, but is in fact definitive of non-substances, which can be handled either way. I suspect that Bennett's point is that any putatively adjectival handling of my self would have to occur within a context which presupposes that my self is in fact substantial (he does say that 'I cannot escape giving my concept of myself a substantival role, and so I must regard myself as substance'). If this is the case, then the definition of substance could be amended along these lines:

Substances, unlike non-substances, must either be handled substantivally or handled adjectivally within the scope of an instance of their substantival handling.

Of course, Bennett does not say why any adjectival handling of my self-concept must occur within the scope of a substantival self-concept. It is important to underscore that the point is not whether or not we *do* represent ourselves adjectivally, or even whether or not we can *conceive* of doing so. Rather, what must be shown is that we *must* represent ourselves only substantivally. This Bennett does not attempt to do. Kant does—and we will see the importance of Kant's attempt to show this representational necessity.

For the sake of argument, however, I will concede to Bennett the substantival–adjectival distinction as definitive of substance, and the thesis that 'my concept of myself cannot play an adjectival role'. This gives us what I will call Bennett's S-interpretation of the First Paralogism:

> If the representation of *x* cannot be handled adjectivally, then *x* is a substance;
> The representation of myself cannot be handled adjectivally;
> So I am a substance.[12]

This interpretation is 'mildly confirmed', says Bennett, by two of Kant's own comments about the Paralogisms. First, he says that 'all the [first] paralogism really establishes is that "in thinking my existence, I cannot employ myself, save as subject of the judgment"'.[13] Second, 'the interpretation also fits Kant's general thesis that the Paralogisms rest upon genuine insights into the formal structure of the Cartesian basis' (where the 'Cartesian basis' refers to 'the intellectual situation in which one attends to nothing but one's own mind and its states').[14] There is some plausibility, then, in viewing this as the argument which Kant views (1) as valid, and (2) as having an inflatable conclusion. Scepticism stemming from the fact that it is an argument which no rational psychologist ever actually advanced is dispelled by Bennett, who says that 'perhaps Kant thought that some philosophers had been nudged towards viewing the soul as a substance by a subliminal awareness of' this argument.

Two qualms about this interpretation should be expressed. The first I will mention in passing: it does seem odd that Kant would defuse an argument never argued, and to suggest that he perhaps viewed this argument as one which seduced 'some philosophers' is to speculate about certain of Kant's speculations (for which we have no independent evidence) about the tacit intellectual seductions of unnamed philosophers. Second, Bennett's interpretation completely ignores the first clause of Kant's second premiss, that 'I, as a thinking being, am the absolute subject of all my possible judgments.' Bennett concedes this, and preserves his interpretation by dismissing the clause as unnecessary and, indeed, the result of a confusion. Bennett does not present these claims without argument, and it is necessary that we examine these arguments closely to see that Kant's use of this clause is actually neither confused nor unnecessary, and must be understood for us to grasp the source of the error Kant exposes in each of the Paralogisms.

Bennett considers four possible interpretations of Kant's claim that 'I, as a thinking being, am the absolute subject of all my possible judgments.' The first interpretation, in which Kant makes a radically solipsistic claim, is—as Bennett says—clearly implausible, as is the second, reading Kant as having phenomenalized all his language except the substantival 'I'.[15] The third interpretation seems more promising: Bennett says that 'the clause reflects Kant's doctrine about self-consciousness, namely that any judgment I make can be accompanied by an "I think ...".'[16] This certainly seems more appropriate, given that the sole basis of the Paralogisms is, according to Kant, the 'I think'. But Bennett rejects this, since the 'absolute subject' clause claims more than does Kant's 'doctrine' of self-consciousness. He says that

the self-consciousness doctrine does not say that all my judgments *are* of the form 'I think ...', as though my judgment *that P* were really an ellipsis for my judgment *that I judge that P*. The doctrine makes no such absurd claim, but merely implies that given any judgment (P) which I make there is a *correlated* true judgment with myself as its subject-matter (I judge that P). That falls far short of 'I am the subject of all my possible judgments'.[17]

Given that these three readings are rejected, Bennett suggests a fourth reading, whereby 'what the clause means ... is merely that all my judgments are *mine*: not that I am their topic or subject matter, but just that they are states of myself or episodes in my history'.[18] And if this is all that is meant by saying that 'I, as a thinking being, am the absolute subject of all my judgments', then it is completely unclear just how this clause can get us from the *definition* of substance to the assertion that *I* am a substance. That all my judgments are mine does not in any obvious way say anything about whether or not I can represent myself adjectivally, as a determination of something else. The second clause, as Bennett points out, is where this work gets done. So the first clause is completely unnecessary to Kant's Paralogism.

Why, though, does Kant insert this clause at all? Bennett suggests that it is because he confuses two senses of the expression 'subject of a judgment', viz., (1) 'topic of a judgment', and (2) 'maker or bearer of a judgment'. In saying that 'all my judgments are mine', I am referring to myself as the bearer of judgments (2); when saying that 'in all our thought the "I" is the subject', I am referring to myself as the topic of judgments (1).[19] For the sake of brevity, I will refer to the subject-as-topic as subject(1) and to the subject-as-bearer as subject(2). Bennett, then, goes on to say that subject(1) refers to concepts and judgments which are 'logico-linguistic' entities, while subject(2) refers to items in the world. This distinction explains two things in Kant's account, according to Bennett. First, it sheds light on how the 'I' which thinks 'is known only through the thoughts which are its predicates': thoughts are not logico-linguistic predicates but are properties—which exist in the world. Second, it explains what Kant means in the second premiss when he refers to 'this representation of myself'. Bennett says that 'all the other premiss-material does concern the role within a judgment of a certain concept or representation; but the clause which has given us difficulty is not about my representation of myself—it is about myself'. In other words, the first clause is about myself as subject(2) rather than as subject(1), while the second clause is about myself as subject(1). To summarize Bennett's account of the second premiss: when Kant says that 'this representation of myself cannot be employed as predicate of any other thing', he is referring to the self as subject(1) = the (logico-linguistic) topic of judgments. And since from the first premiss we know that those topics of judgments which cannot be employed as predicates are substances, we can infer from the character of the self as topic, as subject(1), that it is a substance. The first clause, which asserts that I am the absolute subject(2), or bearer, of all my judgments, is here superfluous, and was only inserted by Kant due to his conflation of subject(1) and subject(2).

If, however, the key clause is taken to be the first, or subject(2), clause, then Kant's First Paralogism would, according to Bennett, at least resemble an actual argument as presented by one of Kant's antagonists. Read in the light of this clause as interpreted, the Paralogism is a version of an argument presented by Descartes.[20] Roughly, it would be of this form:

All accidents inhere in substances;

> All my thoughts (which inhere in me) are accidents;
>
> So my thoughts must inhere in a substance = me.

But, Bennett says, the fact that Kant warns us against the inflation of the conclusion should support his S-interpretation rather than this, which I will call his A-interpretation. It is not clear why this warning should support S rather than A; Bennett says that the inflation which Kant is wary of is that which would lead us from the conclusion that the soul is substantial to the conclusion that the soul is imperishable. Apparently this inflation would be motivated by the idea that since substances are 'sempiternal' and the soul is a substance, the soul is imperishable.[21] So the inflation is in fact an additional syllogism, with the conclusion of the First Paralogism as its minor premiss:

> Substances are sempiternal (and thus imperishable);
>
> My soul is a substance;
>
> Therefore my soul is sempiternal (and thus imperishable).

But it seems obvious that the conclusions of Bennett's S and A could each provide a plausible basis for this inflation. Both conclusions assert that the soul is a substance, and thus provide the minor premiss of this syllogism (which I will call the W-argument); neither asserts that the soul is sempiternal, and thus neither provides the W-argument's major premiss. So the inflation of the Paralogism's conclusion does not in any obvious way lend support to Bennett's endorsement of S over A.

As Bennett points out, Kant does not show us just how the rational psychologist establishes what I have called the major premiss of W, that is, the claim of sempiternity for substances in general.[22] So, though both S and A argue for the soul's substantiality, neither argues for its immortality.[23] And in his own comments amplifying the First Paralogism, Kant does after all focus on putative immortality-claims that involve viewing the soul as substance, but he does so without showing how the move from substantiality to immortality should be made. This leads Bennett to offer a third interpretation of the Paralogism, one taken from Goethe:

every possibility is the possibility of my knowing that such and such; anything which excludes my existence is impossible; therefore I must always exist.[24]

Bennett correctly remarks that this argument is 'no good', and suggests that Kant's presentation of it reveals an unfortunate charity on Kant's part in dealing with the rational psychologist. He says that Kant

writes as though the judgment that I am sempiternal has content, is experience-dividing, involves using a certain concept empirically *in concreto*, even at the level where one has the Cartesian basis with nothing erected upon it. At any rate, he seems not to have noticed how very far from true that is.[25]

As it stands, there does not seem to be any reason to accept that Kant's First Paralogism is in fact a syllogistic variant of Goethe's invalid argument. Apart from any other considerations, the two arguments have nothing in common beyond the questionable and theory-laden synonymy of 'every possibility is the possibility of my knowing that such and such' and 'I . . . am the absolute subject of all my possible judgments' which Bennett would presumably invoke given the 'Cartesian basis'. The conclusion of the Goethe argument is the conclusion of W, which Bennett indicates is the inflated conclusion of S, and so this would account for Kant's warning regarding the potential inflation of the conclusion. But at the same time it completely ignores Kant's emphasis on substance in the First Paralogism. Bennett can say that this focus is a product of Kant's not having made the linguistic turn, and thus presenting the linguistic insight of S in the best way that he can given his terminology, but the Goethe argument evades this linguistic point as well, and so seems to have at most a tangential contact with Kant's argument.[26]

To summarize, then, the state of play: Bennett rejects Kant's assertion that the First Paralogism is a fallacious argument resting on an ambiguous middle term. Bennett suggests—but does not make good the claim that—the self must be handled substantively, and also suggests that this is the point made by Kant in the second clause of the Paralogism's minor premiss. This leads to his S-interpretation of the Paralogism, which rests on the self as subject (1) of judgments = the topic of a judgment. The first clause of the minor premiss merely makes the point that my experiences are necessarily mine, appealing to the notion of the self as the subject (2) = the bearer of a judgment. This clause is unnecessary to the S-argument but is the key to Bennett's A-argument, which rests on the notion of thoughts as accidents inhering in a substance (= my soul). It was pointed out that, *contra* Bennett, each of these arguments lends equal weight to the inflation of the conclusion into a claim about the soul's immortality, since each supplies the minor premiss of the W-argument, which establishes the immortality of the soul on the basis of the 'sempiternity' of substance. Since neither the S-argument nor the A-argument supplies the major premiss— that substances are sempiternal—Bennett suggests a third inter- pretation, after Goethe, of the Paralogism, which rests on the inconceivability of my non-existence by me. Bennett, however, fails to make plausible the claim that this argument is in fact Kant's First Paralogism.

THE SUBJECTIVAL REPRESENTATION OF THE SELF

To see what is really afoot in the First Paralogism, we should consider again that Bennett does not succeed in showing why the self must be represented subjectivally (or as occurring within the scope of a substantival representation). It should also be recalled that Bennett dismisses the first clause of Kant's second premiss as unnecessary to the argument. If we accept that there is something to be said for Bennett's S-argument as a reading of Kant, then it seems reasonable to look at this clause to see if it is necessary—to see, in short, if it provides that demonstration of subjectival necessity which Bennett does not, and which the S-argument manifestly requires. And of course this is precisely what the first clause does do, or is at any rate what it points to. By asserting that 'I, as a thinking being, am the absolute subject of all my judgments', Kant is invoking his theory of the transcendental unity of apperception, as it was presented in the Transcendental Deduction of the Cate- gories. The 'I think', which is the representation of 'I, as thinking being' (and thus of the transcendental unity of apperception) 'is not itself an experience, but the form of apperception, which belongs to and precedes every experience' (A354). Conceptual experience requires both synchronic and diachronic syntheses in order to be conceptual (or, for that matter, experience) at all: Kant says, 'Knowledge is a whole in which representations stand compared and connected' (A97). The key to the transcendental unity of apperception is that these representations must be compared and connected within the framework imposed by the representation of them as representations of a unitary subject. Kant says that 'we demand this absolute unity of the subject of a thought, only because otherwise we could not say "I think" (the manifold in one representation)' (A354). So the 'I think' is posited as a subject of all my representations—in effect, it is a subject which groups the data, brackets it together so that it can be 'compared and connected', synthesized into a course of objective experience. Thus all my thoughts occur within the framework imposed by this 'absolute unity of the subject' = the 'I think', and this is what Kant intends when he says that 'I, as a thinking being, am the absolute subject of all my possible judgments.' That this essentially subjectival 'I' is a necessary condition of all my possible experiences—and thus of any given experience—is a result of the requirements of experiential synthesis. And if this subjectival 'I' is a necessary condition of any possible experience of mine, then it is a necessary condition of any putatively adjectival representation of myself which I somehow succeed in representing. Thus it can be demonstrated why, even if all my representations of myself are not necessarily subjectival, at least it is the case that all of them must occur within the scope of a representation of myself which is subjectival (= the 'I think' of transcendental apperception). The point of Kant's saying that 'I, as thinking being' am the absolute subject of all my judgments is that all my judgments must occur within the scope of the transcendental unity of apperception, or, more accurately, within the scope of the subjectival representation of this unity, the 'I think'.

How does this relate to Bennett's construction of the first clause, that all it really says is that 'my judgments are mine'? It turns out that in a sense Bennett is right—but he underestimates the implications of attributing all my judgments to me. In other words, Bennett has largely ignored the necessary conditions of being a subject(2), a 'maker or bearer of judgments'. It is these conditions, not surprisingly, that Kant is preoccupied with in the Subjective Deduction. Pre-eminent among these conditions is that to be a maker/bearer of judgments one must be just that—*one*. Kant says that 'apperception is itself the ground of the possibility of the categories, which on their part represent nothing but the synthesis of the manifold of intuition, in so far as the manifold has unity in apperception' (A401). For the manifold of experience to be unified (for all my experiences to be mine in any significant sense) requires that the subject(2) of these experiences itself be unitary ('in all consciousness must be one and the same') (B132). Thus the 'I think' is 'represented as an object which I think, namely, I myself and its unconditioned unity' (A398— Kant, as will be seen, is here using 'object' in a dangerously misleading way).

So the necessary mode of unitary experience must be that of experience as had by a *something* rather than by, so to speak, a *such that*, since qualities/determinations/predicates (those entia which are represented adjectivally, broadly speaking) do not individuate as do substances/determined objects/subjects (those entia which are represented subjectivally). So it follows that the subject(2) of judgments (= the 'I' as thinking being) must be represented as something which is itself properly represented subjectivally, that is, as a substance. It is worth noting that there are non-substantial subjectival representations as well, such as classes; that the representation of the 'I' of transcendental apperception is not a representation of a class of items is defended by Kant in the Second Paralogism. For now, we know that its representation must be subjectival and that it is represented as substance; why the latter is true can only be taken up within a detailed consideration of the alleged simplicity of the soul. But that is beyond the scope of the First Paralogism.

It is important to bear in mind two qualifications which Kant places on this subjectival representation of the 'I' of the 'I think'. First, Kant emphasizes that it is only the representation of myself as subject(2) that must be subjectival/substantial, rather than myself apart from any such representation. This is, of course, merely a recapitulation of Kant's point that the noumenal self, the self as it is in itself and not as it appears, is unknowable.[27] What I do know is that my experience is had as if it were that of one subject; with regard to the actual substantiality of the subject(2) apart from my experience I can know nothing. The second qualification made by Kant is that the 'I think' is a 'bare representation' which has no experiential content: in other words, it is not an intuition (A117n.). Kant says that 'this "I" is . . . as little an intuition as it is a concept of any object, it is the mere form of consciousness' (A382, cf. also A23/B37). In other words, the 'I' which is the absolute subject of all my judgments is not perceived as an object; it is not a representation which has any sense-content at all. Rather, it is the necessary mode of consciousness, a way of structuring experience by framing it as had by one subject. It is not a thing which can be pointed to or characterized except in terms of its function, for it is merely a (necessary) function of conceptualized experience. As will be seen, these two qualifications regarding the subject(2) of thoughts are Kant's main weapons against the doctrines of rational psychology.

From this discussion, it becomes clear that the two clauses of the First Paralogism's minor premiss are not unrelated. The first clause, by invoking the transcendental unity of apperception, suggests Kant's way of arguing that the 'I, as a thinking being' is necessarily subjectival. The second clause underscores the subjectival role by indicating its priority (or, to put it another way, its broader scope) over all other representations. Bennett's failure to see this is at least in part due to his misreading of what he calls the 'self-consciousness doctrine'. It should be recalled that Bennett does not believe that the first clause is derived from that doctrine, because 'the self-consciousness doctrine does not say that all my judgments *are* of the form "I think" . . . but merely implies that given any judgment (P) which I make there is a *correlated* true judgment with myself as its subject-matter (I judge that P)'.[28] Of course, Kant's 'doctrine' of the transcendental unity of apperception does say that the 'I think' in fact 'belongs to and precedes every experience' (A354). If this means that all my judgments are thought as 'I judge that P', then this would indeed be a false claim. But Kant says that with regard to this 'I' of the 'I think', 'whether it ever actually occurs, does not here concern us' (A117n.). On the face of it, these two assertions are mutually exclusive, but actually they point to an important distinction which is obscured by Kant's confusing terminology of the self: that the 'I' of such thoughts as 'I think that it is snowing' or 'I ache all over' is the 'I' of empirical apperception, and the 'I' of the 'I think'—as the logical form of consciousness—is that designated by the transcendental unity of apperception. Considered as such, the latter 'I think' need never occur as a thought itself, but only as a formal constraint on thoughts, that is, the constraint that coherent experience must be (meta)-represented as that of a substantially represented subject. Kant does say that 'all my judgments are of the form [or occur within the framework of] "I think" [= the transcendental unity of apperception]' but definitely does not say that all my judgments incorporate—as cognized subject—'I think' (= empirical apperception). Bennett is, of course, right that for any judgment of mine *p* there is a correlated true judgment 'I judge that *p*'. But Kant's theory of transcendental apperception has less trivial aspirations than the mere isolation of truisms; that its terminology is prima facie ambiguous does not make this as clear as could be wished.

Does Kant confuse the subject of a judgment as subject(1), or topic of a judgment, with the subject of a judgment as subject(2), or maker/bearer of a judgment? The distinction is clearly a good one, and one that the expression 'subject of a judgment' (or 'logical subject') obscures in a thoroughly confusing way. But on the reading of Kant I have given, the entire minor premiss seems to focus only on the 'I' as subject(2). And the major premiss seems clearly to focus on substances as subjects(1), as the topics of attributive judgments. Is Kant confused? The answer is this: there is certainly an ambiguity in the notion of a subject, but it is not an ambiguous usage of which *Kant* is guilty, though his presentation of the First Paralogism is obscure enough to make his usage suspect. Kant is in fact aware of the ambiguity and in effect points it out. What Kant intends as the moral of the First Paralogism is something like the following. Those things that in experience are the subjects(1) of judgments and are themselves never attributed to other subjects(1) are substances. The 'I' of the transcendental 'I think' is a subject(2), a maker/bearer of judgments, which does not imply its being a subject(1) (or vice versa). But the key point, again, is that, as a formal condition of unitary consciousness, the 'I' as subject(2) must be viewed as a subject(1)! This is what Kant means when he says that the 'I' is 'in concept substance'—it must be conceived as a substantial (and unitary and persistent) entity, even though it is not known to be a substance (as would be the case with an ordinary subject(1))(A400). This conception of the subject(2) as being a subject(1) is 'the illusion which leads us to regard the unity in the synthesis of thoughts as a perceived unity in the subject of these thoughts' (A402). In other words, the formal condition of a course of orderly experience, which is that it must be experienced as that of a unitary subject, inherently involves an illusion, which is that I can perceive that my experiences are had by a genuinely unitary subject. This hypostasis of a necessary mode of experience Kant calls '*apperceptionis substantiatae*' and the 'subreption of the hypostatised consciousness' (A402). And it is a necessary illusion, since if my experience must be had as *by* a unitary subject, then (in a sense) I must consider myself to *be* a unitary subject. In other words, ordered experience requires that the subject (2) be in concept a subject(1) as well. Properly speaking, of course, Kant should not say that it is an illusion that the self has in itself certain characteristics—for all he knows it may. What is illusory is believing that one knows the self to have these characteristics, rather than that one knows the self to be represented as having them. And for Kant it makes no sense to speak of substance in itself in the first place—but this is anticipatory.

Given these, and earlier, comments on the transcendental unity of apperception, we can note (for now merely in passing) one of the keys to understanding Kant's strategy in the Paralogisms: for Kant, the fallacious reasoning which characterizes the Paralogisms arises—at least in part—from a tendency to become confused about whether the self is being considered as phenomenon or as noumenon. This confusion, of course, poses a danger to Kant's general epistemological project if it is not exposed and dealt with, and Kant has no intention of countenancing (putative) deductions which demonstrate our ability to traffic in noumena, to explore the nature of the self beyond the bounds of our experience. But Kant proposes to go beyond merely pointing out this pervasive confusion, and resultant ambiguity, in our talk about the self as noumenon and as phenomenon: he traces this confusion to its very source. As is true of many of Kant's concepts, we can speak of the self both empirically—in terms of empirical apperception—and transcendentally—via the 'I' of the 'I think'. That we can speak of the self in both of these ways, however, leaves us vulnerable to a philosophically dangerous temptation: we recognize, after a fashion, that we need to speak of the 'I' transcendentally, but we are not clear about just what this does—and, importantly, does not—involve. Thus we are tempted to confuse, or even conflate, the legitimacy of speaking about the 'I' in a transcendental way with a supposed licence to speak about the 'I' as noumenon: characterizing the 'I' as it exists outside our possible knowledge of it. When we fall prey to this temptation, says Kant, we have been victimized by the tendency to hypostasize (reify) the 'I' of the transcendental unity of apperception into a (noumenal) object—which, given proper reflection, it clearly is not. Thus, though the specific errors committed in the Paralogisms vary considerably, it will be important to bear in mind that generally these errors can be traced to (*a*) the confusion between construing the self as noumenon and as phenomenon, and, more fundamentally, (*b*) between speaking (legitimately) about the self transcendentally and speaking (illegitimately) about the self as noumenon, on the basis of a reification of the 'I' of the 'I think'.

To return to Bennett's criticism of Kant: bearing the interpretation above in mind, we can avoid another difficulty in Bennett's reading. As was pointed out, Bennett alleges the Paralogism to be a valid argument with true premises, thus yielding a true conclusion. But the conclusions of both his S-argument and his A-argument assert that the self is a substance, and Kant for one denies that we can know this to be true. It is clear, though, that Kant is to be taken at his word, and that the Paralogism is fallacious, trading on an ambiguous middle term. The ambiguous term, it turns out, is 'subject', and the ambiguity is a version, with variations, of that pointed out by Bennett, between subject(1) and subject(2). A more perspicuous way of putting Kant's point is that the ambiguity is between 'being a subject(1)' and 'being represented as a subject(1)'. To put this in syllogistic form (not far removed from Kant's own):

> That which is a subject(1) is substance.
>
> The 'I' of the 'I think' (= subject(2)) must be represented as a subject(1).
>
> Therefore the 'I' of the 'I think' is substance.

Clearly this syllogism is fallacious or paralogistic: just because the 'I' is necessarily represented as a subject(1), it does not follow that it is a subject(1), and so it does not necessarily follow that whatever is true of a subject(1) is true of the 'I'. Yet, as Kant says, both premises are true, and though the conclusion is false, it is 'an inevitable illusion' and is 'not fictitious and [has] not arisen fortuitously, but [has] sprung from the very nature of reason' (A339/B397). It is inevitable, because it has a transcendental ground, that is, it is an aspect of the formal condition of having an orderly course of experience (A341/B399). Thus Kant suggests that even once we have recognized the fallacy of the Paralogism as such, we cannot at one level abandon the illusion of the substantiality of the soul. His description of this inevitable illusion is remarkable for its force and almost tragic presentation:

Even the wisest of men cannot free himself from [this illusion]. After long effort he perhaps succeeds in guarding himself against actual error; but he will never be able to free himself from the illusion, which unceasingly mocks and torments him. (A339/B397)

And Kant might well view this illusion as unrelenting mockery, since even though one is aware that the self is not known to be substance, it is a necessary condition of this awareness that one's thoughts be had as by a substantial self. If one holds to the Cartesian injunction to accept only what one knows to be true—as Kant usually does—then it is quite plausible that these necessarily accepted and yet unknowable ways of looking at the self are a source of epistemic torment.

TWO WAYS OF INFLATING SUBSTANCE

Having seen the role of ambiguity in the Paralogism, we can now ask what Kant is talking about when he warns against inflating the Paralogism's conclusion. It has been shown that Kant's suggestion of a *sophisma figurae dictionis* was accurate: so what does this have to do with some philosophically misleading inflation of the syllogism's conclusion? A reconstruction of Bennett's account showed that the inflation he discovers is what was called the W-argument, a further syllogism using the conclusion of the Paralogism as minor premiss which establishes the soul's immortality. I suspect, however, that there are actually two inflations against which we are being warned by Kant. The first is that which contributes the ambiguity on which the Paralogism trades: the soul in concept substantial is inflated into the soul substantial in fact. The second inflation is related to that discovered by Bennett, but is actually a good bit more complicated than his reading would indicate. This inflation, resting on an ambiguity in the notion of 'substance', is the transformation of the soul as substance, where 'substance' is understood as the Kantian category (either schematized or not), into the soul as substance, where substantiality implies what Bennett calls 'sempiternity'. To see what is inflated into what, it is necessary to consider what Kant means by 'substance'. As a pure unschematized category, and thus as 'the function of thought in judgment', 'substance' indicates an entity which is necessarily subjectival and not adjectival, that is, which can have qualities but cannot itself be a quality of something else (A70/B95). And 'entity' is here used as vaguely as possible, since, as an unschematized category substance has no experiential content at all; it should not, for instance, be thought of as an object, which is a concept only properly applied in experience. As Kant says, substance, 'when the sensible determination of permanence is omitted, would mean simply a something which can be thought only as subject, never as a predicate of something else' (A147/B186). Here too, Kant's 'something' should be read as implying no experiential content, no 'sensible determination'. Kant goes on to say that 'the categories . . . without schemata, are merely functions of the understanding for concepts; and represent no object' (A147/B187). What Kant means by the sensible determination 'of permanence' is the key to substance considered as a schematized category. He says that 'the schema of substance is permanence of the real in time, that is, the representation of the real as a substrate of empirical determination of time in general, and so as abiding while all else changes' (A143/B183). At least part of what this means is that substance, the notion of a something that is necessarily subjectival, is applied in experience as the notion of enduring items in the phenomenal world. Given the notion of enduring experiential items, which in various ways persist through observed alterations, experience is orderly. Without going into detail, Kant argues in one passage in the First Analogy that the very possibility of a course of experience ordered in a unitary time-structure presupposes the representation of permanence in that which is experienced (A188/B231). As he says, substance (schematized into the concept of something enduring in experience) 'is . . . the substratum proper of all time-determination' (A185/B228). What endures in experience is matter, which Kant calls '*substantia phaenomenon*', or substance in the realm of experience (A277/B333). Thus we can summarize Kant's theory of substance—albeit in a somewhat cavalier fashion—in this way: substance as a function of judgment is the concept of a bare something which is necessarily represented subjectivally, and not adjectivally. Applied in experience, this concept gives us the concept of something which persists through experientially perceived changes (accidents), thus something which provides an abiding framework for structuring the time-order of experience itself. This something is matter, which in experience persists through empirical transitions.

One caution is important here. In common usage, the words 'substance' and 'reality' have a solid feel about them, evoking thoughts of things in themselves and not merely things as they appear. This is far from what Kant intends to convey by using these terms. 'Substance' for Kant is at its most abstract a mere logical form used in judgment: the form of something inherently subjectival. Indeed, even 'something' seems too loaded a term for unschematized substance, since a good case could be made for the concept of a thing's being logically parasitical on the concept of an object. When schematized, substance is the 'substratum' of the real, and this certainly has a thing-in-itself ring to it. But the real for Kant consists merely of the contents of empirical intuition, and the substratum of these contents, that which allows their being experienced within a unitary time-order, is matter, which is posited as persistent through the flux of appearances. As such, matter is not a thing in itself but a necessary way of representing appearances. Thus the 'permanence of the real', which Kant calls schematized substance, is merely a permanence within the bounds of experience. It simply indicates that my experience is in part experience of entities which persist in some way through time.

And now it is possible to see the source of the second inflation which Kant attacks. This inflation, that of transforming Kant's notion of substance into that of substance as sempiternal, actually has two aspects as considered by Kant, since Kant considers there to be two working concepts of substance, schematized and unschematized. I will deal with the inflation of unschematized substance first, as does Kant. It is clear from the major premiss of the Paralogism that the first inflation was of the self represented as unschematized substance into the self represented as schematized substance. But if this vitiating ambiguity were allowed to stand, yielding the conclusion that the self is unschematized substance, what possible use could be made of this conclusion? Kant says that the conclusion that 'I . . . do not in any natural manner either arise or perish, can by no means be deduced from it' (A349). If the self is unschematized substance, all this says is that it is necessarily subjectival. Recalling Bennett's W-argument, what would be needed is a demonstration of the truth of the major premiss, that is, that unschematized substances are sempiternal. As Bennett points out, Kant here gives us no argument which would establish this premiss. But this is not a flaw in Kant's argument. Rather, it is one of the points of it: even were the First Paralogism sound—which it is not—it would not supply us with anything more than the minor premiss of an argument for the soul's sempiternity. To believe that it also provides the major premiss is to inflate intolerably the content of the unschematized category of substance. If the rational psychologist cannot legitimately infer the sempiternity of substance from the pure category of substance, though, then perhaps he can make this inference from the schematized category of substance. This Kant now considers.

It is interesting to observe the strategy of demolition undertaken by Kant here against the rational psychologist, for it is one that recurs throughout the Paralogisms.[29] First, Kant has shown that the Paralogism is fallacious, and so it does not succeed in proving that the soul is substance. But then he provisionally grants that the conclusion is proven and asks what this proof has accomplished. If sound, it has proven that the soul is unschematized substance. But this only supplies one of the two premises it would need to prove the soul's immortality, which is assumed to be the goal of the rational psychologist's arguing that the soul is substance. So the proof, were it to be sound, would not demonstrate that which is its ultimate object. The rational psychologist, then, must demonstrate that the soul is schematized substance, for this is the only other intelligible notion of substance available: perhaps this proof would establish the sempiternity of the soul. Of course, the Paralogism itself does not prove any such thing as that the soul is schematized substance, and it is very hard to see how it could, since the major premiss, defining substance, would in this case be something like 'that which is the substratum of all that is real is (schematized) substance'—and it is unclear what assertion about the soul in the minor premiss could lead to the conclusion that the soul is (schematized) substance. But Kant here is not just refuting the initial argument of the rational psychologist; having done this, he is also allowing the rational psychologist enough rope to hang himself twice over.

So Kant considers whether or not it is possible for an argument to be constructed with the conclusion that the soul is schematized substance. And he concludes that any such argument would be fundamentally incoherent: it would in effect require the commission of a category-mistake. As was pointed out, unschematized substance is not objective, since it is a pure category 'by which I do not think a determinate object' or even, strictly speaking, 'the concept of an object' (A399). To have an idea of objective substance requires that substance be schematized, thought as enduring matter, which is the content of empirical intuition. So the proposition that the soul is schematized substance implies the proposition that the soul is representable as empirical intuition. Kant says that to say that something in experience is a (schematized) substance, I must judge 'predicates of its intuition', that is, it must be an intuition, something of which I am aware as a 'this-such' (A399–400). In other words, I must be able to pick out the putatively schematized substance and say something about it. But this is precisely what I cannot do with the

'I' of the 'I think'. As Kant says in the Refutation of Idealism, 'the consciousness of myself in the representation "I" is not an intuition, but a merely *intellectual* representation of the spontaneity of a thinking subject. This "I" has not, therefore, the least predicate of intuition' (B278). Indeed, the very illusion which led to the ambiguity of the Paralogism itself is at work here as well: *apperceptionis substantiatae*, the hypostasis of a mode of representation, leading to thinking of the 'I' as an object. Kant says that 'all illusion may be said to consist in treating the subjective condition of thinking as being knowledge of the object' (A396). More perspicuously, Kant says that

the synthesis of the conditions of a thought in general . . . is not objective at all, but merely a synthesis of the thought with the subject, which is mistaken for a synthetic representation of an object. (A397)

And now we are brought back to an earlier point regarding the natural slippage from the self considered non-empirically, or transcendentally, to the self considered as noumenal object: we need, according to Kant, to speak of the self in a sense transcendentally, via the transcendental unity of apperception. And there is a natural tendency, when speaking of the 'I think', to fall prey to *apperceptionis substantiatae*, the reification of the 'I think' into an object—particularly, a noumenal object. And if I am disposed to regard the 'I' as an object, it follows that I am disposed to regard it as an intuition, that is, as something which I can pick out and about which I can say something (via 'predicates of its intuition'). It is, then, the transcendental unity of apperception, with its inevitable hypostasis of the logical form of all judgments into the 'I' of the 'I think', that is the source of the illusion that the self is at the same time noumenal and intuitable. That there is no such object we can possibly experience is the moral of Hume's thought-experiment in which he does not stumble over himself; it is also the source of Descartes's finding the 'I' immune from his otherwise universally effective hyperbolic doubt. The 'I' of apperception is not encountered in the world, and therefore, says Kant, it is illegitimate to speak of this 'I' as an object encountered in the world, and in doing so to invest it with both noumenal and phenomenal characteristics. And, to relate this to the inflation of substance, it is also unintelligible to assert that the 'I' is schematized substance, which is, as schematized category, descriptive only of those things that are so encounterable.

Thus Kant rejects the possibility that the 'I, as thinking substance' is schematized substance. This is his point when, in rejecting the rational psychologist's last potential inflation, he says that

The 'I' is indeed in all thoughts, but there is not in this representation the least trace of intuition, distinguishing the 'I' from other objects of intuition. Thus we can indeed perceive that this representation is invariably present in all thought, but not that it is an abiding and continuous intuition, wherein the thoughts, as being transitory, give place to one another. (A350)

Since we cannot perceive that the 'I' is 'an abiding and continuous intuition'—because it is not an intuition at all—we cannot ascribe to it the permanence which is constitutive of schematized substance. If we attempt to do so, says Kant, 'we are thus making an empirical, but in this case inadmissible, employment of the category' (A403). So Kant has shown that if the soul is proven to be unschematized substance, this is not sufficient to prove its sempiternity, since sempiternity is not implied by unschematized substantiality. And it is an inadmissible use of the notion of schematized substance to apply it to the soul at all. So even if the idea of schematized substance did somehow provide a way of demonstrating that such substances are sempiternal, it is not possible to demonstrate that the soul is a substance of this kind, since by definition it cannot fall under the category of schematized substance. Recalling the W-argument, we can see that any such provisional concession would be worthless to the rational psychologist. The inflation of the soul as *in concept* unschematized substance into the soul as *in fact* unschematized substance gives us the minor premiss of W, but not the major premiss. And even if the idea of schematized substance can be shown to imply sempiternity, and thus give us the major premiss of W, this same idea coupled with the nature of 'I, as thinking being' precludes the true assertion of the minor premiss. Given no other intelligible notions of substance, however, it follows that even if the soul were in some sense substance, this fact 'does not carry us a single step further' towards proving the sempiternity of the soul (A350).

Finally, does Kant think that the judgment that I am sempiternal has content even at the level of what has been called Kant's methodological solipsism? On the basis of the reading of Kant just given, it seems clear that Kant in fact explicitly denies content to such a judgment: for Kant it can only have experiential content if it relies on empirical intuition. But the 'I' of the 'I think' does not meet this criterion. What about sempiternity? Within the context of the First Paralogism Kant utterly rejects the inference of the soul's sempiternity from the hypothesis that the soul is substantial. He rather pointedly rejects the idea that the judgment 'I am sempiternal' is one which, in Bennett's phrase, 'involves using a certain concept empirically *in concreto*'.[30] Kant does say that to assert that the soul is schematized substance is to make an 'empirical ... employment of the category'—but he says explicitly that it is 'in this case inadmissible' (A403). Curiously, Bennett cites this very passage as support when he says that Kant 'clearly implies that the judgment "I shall last forever" *does* use the concept of substance in a manner that is empirically serviceable. Arguably it does not.'[31] But it seems clear that *Kant* argues that it does not—and he does so as forcefully as this point can be argued. When Kant says that this judgment is 'empirical, but in this case inadmissible', he is merely saying that the concept is empirical and cannot coherently be applied to this item, the 'I, as thinking being'. But is that not what Bennett maintains as well? Kant does concede the use of 'substance' in this judgment to be 'empirical', which in an explicitly verificationist climate would presumably imply that the judgment is meaningful. But Kant is not part of this later framework erected around the empirical employment of concepts, and his point is clearly that the use of (schematized) 'substance' in this connection is completely illegitimate.

Were Kant to be writing within this later framework, he would surely not say that this judgment is an empirical employment of the category but rather that it is an attempt to apply an empirical concept to a non-empirical subject, and so is as meaningless as saying that 'the number four is round and heavy'. But Kant is also aware that such judgments as 'I am sempiternal', though illegitimate, have a significance that is obscured by their mere dismissal as being meaningless in the way that 'the number four is round and heavy' is meaningless. Kant's genius in the Paralogisms lies not in his pointing out the unencounterability of the thinking self in experience, for that had been pointed out by Hume and others (Leibniz, again: 'Nihil est in intellectu, quod non fuerit in sensu, excipe: nisi ipse intellectus.'[32]) Nor does it lie in rejecting as illegitimate the application of empirical categories to non-empirical entities, for that point dates back at least to Hobbes, if not to Aristotle.[33] Rather, it lies in the fact that Kant saw the source of both the thinking self's unencounterability and this

3

The Self as Simple:
The Second Paralogism

In the Second Paralogism, Kant considers the rational psychologist's claim that the soul is simple, a claim which he says is bolstered by an argument which is 'the Achilles of all dialectical inferences in the pure doctrine of the soul' (A351). It is not clear that Kant takes the Second Paralogism itself to be this dialectical inference: immediately after the formal presentation of the Paralogism he proceeds to formulate another—albeit related—argument for the conclusion that the soul is simple (this argument will be examined shortly). In fact, although the Second Paralogism as presented in A has a structure which is, at least on the face of it, similar to that of the First Paralogism, Kant's discussion of it is far from straightforward, and has generated widely divergent interpretations. Bennett seems to find one argument against the rational psychologist in the text; Broad finds two; and Kemp Smith comes up with three.[1] I will argue here that Kant actually presents five arguments in his discussion of this Paralogism. The first argument is directed, interestingly, against a constructed opponent of the rational psychologist and appears in the third to sixth premises of Kant's reformulated version of the Second Paralogism—that version of the Paralogism which he presents, with comments, after its formal, syllogistic, version.[2] The remainder are directed against the rational psychologist himself: the second is a *refutation* of the reformulated version of the Paralogism,[3] and the third[4] and fourth[5] are parallel to those which Kant advances against the two inflations of the First Paralogism. I will then show that, in the second edition, Kant presents yet a fifth, and remarkably intricate, argument intended to defuse the significance of the 'Achilles of all dialectical inferences'.

The formal structure of the Second Paralogism is presented as follows:

> That, the action of which can never be regarded as the concurrence of several things acting, is *simple*.
>
> Now the soul, or the thinking 'I', is such a being.
>
> Therefore, etc. (A351)

On the face of it, this syllogism's structure is obviously similar to that of the First Paralogism. But Kant, after saying that it is 'no mere sophistical play' but actually quite persuasive, immediately offers a reformulation (in paragraph 2) that is not in any obvious way equivalent to the syllogism. He begins by constructing an argument, ostensibly presented by an opponent of rational psychology, to the effect that the soul may well be composite. For the sake of clarity, I will call this opponent the 'anti-rationalist', in order to distinguish his criticism of rational psychology from that presented by Kant.[6] The anti-rationalist's argument goes like this:

(1) Every composite substance is an aggregate of several substances, and the action of a composite, or whatever inheres in it as thus composite, is an aggregate of several actions or accidents, distributed among the plurality of the substances.

(2) Now an effect which arises from the concurrence of many acting substances is indeed possible, namely, when this effect is external only (as, for instance, the motion of a body is the combined motion of all its parts). (A352)

In other words, those properties which we predicate of any composite substance are properly predicable of both the whole substance and of its parts. In this case, the property predicated of the whole substance is actually analysable into—or, better, *reducible* to—what is predicable of the parts of the whole, that is, the properties of the various substances which make up the composite. Furthermore, it is entirely conceivable that a composite substance can have a property that appears to be predicable merely of the composite itself and is actually predicable of the composite's constituents. Kant's example is that of a body in motion, and it seems reasonable, if a bit tortuous, to concede that the conjoined movement of the various parts of a body appears to be, but is not, a simple movement by the body itself. And if this is possible, then it is also possible that the soul itself may be a composite substance, and its 'actions' (thoughts, desires, etc.), though ostensibly those of a simple substance, are actually the result of the conjoined 'actions' of the constituent substances which make up the soul.

The rational psychologist, says Kant, responds to this by pointing out that though a composite substance can produce simple effects in the case of 'extentional' properties, this is not true of 'intentional'—mental—properties. The rational psychologist shows that this is true (though for Kant only in the case of the *perceived* simplicity of the soul) by using what is in effect a *reductio* of the conclusion[7]:

(3) with thoughts, as internal accidents belonging to a thinking being, it is different [from the case of 'external' accidents].

(4) For suppose it be the composite that thinks:

(5) ... then every part of it would be a part of the thought, and all of them taken together would contain the whole thought.

(6) But this cannot consistently be maintained. For representations (for instance, the single words of a verse), distributed among different beings, never make up a whole thought (a verse) ...

(7) ... it is therefore impossible that a thought should inhere in what is essentially composite.

(8) It is therefore possible only in a *single* substance, which, not being an aggregate of many, is absolutely simple.

Before going into this rebuttal of the anti-rationalist's argument, it should be noted that it is far from obvious just why either Kant or the rational psychologist would take any pains to refute the anti-rationalist at all. As Broad has correctly pointed out, premiss (1) is simply false: though it certainly seems true that some properties of some composite substances are themselves mere aggregates of properties of the constituent parts of the substance, this is certainly not true of all properties of composites. Broad says that it is in particular false with regard to the obvious case of a chemical compound:

The fundamental premiss of the argument is that any property or act of a compound substance must be a compound property or act composed of properties or acts each of which belongs to a different one of the component substances. This is certainly false. A chemical compound, such as chloroform, has properties, such as producing loss of consciousness, boiling at 61 degrees C etc., which are in no sense composed of the properties of its elements, carbon, hydrogen, and chlorine. [8]

In contrast to the anti-rationalist's model of the properties of composite substances, we should also consider, along with Broad's example, the example of a symphony orchestra: the anti-rationalist will presumably want to say—on pain of having to abandon premiss (1)—that the sound of the symphony is an aggregate of the sounds of the individual instruments. But the fact that composers use principles of orchestration indicates that there are properties of orchestral music which emerge when the constituents of the orchestra are put together in certain ways, and that these properties are not simply an additive compilation of the properties of those constituents. Premiss (1) assumes that all those properties which we can predicate of complex substances are *reducible* properties, properties we can predicate of the parts of those substances. And clearly, given consideration of Broad's chloroform and my symphony orchestra, the range of properties which are so predicable of composite substances is not this straightforward.

In a word, what premiss (1) neglects is the possibility of a composite having *emergent* properties = properties predicable of the composite which would not be properties predicable of any proper subset of the composite's constituent parts. Circularity, for example, is a property which is clearly emergent: since the arcs are themselves, obviously enough, not circular, circularity is not predicable of those arcs which are the parts of a circle. At least it is usually not: to make the point more precise we should here consider the case of a circle which is itself made up of a ring of smaller circles. The key is that even in this case circularity is an emergent property, since the circularity predicated of the circle is not analysable into the circularity of each of the parts. That is to say, the circularity of the circle does not consist in the circularity of each of its parts. In any case, the relevant point here is that by assuming that the properties predicable of a composite substance must be reducible properties, properties predicable of the parts of the composite, the anti-rationalist has understated the complexity of the range of predicable properties. In doing so, he has argued from a premiss that, as Broad argues, we should not be inclined to accept.

In any case, what is important here is not whether or not the anti-rationalist properly describes the possible properties instantiated by composite substances, or concomitantly whether or not he is justified in asserting premiss (1), but rather what the rationalist's reason is for saying that the soul itself cannot, given its properties, be a composite substance. And this reason is precisely that 'representations (for instance, the single words of a verse), distributed among different beings, never make up a whole thought (a verse)'. As we have seen, one key point in Kant's Subjective Deduction is that for me to have intelligible experience, that experience must be synthesized, brought together as *my* experience. Part of what this means is that any given succession of representations which I experience as such must be representable as belonging to the same unitary subject—otherwise they are simply unrelated representations. To show this, Kant cites the case of 'drawing a line in thought', and argues that, unless each representation of a part of the line were synthesized with those that precede it, 'a complete representation would never be obtained' (A102). But this synthesis is—necessarily—a grouping of the successive representations as representations of a diachronically unitary experiencing subject. The synchronic counterpart to this diachronic unity is that which is required for having 'a whole thought': if a complex thought (requiring synthesis) is to be possible at all, it must be possible for all its parts to be had by the same subject. This is perhaps not obviously true, however, in the case of a verse: imagine a group of people who deem it puckish to speak the words of a poem in sequence, such that one says the first word of the poem, the second says the second, and so on: they would (in a sense) be reciting verse. Kant's point is more clear if we consider the case of a *judgment*: as William James—following Kant—pointed out,

Take a sentence of a dozen words, and take twelve men and tell to each one word. Then stand the men in a row or jam them in a bunch, and let each think of his word as intently as he will; nowhere will there be a consciousness of the whole sentence.[9]

And this is certainly true: given three subjects A, B, C such that A thinks 'Snow', B thinks 'is', and C thinks 'white', we do not have an instance of the judgment that snow is white. If the thinking self is composed of several different consciousnesses, then presumably by definition these different consciousnesses in no way have direct access to each other's representations, and so if the soul were composite in this way it would no more be possible for these various non-communicative souls to generate a whole thought out of their independent thoughts than it would be possible for *A*, *B*, or *C* to judge whether or not snow is white merely on the basis of the three of them having their own representations of 'snow', 'is', and 'white'. And if the anti-rationalist insists that the separate consciousnesses are not necessarily non-communicative, the burden is on him to explain how he individuates consciousnesses. In other words, he must show in what way consciousnesses which have each other's thoughts are properly called 'separate' consciousnesses at all.

Thus we have Kant's first argument in the discussion of the Second Paralogism. From this discussion it should be clear that the point being made against the anti-rationalist has a distinctly Kantian air, at least inasmuch as premisses (3)–(6) demonstrate the transcendental justification of the synchronic unity of the self in much the way that Kant himself argues for the diachronic unity of the self in the Subjective Deduction. What, then, is Kant's objection to this rationalist argument, given that he at least seems to accept the truth of some of the premisses? The key, of course, is *which* premisses he accepts. It is not clear whether or not he accepts (1)—though it is clear from the above discussion that he should not. Clearly he does not accept the anti-rationalist's conclusion = (2). And (3)–(6) are in effect Kant's own argument establishing the necessity of the represented synchronic unity of the self. In paragraph 3, however, Kant says that 'The so-called *nervus probandi* of this argument lies in the proposition, that if a multiplicity of representations are to form a single representation, they must be contained in the absolute unity of the thinking subject' (A352). This proposition, of course, is not itself a premiss of the argument, but it seems to be an elision of premisses (6)–(8). Presumably the key to his objection to this proposition, and thus to the argument itself, lies in its use of the word 'absolute', in so far as this implies a claim about the self in itself. The rational psychologist is taking this argument to prove that the soul in itself must be non-composite, and it is certainly part of Kant's design to disabuse the rational psychologist of the illusion that he can prove anything whatsoever about the soul's noumenal state. So we can say that *Kant* endorses premisses (3)–(6) of this argument but parts company with the rationalist when he goes beyond describing what is necessarily true of how a thinking being is represented and begins making claims about the soul in itself. And premisses (7) and (8) appear to make such claims, if we take '*essentially* composite' and '*absolutely* simple' to refer to properties of things in themselves. How, then, does Kant rebut that part of the rationalist response which he is unwilling to accept?

Kant's refutation of the rationalist's argument (= his own argument, with the objectionable addition of premisses (7) and (8)) provides us with his second argument. Kant recalls that there are three ways that a judgment can be determined to be true: analytically, empirically, or by establishing the judgment to be synthetic *a priori*. Kant begins by pointing out that the judgment 'A thought can only be the effect of the absolute unity of the thinking being' (which he takes, not problematically, to be equivalent to 'If a multiplicity of representations are to form a single representation, they must be contained in the absolute unity of the thinking subject') cannot be analytically true:

For the unity of the thought, which consists of many representations, is collective, and as far as mere concepts can show, may relate just as well to the collective unity of different substances acting together (as the motion of a body is the composite motion of all its parts) as to the absolute unity of the subject. (A353)

In other words, it may well be that a complex thought is itself the result of a complex of substances acting in concert—in any case, there is nothing implied by the mere concept of a thought that dictates the impossibility of such a thesis. It should be noted that Kant is *not* making the claim here that a number of thinking substances (= consciousnesses) may have the thought in the sense (discussed above) of each consciousness having part of the thought, and the 'collective unity' of thinking beings having the unified, complex, thought. For Kant, as we have seen, such a collective unity of different thinking beings is logically impossible. What Kant is pointing out instead—and what will become a well-worn theme in the Paralogisms—is that there is nothing in the concepts of thought or of the thinking 'I' that rules out the possibility that 'the thing which thinks'—at the noumenal level—may well be complex. Interestingly, Broad takes Kant to task for not having made this point against the rationalist:

The fact that, if each of the words of a sentence were heard and understood by a different person, no one would be hearing or understanding the sentence as a whole, is completely irrelevant for the purpose. At most it would show that, *if* a human ego is a compound substance, then it does not consist of a number of other egos interrelated in the sort of way in which the egos of different human individuals are interrelated. This leaves it quite possible that a human ego is a compound substance whose components are not egos.[10]

Kant, of course, would obviously disagree that premiss (6) is 'completely irrelevant', since it is this very case which shows the necessity of the synchronic unity of consciousness. But the objection that the soul may be—at the *noumenal* level—'a compound substance whose components are not egos' is precisely the point that Kant is making against the rational psychologist at A363.[11]

Kant also denies that this 'proposition allows of being known synthetically and completely *a priori* from mere concepts—not, at least, if he [the rational psychologist] understands the ground of the possibility of *a priori* synthetic propositions, as above explained' (A353). All that a synthetic *a priori* truth can express is a fact regarding what constitutes a necessary condition of experience: for Kant, it cannot express anything about the absolute, noumenal, unity of the subject at all. And Kant points out that 'it is likewise impossible to derive this necessary unity of the subject, as a condition of the possibility of every thought, from experience. For experience yields us no knowledge of necessity, apart even from the fact that the concept of absolute unity is quite outside its province' (A353). Given that the crucial proposition makes a claim about what must be the case, it is not an experientially verifiable claim at all, since experience does not reveal necessity. So if this crucial proposition cannot be an analytic, synthetic *a priori*, or empirical truth, it cannot be known to be true at all, and the rationalist's response to the anti-rationalist challenge is based on an empty claim.

Having refuted the restated version of the Second Paralogism, Kant, apparently inexplicably, shifts his focus in paragraphs 5 and 6 to making some remarks about how we represent thinking beings to ourselves—specifically, how we represent *other* thinking beings to ourselves. He says that there is only one way to do so:

I must put myself in his place, and thus substitute, as it were, my own subject for the object I am seeking to consider (which does not occur in any other kind of investigation). . . . we are not in a position to represent such being to ourselves save by putting ourselves, with the formula of our consciousness, in the place of every other intelligent being. (A353–4)

Interspersed with these comments about the representation of other minds are reiterations of premiss (6) above (for example, 'although the whole of the thought could be divided and distributed among many subjects, the subjective "I" can never be thus divided and distributed'). There are thus two exegetical problems here: (1) why has Kant abruptly turned his attention to the problem of other minds, and (2) what is the relevance of premiss (6) to this problem? The answer to (1) will be given in due course. As I will now show, however, we in effect have the answer to (2) already. On the face of it, there is no particularly good reason why we cannot represent other thinking beings to ourselves non-analogically. Consider the extreme case of a radically different kind of thinking being: although Nagel has argued that we cannot know what it is like to be a bat, and that the closest we can get to knowing this is by some kind of analogical extrapolation from our own consciousness (which Nagel suggests is bound to be only dimly successful), it is arguably true that Nagel is here confusing (1) knowing what bat experience is like, and (2) actually having the experiences of a bat.[12] Obviously the former is not the same as the latter, and it is asking far too much of knowledge of bat experience to expect it eventually to *become* bat experience. Similarly, if Kant is saying that I cannot represent others' mental activity at all, he too seems to be trading on a confusion between, on the one hand, knowing (or representing) something about another thinking being *qua* thinking being and, on the other hand, actually having this thinking being's thoughts. On these grounds, and recalling the formal presentation of the Paralogism, it seems that Kant's minor premiss is, in fact, false: consider 'the soul, or the thinking "I", [can never be regarded as the concurrence of several things acting]'. This is simply not true: I can well imagine myself (as a thinking being) to be a human organism, having a complex and composite nervous system which is the source of all my thinkings—in short, I can be a central-state materialist. And there is no reason to think that a central-state materialist cannot view himself as such a physical, composite, object.

It seems that Bennett's reading of Kant's argument endorses this same mistake. He says that

If something is to be viewed as composite, some mind must unite its constituent parts by an 'intellectual synthesis' ... My basic notion of compositeness is that of a number of elements united by my judgment: it pre-requires myself, my synthesizing self, to judge that the elements are so interrelated as to *compose* a whole. I therefore cannot bring this notion to bear *upon* myself . . .'[13]

But again, it is by no means obvious that I cannot apply the notion of compositeness to myself, and if I am a materialist, it is conceivable that I do so with possibly uncomfortable regularity. This, however, is not Kant's point—nor is it (presumably) Nagel's. What Nagel would (or at least should) say in response to the charge that he is confusing knowing about an experience with having that experience is that there are kinds of knowing about an experience that are not accessible from the outside. In other words, to know certain things about an experience requires actually having the experience itself. This, of course, leads directly into Nagel's distinction between subjective and objective points of view, and to his thesis that there is cognitive content accessible from each point of view that is not accessible from the other. This is not the place to examine Nagel's position in any detail, but it does help to illuminate Kant's point. Kant is not saying that I cannot view myself as thinking being in terms of compositeness: a brief look ahead to B415–18, and Kant's intentionally fanciful suggestions there of how I *can* view human consciousness, should make it clear that Kant believes that I can view thinking beings in almost any way that I please. What he is saying, though, is that these representations of myself and of others as thinking beings are (in Nagel's terminology) *objective*: they are representations of thinking beings from a third-person point of view. From a *subjective* standpoint, however, the story is entirely different. In the case of myself, I cannot view my own representings as those of a composite being, since—recalling the Subjective Deduction—I must represent my representings as though they were those of a unitary, and simple, being.[14] Why can I not represent the representings of other thinking beings from a subjective standpoint as the representings of a composite being? The answer was implicit in premiss (6), namely, that if I am to represent the experiences of a thinking being from the subjective standpoint, then I am, by definition, actually having those experiences *myself*. And if I am having those experiences, it becomes extremely problematic to say just how those experiences could possibly not be simply *mine*. So Kant's point is this: if I am to represent another thinking being 'from the inside', that is, to represent a thinking being *qua* thinking being, I must do so analogically, by projecting my own subjective states on to those of another, by 'putting myself in his place'. And given that when Kant speaks of representing a thinking self he is exclusively referring to (again in Nagel's terminology) a *subjective* representation, it follows that for Kant the only kind of non-analogical experience of a thinking being I can have is that experience I have of myself. And as we have seen, Kant argues that what I cannot do is view my representings, from this subjective standpoint, as those of a composite being. So if I am to represent the representings of another thinking being (in the attenuated sense in which I can do this at all), I cannot represent these representings as those of a composite being. Thus we see the relevance of premiss (6) to Kant's digression; the purpose of this digression itself will be seen shortly.

Kant now proceeds to refute the Paralogism in its formal presentation. Thus we have Kant's third argument; his refutation here (in paragraphs 7–9) essentially parallels the refutation of the First Paralogism in A. As was pointed out there, the fallacy of the Paralogism is that of appealing to an ambiguous middle term. The major premiss is a categorial proposition, expressing an analytic truth which is also in some way a necessary component of our conceptual structure. The minor premiss is ambiguous, such that on one reading it asserts something which is analytically true of the self, given the self's role in synthesizing representations—specifically, it describes an aspect of how the self is necessarily represented. On the other reading, it is a synthetic *a priori* judgment, typically asserting that something is true of the self in itself. The important point is that if the first reading of the minor premiss is accepted, then the Paralogism is itself invalid: the major premiss asserts that everything that has a certain property is X, and if the minor premiss only asserts that the soul is *represented as* having that property, then it does not follow that the soul is X. If, of course, the second reading of the minor premiss is accepted, then the Paralogism is a valid syllogistic inference—but Kant argues strenuously that we are not entitled to this reading of the minor premiss, given the 'ground of the possibility of *a priori* synthetic judgments': all that synthetic *a priori* judgments can tell us is what must necessarily obtain given what we know about the character of our own experience. It is also worth recalling that, given the 'represented as' reading of the middle term, and importing this reading into the conclusion, we get (on Kant's view) a true conclusion to the effect that the soul is represented as X.

In paragraph 8 Kant gives his parallel refutation of the Second Paralogism. He says that

the simplicity of the representation of a subject is not *eo ipso* knowledge of the simplicity of the subject itself, for we abstract altogether from its properties when we designate it solely by the entirely empty expression 'I', an expression which I can apply to every thinking subject. (A355)

And this is the point which Kant makes in the First Paralogism as well: the inference that the self is substantial trades on an illicit shift from a claim in the major premiss about what properties a substance has, to a claim in the minor premiss about what properties the self is represented as having. Here, similarly, he is noting that, although we know that the representation of the self is (necessarily) the representation of something as simple, this does not entitle us to say that the self itself is simple, and in fact we can know nothing whatsoever (according to Kant) about the self as it is in itself. The illusion that we can know the self itself to be simple (or substantial) derives from this fact, noted by Strawson: 'just because we have nothing left but the bare *form* of reference, it will appear that the object of this reference must be an object of singular purity and simplicity—a pure, individual, immaterial substance'.[15] Once we assume that the thinking self is an object—which Kant and Hume have taken pains to show us that it is not—then given the fact that the 'I' of the 'I think' is 'the bare form of representation', we will tend rather naturally to infer from the fact that the *representation* 'I' is not composite, accidental, or a plurality that the *self* is in fact simple, substantial, and unitary. Kant says that

It is obvious that in attaching 'I' to our thoughts we designate the subject of inherence only transcendentally, without noting in it any quality whatsoever—in fact, without knowing anything of it either by direct acquaintance or otherwise. It means a something in general (transcendental subject), the representation of which must, no doubt, be simple, if only for the reason that there is nothing determinate in it. Nothing, indeed, can be represented that is simpler than that which is represented through the concept of a mere something. (A355)

Thus the source of what Strawson has called the Cartesian illusion is in essence an illicit shift from the observation that the 'I' is *not* represented as a *composite* determinate object to the observation that the soul *is* represented as a *simple* determinate object, while in fact the 'I' is not represented as a determinate object at all.[16] It is represented, however, as having what Kant calls 'indivisible unity', and as the bare form of consciousness it is naturally enough taken to be both simple and unitary (A355). And the Second Paralogism trades on precisely this illicit shift, or 'inflation', from the notion of being represented as X to that of being X. So if the Second Paralogism is to be valid, we must have grounds for accepting the minor premiss as a true judgment about the self *an sich*, and this Kant says we do not have. And if we rightly take the minor premiss to be a true judgment about the (necessary) representation of the self, then the Paralogism is simply invalid.

What should we say, then, about the *second* inflation of this Paralogism? In the case of the First Paralogism, the second inflation was that of inflating the conclusion: if the conclusion was read to mean that the soul is represented as unschematized substance, then it was taken to be true, but for it to do the rational psychologist any good, it was necessary that it be 'inflated' to the claim that the soul is represented as schematized substance (though, as Kant argued, even this inflation is inadequate for the rational psychologist's programme). In effect, this inflation was a category mistake, trading on an ambiguous usage of schematized and unschematized 'substance'. On the face of it, the same kind of charge of inflation in the case of the Second Paralogism does not seem to be available to Kant, since 'simplicity' is not a category for Kant at all. The Paralogism is placed, under Kant's often problematic architectonic, under the Categories of Quality in A, which include Reality, Negation, and Limitation, and under the Categories of Relation in B, which include Substance and Accident, Cause and Effect, and Reciprocity.[17] Certainly simplicity *per se* is not a Kantian category, and it would be more or less futile to attempt any post-Kantian gerrymandering to see what is likely to be a strained relation in any case. But, interestingly, Kant does treat simplicity as a concept which is used with what looks like a schematized–unschematized distinction. In paragraph 9 he says that

through the 'I', I always entertain the thought of an absolute, but logical, unity of the subject (simplicity). It does not, however, follow that I thereby know the actual simplicity of my subject. (A356)

This notion of 'an absolute, but logical' simplicity is contrasted with 'actual' simplicity, and can be taken to be the same contrast as that between an unschematized and a schematized category. In the case of a representation having logical simplicity there is no spatial content to the representation at all. That which is taken to be (logically) simple is so only in so far as its representation is not that of something composite, as opposed to that which is (actually) simple by virtue of its having extension but not being divisible. So the second inflation of the Second Paralogism appears to be that of taking the conclusion to assert not merely that the soul has *logical* (unschematized) simplicity but that it has *actual* simplicity: that it is a contentive, extended representation of an indivisible object. Kant makes this reasonably explicit by pointing out that we can apply 'substance' to ourselves, but only as pure (unschematized) category and not empirically, as schematized category. He makes precise the parallel between attributions of substantiality and attributions of simplicity, linking the two putative properties of the thinking self together and saying

I may therefore legitimately say: 'I am a simple substance', that is, a substance the representation of which never contains a synthesis of the manifold. But this concept, as also the proposition, tells us nothing whatsoever in regard to myself as an object of experience, since the concept of substance is itself used only as a function of synthesis, without any underlying intuition, and therefore without an object. It concerns only the condition of our knowledge; it does not apply to any assignable object. (A356)

Thus there is for Kant a sense in which I can say that the self is simple: it is *logically* simple, inasmuch as it is not contentive/determinate at all, and is merely an operator, whose function is to synthesize representations as those of a unitary subject. But this tells us nothing about the claimed actual—*experiential*—simplicity of the thinking self, and to appeal to the logical simplicity of the 'I' in support of these claims is to commit, quite literally, a category mistake.

Given this second inflation, Kant announces—at the end of paragraph 9—that 'We will test the supposed usefulness of the proposition by an experiment,' and he thereby leads into his *fourth* argument (A356). In paragraph 10 he asks what the rational psychologist's point is in arguing that the soul is a simple substance, and suggests that

the assertion of the simple nature of the soul is of value only in so far as I can thereby distinguish this subject from all matter, and so can exempt it from the dissolution to which matter is always liable. (A356)

That is to say, the only purpose that can in any obvious way be served by demonstrating that the soul is actually simple is that this premiss can itself be used to argue that the soul is immortal. To see how such an argument could go, we need look no farther than Plato's *Phaedo*, where Socrates says that

What kind of thing is likely to undergo . . . dissolution . . . and what kind of thing is not liable to it? . . . mustn't we further ask to which of these two kinds soul belongs, and then feel either confidence or fear for our own soul accordingly? . . . what has been put together and is naturally composite is liable to undergo [dissolution], to break up at the point at which it was put together; whereas if there be anything incomposite, it alone is liable, if anything is, to escape [dissolution].[18]

And having established the intuitive link between being composite and being destructible, Socrates proceeds to develop an intricate argument to show that the soul is actually simple: to prove what is in fact the inflated conclusion of the Second Paralogism. Kant stresses that the rational psychologist, in trying to distinguish the soul from that which is *composite*, in practice focuses his efforts on driving a wedge between the soul and *matter*. In effect, then, the proposition 'The soul is simple' is 'generally expressed as "The soul is not corporeal"', and it is this latter formulation of the inflated conclusion which is used by the rational psychologist to argue for the soul's immortality (A356–7). It should be noted that Kant need not accept this formulation, since being simple and being non-corporeal are fairly obviously not equivalent properties. The set of natural numbers, for example, is presumably both non-corporeal and composite; and Kant does not rule out the possibility of there being simple extended (and hence presumably corporeal) substances: this, presumably, is what Kant means by 'actual' simplicity.[19] But Kant does provisionally grant the equivalence of these two formulations of the Paralogism's conclusion. Having done so, he now (in paragraphs 11–16) considers the 'usefulness' of this inflated conclusion, were we to know it to be true. And the point of doing so is parallel to that of granting the inflated conclusion of the First Paralogism: that 'although we allow full objective validity' to this proposition 'we still cannot make the least use of this proposition in regard to the question of its dissimilarity from or relation to matter' (A357).

In one sense, Kant says, we do have reason for saying that 'the soul is non-corporeal'. Recalling the Transcendental Aesthetic, he notes that those things which *are* corporeal—bodies—are only appearances of outer sense. And the soul, however it is represented, is not represented as such an appearance. To the extent that it is an object at all, 'it is represented by us as object of inner sense' and so 'it cannot, in so far as it thinks, be an object of outer sense, that is, an appearance in space' (A357). It is important to note that here Kant is by no means saying that either the self in itself or the self of transcendental apperception is represented as any kind of object at all—rather, he is referring to the self of *empirical* apperception = the 'flux of appearances' which comprises the Humean bundle of perceptions. And Kant's point in part is that the contents of such representations are not extended. Thoughts are not spatially represented, and to the extent that such appearances are themselves represented at all, they are represented as objects of inner sense. Since, then, we do not ever in practice encounter thinking selves as extended, corporeal objects, we are 'justified in saying that our thinking subject is not corporeal' (A357). So here we finally see the reason for Kant's (misplaced) comments above regarding the impossibility of representing a thinking being's experience from the outside: in arguing for this impossibility, he is supporting his claim that thinking beings are only objects of inner sense and that at least in one sense we can reasonably say that 'the soul is non-corporeal' = 'the soul is never an object of outer sense'.[20] Indeed, the perception that, in the realm of appearances, souls are not experienced in the same way that bodies are is 'so natural and so popular that even the commonest understanding appears ... from the earliest times, to have regarded souls as quite different entities from their bodies' (A357–8). It is important to note, however, that Kant does not say that it follows from this 'natural' and 'popular' perception that souls and bodies are distinct even at the phenomenal level—but on the other hand it is not clear what it would mean were one to say that they are not phenomenally distinct. So at the phenomenal level, souls are obviously enough non-corporeal, and in this sense Kant can grant the rational psychologist his 'non-corporeal' formulation of the Paralogism's conclusion.[21]

Does this attenuated sense in which we can with reason say that the self is non-corporeal provide the rational psychologist with what he needs to demonstrate the soul's immortality? Kant now (paragraph 12) argues that it does not. It must be remembered, says Kant, that all we have been talking about is thoughts and bodies, which are phenomenal representations, and knowledge of such representations does not lead us, at least not legitimately, to knowledge of things in themselves. He says that the conceded sense of 'the soul is non-corporeal' leaves open the possibility that

the something which underlies the outer appearances and which so affects our sense that it obtains the representations of space, matter, shape, etc., may yet, when viewed as noumenon (or better, as transcendental object), be at the same time the subject of our thoughts. (A358)

So it is not inconsistent with the phenomenal distinctness of thoughts and bodies that in fact there is a noumenal substrate of the phenomenal body which is itself the subject—here, a subject(1)—which has my thoughts.

Kant says, provocatively, that it is even possible that this substrate of matter is itself *simple* (A358). If this is possible, then even if we concede that the self is phenomenally simple, and that we can distinguish our thinking selves from bodies as outer appearances, it is still the case that we cannot distinguish the thinking self—in itself—from whatever it may be that underlies matter as outer appearance. And, says Kant, this is true 'even granting the soul to be simple in nature' (that is, assuming that the soul is in itself simple), since matter may be 'in itself simple' as well (A359).[22] Given the possibility that matter itself may well have a simple substrate, and that we do not know what underlies the thinking self, Kant raises an interesting possibility:

I may further assume that the substance which in relation to our outer sense possesses extension is in itself the possessor of thoughts, and that these thoughts can by means of its own inner sense be consciously represented . . . Accordingly, the thesis that only souls . . . think, would have to be given up; and we should have to fall back on the common expression that men think, that is, that the very same being which, as outer appearance, is extended, is (in itself) internally a subject, and is not composite, but is simple and thinks. (A359–60)

Since we do not know what underlies either empirical apperception or extended bodies, it is completely plausible that there is some substantial entity which is—in itself—simple, and which has the (phenomenal) properties of thought and extension. In other words, it may be that at the level of things in themselves what is the case is something very like what we are getting at when we say that persons, rather than souls (or bodies) are the subjects(1) of thoughts.[23] But it is essential to remember that this is for Kant nothing but imaginative speculation, since we cannot know what the substrate of either the thinking self or of an extended body in fact is. Kant's point is merely this: it is granted that the soul as it appears in empirical apperception is distinguished from the appearances of corporeal/material entities. And the soul in itself is distinct from matter as well: in paragraph 14 Kant says that asking whether or not the soul in itself is 'the same in kind as matter . . . is by its very terms illegitimate', since matter is not a thing in itself (A360). But this tells us nothing about whether or not the soul *itself* is different from whatever underlies matter. And the key is this: we do not know if the substrate of the thinking self—or of matter—is itself composite, and hence subject to dissolution.

At this point (paragraph 15) Kant reverts, confusingly, from talking about the self of empirical apperception to talking about the 'I' of transcendental apperception ('das denkende Ich'), and makes the same point with regard to our not being able to distinguish the substrate of this 'I' from the substrate of matter. And in paragraph 16, he seems to refer to the illusion derived from the form of the transcendental 'I', saying that 'The simple consciousness is not, therefore, knowledge of the simple nature of the self as subject, such as might enable us to distinguish it from matter, as from a composite being' (A360). This seems to be a confusion between the two inflations, the first being that of mistaking the logical simplicity of the transcendental unity of apperception for the actual simplicity of the soul, and the second being that of mistaking the non-corporeality of the self of empirical apperception for the self's being in itself non-composite. But the point of Kant's first argument is related to the concession that the (representation of) the self in empirical apperception is non-corporeal: given that the transcendental 'I' is such that its representation is that of a simple being, we cannot infer from this that the self is in itself simple—and we cannot infer that it is non-composite, nor that it does not have the noumenal corollary of corporeality. Even if we grant, then, that those substances which are simple in themselves are immune to dissolution, and hence immortal,[24] we cannot infer that the soul is such a substance merely on the basis of saying that 'the soul is non-corporeal'—at least not in the sense of this expression which Kant is prepared to concede. So even if we grant the rational psychologist the inflated conclusion that 'the soul is non-corporeal', he is not able to distinguish the soul from, in Socrates' words, the 'kind of thing [that] is liable to undergo . . . dissolution'. And the rational psychologist seems to have failed in his ultimate goal of proving the soul's immortality from its non-corporeality.

So far, we have seen Kant deploy four arguments in the A version of the Second Paralogism. First, he argues against the anti-rationalist that the representation of the self must be a representation of something which is simple, or it would not be possible for the thinking self to have complex thoughts at all. Second, he argues against the rational psychologist that the proposition 'A thought can only be the effect of the absolute unity of the thinking being'—a proposition which is crucial to the restated version of the Paralogism—is itself unprovable. Third, he argues that the Second Paralogism itself trades on an ambiguity between, on the one hand, the concept of 'being simple' = being actually simple and, on the other hand, 'being represented as simple' = having logical simplicity, such that logical simplicity is inflated into actual simplicity. Fourth, Kant concedes to the rational psychologist the proposition that 'the soul is non-corporeal' (but in a fatally attenuated sense) and shows that this concession gains him nothing in his attempt to prove the soul's immortality. Kant, however, is not yet done with the rational psychologist, as can be seen by consideration of the fourth argument. As was pointed out, in paragraph 10 Kant suggests that 'The soul is simple' is taken (in the context of rationalist arguments) to be equivalent to 'The soul is non-corporeal', and though Kant does not need to concede this putative equivalence, he does so in order to show the uselessness of the inflated conclusion of the Paralogism for the rationalist's aims. And he shows this by pointing out that 'The soul is non-corporeal' tells us nothing about the soul (or body) in itself, and so cannot tell us that the soul is such that it cannot undergo the dissolution to which all corporeal substances, presumably, are prey. Given Kant's strategy, 'The soul is non-corporeal' is not obviously a weaker claim than its presumed equivalent, that 'The soul is (actually) simple', since 'actual' simplicity is a property of phenomenal entities. That a representation of the soul has such a property tells us no more about the nature of the soul in itself than does the assertion that it is non-corporeal. But brief consideration will show that this is not true of yet a third inflation of the Second Paralogism's conclusion: that 'The soul is *in itself* simple.' Were the rational psychologist to establish this as the conclusion of the Second Paralogism, Kant's arguments against the inflation of the Paralogism would not hold, since 'The soul is in itself simple', unlike

'The soul is (actually) simple' and 'The soul is non-corporeal', *does* tell us something about the nature of the soul in itself. And if Kant objects that we do not thereby know that the substrate of matter is not also simple, the rational psychologist may well concede the point, but will also ask why that is damaging to his case. If we can infer from the soul's simplicity that the soul is indestructible, then the rational psychologist has succeeded in achieving his aim; all Kant's objection would establish is that the substrate of matter may be indestructible as well. Of course, the rational psychologist has not proven that 'The soul is in itself simple', and, from Kant's perspective, such a proof would be impossible. What seems true, though, is that the claim 'The soul is in itself simple' appears to provide an adequate ground for establishing the soul's immortality; in any case, it is the conclusion to which the rational psychologist aspires and it is the linchpin of Plato's affinity argument. Were Kant to grant the rational psychologist this inflation of the Paralogism's conclusion, and were he to show that even equipped with this piece of noumenal self-knowledge, the rational psychologist cannot prove the soul's immortality, then Kant would have thoroughly destroyed any possible importance the Second Paralogism could have for the rational psychologist's programme. And this is precisely what Kant does do, but not until the second edition, in his 'Refutation of Mendelssohn's Proof of the Immortality of the Soul'.

MENDELSSOHN'S PROOF

To restate the obvious, it is part of Kant's design in the *Critique of Pure Reason* to show the indemonstrability of the immortality of the soul. As we have seen, and as Kant well realizes, there is a long tradition of attempts to prove the immortality of the soul on the basis of the soul's being a 'simple substance'. And in the First and Second Paralogisms, Kant goes to considerable trouble to deprive these purported proofs of their foundation: he argues forcefully that we cannot know the soul to be either simple or substantial. Having done this, however, he goes one step further and produces a demonstration that suggests the impossibility of proving the soul's immortality even given the premiss that the soul *an sich* exists as a 'simple substance'. For the purposes of this demonstration, Kant considers an argument of Moses Mendelssohn:

This acute philosopher soon noticed that the usual argument by which it is thought to prove that the soul—if it be admitted to be a simple being—cannot cease to be through dissolution, is insufficient for its purpose, that of proving the necessary continuance of the soul, since it may be supposed to pass out of existence through simply vanishing. In his *Phaedo* he endeavoured to prove that the soul cannot be subject to such a process of vanishing, which would be a true annihilation, by showing that a simple being cannot cease to exist. His argument is that since the soul cannot be diminished, and so gradually lose something of its existence, being by degrees changed into nothing (for since it has no parts, it has no multiplicity in itself), there would be no time between a moment in which it is and another in which it is not—which is impossible. (B413–14)

It seems that Mendelssohn is aware that the soul as a simple substance cannot cease to exist through a breaking up of its parts, since, being without size, it has no parts to have broken up. As we have seen, this is the standard move made by those Kant calls rational psychologists, and is borne out in Mendelssohn's *Phaedo*. But Mendelssohn is also aware that there is another way in which the soul could cease to be, namely, by simply vanishing. In other words, the soul would not 'break up' or diminish in any way, but rather would simply disappear and be gone. This kind of cessation of the soul is not in itself barred by positing the soul as a simple and unitary substance, since there is no obvious reason why a simple substance would be any less susceptible to such a disappearance than any other substance. The force of the objection is that this type of cessation does not require a gradual alteration, in which parts break off, erode, or change. And it is this requirement that makes the notion of the soul as simple substance as philosophically attractive as it is, since viewing the soul as simple eludes the possibility of cessation by dissolution. Cessation by vanishing, however, cannot be dismissed in this way.

Mendelssohn, then, recognizes the need to make another move: he asserts the impossibility of cessation by disappearance with regard to *any* substance. As he says in his *Phaedo*:

dying is the transition from life to death . . . As the body decomposes, nothing is lost. Its disintegrating components continue to exist. They bring about and suffer changes, undergoing new compositions and decompositions until, through an endless change of transformations they change into elements of another natural compound . . . death and life are physiologically not as separated as they appear to our senses. They are but links in a chain of ceaseless transformations, closely interconnected by gradual transitions. There is no exact moment of which we could definitely say, 'Now the animal dies' . . . we realize that in reality life and death are not separated from each other.[25]

Mendelssohn admits that we for the most part do not see changes of states as a continuous process, but he explains this in terms of structuring by our imagination: 'the days of the week, seen as a whole, are indistinguishable. For whatever is continuous and contiguous can be separated into distinct, discrete parts only in our imagination.'[26] This separation by the imagination can be illusory, though, for it belies the actual continuities of alteration in the world. As Mendelssohn says, 'Our mind can well discern . . . that we must not stop where there is no real division.' What we have here is really an instance of Whitehead's 'fallacy of misplaced concrescence': Mendelssohn is pointing out that by bracketing continuous quanta we tend to lose sight of their actual continuity. So, for Mendelssohn, nothing in fact simply vanishes: change from one state to another state does require alteration over time, since change is indeed continuous. For Mendelssohn, any talk about distinct states at all is somewhat illusory, since 'a chain of ceaseless transformations' is the substratum of what is. Since continuity of change is a given, it is a mistake to accept the possibility of an abrupt vanishing of the soul. Any change from one state to another is gradual, and so if the soul does cease to exist, it must do so gradually, by dissolution. As Mendelssohn says:

A sudden or gradual death seem to exhaust all possibilities . . . The first possibility is: the soul perishes suddenly, disappearing abruptly. Such a death would seem to be impossible (since) nature never destroys anything completely . . . Between being and not-being there yawns a terrible abyss, and it is not in the nature of things to leap across this chasm.[27]

Since such an abrupt change is not 'in the nature of things', the only other kind of cessation possible (according to Mendelssohn) is cessation by dissolution. And this too is not possible:

We therefore have to examine only one other question: whether the soul's innate powers might not disappear in the same gradual manner in which the parts of a body's machinery disintegrate . . . (just as the body weakens so the soul) grows gradually weaker. Its emotions become confused, its thinking incoherent . . . Eventually, the body dies . . . The soul may still experience some weak stirrings, creating certain dim notions. But this would represent the limit of its remaining power. Presently, physical decomposition sets in . . . And the soul? . . . have all its inclinations and passions disappeared without the slightest trace? . . . The soul cannot perish in all eternity. For the final step, no matter how long delayed, would still be a leap from being to nothingness, and such a leap is out of character with the nature of either a simple substance or that of a compound. Hence the soul must exist, or endure, eternally.[28]

So, since the soul cannot pass out of existence either abruptly, by vanishing, or gradually, by dissolution, it cannot pass out of existence at all.

Mendelssohn's proof, as it stands, is not clearly that of an 'acute philosopher'. He attempts to show that the soul cannot undergo cessation by either abrupt disappearance or dissolution. But his proof that the soul cannot abruptly vanish rests only on the observation of just how change of states occurs in the world. It is experientially clear that objects do not abruptly disappear but instead undergo transformations over time. This, however, is a contingent truth—at least Mendelssohn has not shown it to be otherwise. It has not been shown to be *impossible* for an object to vanish abruptly. But such impossibility is required by the 'rational psychologist' if he is to demonstrate the necessity of the soul's continued existence, and yet Mendelssohn gives no clear reason to rule out the *possibility* that in fact the soul does vanish as the body dies. And his demonstration of the impossibility of the soul's cessation by dissolution has equally little force. Mendelssohn suggests that the soul does not actually, cannot, cease to be because nothing actually ceases to be; objects undergo change as a constant process, but they do not go out of existence. This, however, tells us no more than that the body does not cease to exist, because its parts endure after undergoing transformation. These transformations are in fact definitive of dissolution. Dissolution does not imply an absolute ceasing to be but a transformation that involves a ceasing to be one thing and coming to be another. So the body ceases to be a body and becomes a group of organic compounds. Similarly, the soul could cease to be (as a soul) and become something else. At best, Mendelssohn has established that if there is something that constitutes a soul, then that something cannot absolutely cease to be.[29] But this is true of the body as well: something stronger is at issue here than that which Mendelssohn has actually—and trivially—demonstrated.

Mendelssohn's demonstration, as shown above, is weak. And it is not the proof which Kant attributes to Mendelssohn (though Kant's statement of Mendelssohn's proof has its genesis in some of what Mendelssohn is getting at). Let us look again at the presentation of Mendelssohn's proof in the Second Paralogism. The soul, according to *Kant's* Mendelssohn, is a simple substance ('for since it has no parts'). As such, the soul has no extensive magnitude, and therefore cannot undergo cessation by dissolution: to dissolve, a thing must have extensive magnitude, must be subject to partition so that it can diminish by gradually losing part of itself until at some point it is no longer such that it constitutes what it was prior to the dissolution. As a non-extensive thing, the soul is not subject to partition and thus cannot cease to be by dissolution. But it is also possible that the soul could cease to be abruptly, by disappearing instantaneously. And this, Kant's Mendelssohn says, is impossible, for 'there would be no time between a moment in which it is and another in which it is not— which is impossible' (B414). Just what is it, however, that is impossible about this kind of cessation? Mendelssohn himself has asserted it to be impossible on the basis of observation, but this assertion, as already noted, lacks logical necessity. Kant is clearly suggesting a more substantial impossibility, one that is best seen by an examination of the Anticipations of Perception.

In the Anticipations, Kant offers what amounts to a criticism of Mendelssohn's basis for the principle of continuity of alteration. He says,

Since all appearances . . . are thus continuous magnitudes, it might seem to be an easy matter to prove with mathematical conclusiveness the proposition that all alteration (transition of a thing from one state to another) is continuous. But the causality of an alteration in general, presupposing, as it does, empirical principles, lies altogether outside the limits of a transcendental philosophy . . . alterableness is to be met with only in certain determinations of appearances . . . whereas the cause of these determinations lies in the unalterable, experience alone can teach what they are. (A171/B213)

In other words, even though we experience objects only as having continuous magnitudes, we experience alteration only in particular 'determinations of appearances'. What causes alteration itself is an empirical matter, and thus is not obviously subject to the necessity of Kant's transcendental philosophy. So we may well experience alteration as continuous—but this is contingent on experience, and is not logically compelling. According to Kant, then, we do not have access to the nature of alteration except through our experience. And this indirect access vitiates the absolute grounds for the principle of continuity of change that Mendelssohn presumes he has established. As Kant says in the Second Analogy of Experience:

How anything can be altered, and how it should be possible that upon one state in a given moment an opposite state may follow in the next moment—of this we have not, *a priori*, the least conception. For that we require knowledge of actual forces, which can only be given empirically. (A207/B252)

So for the principle needed by Mendelssohn to be firmly established, it must be demonstrated in some other fashion.

In the Second Analogy, Kant offers a demonstration of the principle of continuity of alteration that is consonant with the transcendental method of the *Critique*. He says that

apart from all question of what the content of the alteration, that is, what the state which is altered, may be, the form of every alteration, the condition under which, as a coming to be of another state, it can alone take place, and so the succession of states themselves (the happening), can still be considered *a priori* according to the law of causality and the conditions of time. (A207/B252)

In other words, despite the empirical nature of alteration, and the concomitant contingency of our observations concerning it, we can none the less draw *a priori* conclusions about alteration by considering the necessary condition of alteration as empirical phenomenon. It is possible, says Kant, to determine just what is required of alteration for it to be experienced by us. He says:

If a substance passes from one state a, to another b, the point of time of the second is distinct from that of the first, and follows upon it. Similarly, the second state as reality in the (field of) appearance differs from the first wherein it did not exist . . . The question therefore arises how a thing passes from one state = a to another = b. Between two instants there is always a time, and between any two states in the two instants there is always a difference which has magnitude. For all parts of appearances are always themselves magnitudes. All transition from one state to another therefore occurs in a time which is contained between two instants, of which the first determines the state from which the thing arises, and the second that into which it passes. Both instants, then, are limits of the time of a change, and so of the intermediate state between the two states, and therefore as such form part of the total alteration. . . That is the law of the continuity of all alteration. Its ground is this: that neither time nor appearance in time consists of parts which are the smallest (possible), and that, nevertheless, the state of a thing passes in its alteration through all these parts, as elements, to its second state. (A207–9/B253–4)

Kant's strategy is this: we can distinguish two states of a substance in terms of the difference of magnitude experienced in each. Time is a formal condition of experiencing two distinct states, and cannot itself be divided into discrete segments which are the smallest possible, for between any two instants of time there is always some period of time, however small ('Between two instants there is always a time'). So if we are to distinguish two distinct states, we must do so in time. And between these two states, since they are located at distinct instants of time, there is necessarily a period of time, namely, that time between any two instants. It is clear, then, that if any alteration of state takes place in a substance, that alteration of state must take place *over time*. The apparent immediacy of the conjunction of the two states is not relevant, for if we can distinguish the two states at all we have distinguished them in time. And given the nature of time—that it is not reducible to some kind of basic indivisible units—there is a time over which the alteration of states occurs, such that the alteration is continuous. This is necessarily so, given our forms of intuition: if time were not itself continuous in this way, our experience would be fragmented and incoherent in a way that it is not. And since our experience of states of a substance must take place in time—since time is a form of intuition—it is clear that our experience of alteration is necessarily of a continuous phenomenon.

So Kant has (1) shown that the principle of continuity of alteration cannot be demonstrated absolutely, due to the constraints of experience, and (2) offered a transcendental proof of the principle, that is, that it is necessary given the form of our structuring of experience that alteration be continuous. On this basis, Kant can allow Mendelssohn his move countering cessation by disappearance. As Kant says of this move, 'there would be no time between a moment in which it is and another in which it is not—which is impossible' (B414). The point is this: if the soul cannot diminish due to its lack of extensive magnitude, then, Mendelssohn would say, the only alternative would be a cessation by disappearance. But since this cessation is by definition not gradual, it must involve an alteration from one state (existence) to another (non-existence) without any intermediate process. If this is the case, then the alteration does not occur over time; there is no interval of time between the first state and the second state. But this belies the nature of time itself, which is such that there is always an interval of time between any two moments. Correlatively, this would contradict the principle of continuity of alteration. So it is not possible for cessation by disappearance to occur.

Kant, then, has given Mendelssohn's argument a provisional force that it lacks in itself. His purpose in doing this is clear, given the context of his discussion in the Second Paralogism. By taking an argument for the immortality of the soul which proceeds from the premiss that the soul is a simple substance, and by making this proof as forceful as possible, then by refuting this proof, Kant again intends to thwart the philosophers of rational psychology on their home turf. Intending to give Mendelssohn's argument its greatest possible strength, and *then* show its inadequacy, though, Kant provisionally (and tacitly) accepts several points that he in fact rejects. The most obvious, of course, is that the soul is a simple substance. It is also well to reiterate that Kant does not accept the specific *kind* of impossibility that Mendelssohn ascribes to cessation by disappearance. Both Kant and Mendelssohn do accept the principle of continuity of alteration. But they do so on quite different grounds, with Kant explicitly criticizing the type of justification offered by Mendelssohn. It is worth noting briefly that Kant's transcendental version of the principle would in fact not suffice in a 'rational doctrine' proof of immortality: it only establishes continuity as ground of possible experience, and says nothing, can say nothing, about what alteration must be like in itself and when consciousness ceases. In any case, it is well to bear in mind that Kant is allowing Mendelssohn and rational psychology every move that he can—and in doing so is giving Mendelssohn all the rope he needs to hang himself.

KANT'S REFUTATION OF MENDELSSOHN

Mendelssohn states that there are only two ways in which the soul may cease to be, that is, through diminution or disappearance. Since the soul has no extensive magnitude to diminish, and cessation by disappearance (vanishing) is impossible, he draws the conclusion that the soul cannot in fact cease to be. And Kant grants that the soul cannot cease to be by diminution or by disappearance. But, says Kant, there is a third alternative to the first two forms of cessation. He says,

[Mendelssohn] failed, however, to observe that even if we admit the simple nature of the soul, namely, that it contains no manifold of constituents external to one another, and therefore no extensive quantity, we yet cannot deny to it, any more than to any other existence, intensive quantity, that is, a degree of reality in respect of all its faculties, nay in respect of all that constitutes its existence, and that this degree of reality may diminish through all the infinitely many smaller degrees. In this manner the supposed substance . . . may be changed into nothing, not indeed by dissolution, but by gradual loss (*remissio*) of its powers, and so . . . by elanguescence. (B414)

To understand Kant's objection requires a brief digression on intensive magnitude. Though the soul as a simple substance would have no *extensive quantity*, and therefore cannot diminish in terms of its extended parts, it does still have *intensive quality*. As pointed out in the Anticipations, 'In all appearances, the real that is an object of sensation has intensive magnitude' (A166/B207). The category of reality 'in the pure concept of understanding, is that which corresponds to a sensation in general' (A143/B182); so the real involves 'objects of sensation'—those objects that appear to us through the senses. In the appearance, and apart from the intuition of the objects (the real), there is also what Kant calls 'the matter for some object in general . . . appearances contain, that is to say, the real of sensation' (B207). So part of what is involved in an appearance is being affected by 'the real of sensation'—by the sensory encounter with an object. Now sensation is not extensive, since 'the real of sensation' is for Kant a *content* while 'extensive magnitude' is rather a matter of *form*. In other words, 'the real of sensation' is something which *is extended* in some more or less determinate way (for example, a piercing pain *in* my arm), but this notion of extension is not properly applicable to the *sensation itself*: hence the absurdity of the question 'How wide is the pain in your arm?' As Kant says in the Anticipations of Perception, 'since neither the intuition of space nor that of time is to be met with in (sensation), its magnitude is not extensive . . .' (B208). So sensation, not itself having form, does not possess extensive magnitude.

But sensation does have *intensive* magnitude, which is, roughly, the level of influence it can exert upon the senses. This intensive magnitude, like extensive magnitude, admits of degree. Kant says that

Now from empirical consciousness to pure consciousness a graduated transition is possible, the real in the former completely vanishing and a merely formal *a priori* consciousness of the manifold in space and time remaining. Consequently there is also possible a synthesis in the process of generating the magnitude of a sensation from its beginning in pure intuition = o, up to any required magnitude . . . This (intensive) magnitude is generated in the act of apprehension whereby the empirical consciousness of it can in a certain time increase from nothing = o to the given measure. (A166/B208)

In other words, given an experience of a thing, such as a sound, the consciousness of this sound can alter gradually, diminishing from a vivid experiential awareness of the sound as loud, or as bright, to an awareness of the sound as softer, or as more dull and flat. Eventually the sound may fade out entirely, leaving 'pure intuition'. (It is worth noting that by 'pure intuition' Kant means *empty* space and time, 'in which there is nothing that belongs to sensation', in which there is nothing to exert influence upon the senses) (A20/B34). Similarly, the sensory experience of an object may arise out of 'pure intuition' and develop to a given intensity. Thus my experiencing a sound may begin with silence, which is followed by the gradual increase of the sound's volume such that my awareness of it progresses from a vague sense of some sound being made to an awareness of increased volume and of certain aspects of the character of the sound: brilliance, shrillness, etc. My apprehension of the sound has involved generation of an intensive magnitude in sensation, without there being change in any extensive magnitude that is, with intensive magnitude, constitutive of my apprehension. And this intensity increased from 'nothing = o' to a certain magnitude in the process of apprehension. Clearly, then, sensation (and intensive magnitude) admits of degree, continuous from no intensity up to higher degrees of intensity.

Correlative with the intensive magnitude of sensation, says Kant, is an intensive magnitude of the object of sensation (A166/B208). 'The real of sensation' itself has intensive magnitude in so far as it is subject of apprehension. In hearing a loud sound, I feel an intense sensation whose magnitude reflects the intensive magnitude of the sound in so far as it is loud. In this way 'the real that is an object of sensation has intensive magnitude': in so far as an appearance contains a sensory representation as well as an intuitive representation, it involves sensation, which has intensity. And the object of this appearance has an intensive magnitude in that it is represented partly by sensation. Thus Kant speaks of these objects as 'the real in sensation'—the real, considered in so far as it has a sensory representation. And the real, says Kant, has a 'substratum', namely, substance, which is present in that which is real. As substratum, substance is that which is conserved through apparent change. He says, 'the substratum of all that is real, that is, of all that belongs to the existence of things, is substance' (A182/B225). So all substance, as substratum of the real, has itself intensive magnitude. Through sensory apprehension, substance is characterized by an intensity of sensation that is part of its apprehension by the experiencing subject.

Here Kant's refutation of Mendelssohn draws on the Anticipations. If the soul is a simple substance, then as substance it has intensive magnitude. And intensive magnitude, being by nature a matter of 'graduated transition' (or degree), can reduce to no intensity at all. So even though the soul has no *extensive* magnitude that can undergo dissolution to nothing, it does have *intensive* magnitude that can by definition decrease to nothing. If the soul is, as Mendelssohn holds, a substance, then 'we yet cannot deny to it, any more than to any other existence (or substance), intensive quantity, that is, a degree of reality ... and ... this degree of reality may diminish through all the infinitely many smaller degrees' to nothing. So Kant has pointed out a third type of cessation, which Mendelssohn does not account for: in addition to cessation by vanishing, and cessation by dissolution of extensive quantity, Kant suggests the possibility of cessation by *elanguescence*, a 'fading away' by diminution of intensity. If the soul is a simple substance and lacks extensive magnitude, then it is still real to the extent that it has intensive magnitude, reflected in its subjective representation. If its intensive magnitude diminishes to nothing, then it is no longer real. Thus the soul, in losing its intensive magnitude (its 'powers'), can cease to exist. Kant, of course, is not saying that the soul does in fact undergo elanguescence. Rather, he is saying that given Mendelssohn's presuppositions about the soul, and the nature of substance and its intensive magnitude, then there is a third possible form of cessation—elanguescence—that the soul *may* undergo. Mendelssohn has not accounted for this possibility, and, as will be seen, Kant believes that Mendelssohn cannot conclusively discount such a possible cessation of the soul's existence.

In fact, says Kant, the soul as thinking subject—which is the soul of 'rational doctrine'—does indeed have intensive magnitude, at least in so far as it is represented to us: 'For consciousness itself has always a degree, which always allows of diminution, and the same must also hold of the faculty of being conscious of the self, and likewise of all other faculties' (B414–15). In a footnote, Kant argues against the idea that there is one given 'clear' state of consciousness, a clear consciousness of a representation (B415). He argues that even in the case of 'obscure', vague, representations there is consciousness of them as representations, however minimal: if there were no such consciousness we could not differentiate between such nebulous representations when presented together. Kant argues that our ability to distinguish ephemeral or abstract terms ('right' and 'equity', for example), and our ability to distinguish similar events occurring simultaneously (musical chords and discords) indicate a consciousness even of obscure representations. Of course, we may be *aware* of being able to make these distinctions in varying degrees, or we may not be aware of this ability at all in certain circumstances. For instance, there are words with similar yet slightly different meanings that I use in distinct ways, but I am not aware of the difference in use and could not well express it on reflection. And I may be more or less aware of this difference. So consciousness is a matter of 'infinitely many degrees'—and may cease to exist through a gradual reduction in degree of intensity.

ELANGUESCENCE AND DEGREES OF REALITY

In this context, it is interesting to look at a recent criticism, by Chisholm, of Kant's notion of elanguescence. Kant's presentation of this notion, Chisholm says, involves 'a monstrous hypothesis', namely, that

Different things . . . may have different *degrees of reality*. It is possible, (Kant) thought, for the degree of reality of a thing to increase or to decrease in a continuous manner ... he thought that some things could have *more* existence than others. It is as though he thought that one day you may set out from nonbeing and head in the direction toward being with the result that the farther you go in that direction the more being you will have.[30]

Chisholm expresses some surprise that Kant would adopt such a hypothesis, given his disavowal of existence as a predicate, but he believes that 'Kant is to be taken literally here.'[31] Chisholm objects strenuously to this hypothesis, given his own project of attempting to argue that persons are entia *per se*, ontologically real in the sense that 'natural kinds' are real: they are non-reducible entities in the world, and are not subject to degrees of being. As persons they *are* real, and the notion that one person is more real than another is not only intuitively wrong but also calls into question Chisholm's whole theory of persons. Given the goals of his discussion, it is understandable that such a view of degrees of reality is both 'monstrous' and bizarre.

Chisholm argues against the notion of degrees of reality, and what he takes to be elanguescence, by appealing to an intuitively correct notion of being. He says, 'surely there is no mean between being and nonbeing. If something *is* on a certain path, then that something *is*. Or if it *is not* yet, then it cannot be on the path between being and nonbeing.'[32] This clearly seems to be true, and reflects the accepted distinction between the existential and the predicative 'is'. To say that '*x* is more real than *y*' is to conflate, in a way, these two uses, and to make a predicative claim of an existential assertion. Reality is not normally spoken of as a matter of degree, if we believe that something's being real is a matter of that thing's being at all. To say that something is real is what we can say when we mean that it exists. To say that something is more or less real is a lot like saying that a drowned man is more dead than a poisoned one—they are each dead, and that is the end of it. We can say that one is 'more lamentably dead', but how we regard his passing does not tamper with his perpetual inactivity. Similarly, to speak of something being more or less real is mistaking the nature of the language used. It is a case of thinking oneself to be just a little bit pregnant.

This confusion of believing 'real' to have predicative character is summarized well by Chisholm: 'Of course, things may be more or less endowed. But things cannot be more or less endowed with respect to being. What is poorly endowed *is* poorly endowed and therefore *is*.'[33] If a thing has properties, then in some sense it is real, if only in the sense that unicorns are real imaginative fabrications in a way that garbalorps are not. Of course, the objection may be offered that Chisholm's logic allows the following: 'Unicorns are unreal. Therefore unicorns exist.' But this objection trades on the very confusion Chisholm points out with regard to predication. The expression 'is unreal', when taken to refer to real = existent, is simply the negation of an existential assertion. It is not predicative, and does not fit Chisholm's model of something 'poorly endowed'; the logical form of 'Unicorns are unreal' is not 'There exists something, unicorns, which are unreal', $(Ex)(x = p \& Ux)$, but rather 'Unicorns do not exist', $\sim(Ex)(x = p)$. The difference, put like this, is clear. If, on the other hand, one says 'Unicorns are fictitious. Therefore unicorns are', then there is no problem. Unicorns are; they are imaginative fabrications.

Chisholm criticizes Kant on his own ground when he considers the role of reality in relation to sensation. If we accept sensations as real, then 'we have no ground for saying that the feeling which is less intense is *less real* than the feeling which is more intense'.[34] Since both *are*, they are both real, and no more can be said on that account. To say that one is more intense is to engage in a different kind of talk, talk that is predicative. A beagle mix is a dog; so is a purebred Labrador retriever. If the Labrador owner points to my beagle and says 'That's not much of a dog', my response clearly is 'A dog's a dog.' And this would in all likelihood force a bit of better metaphysics: the next thing for the Labrador owner to do would be, I expect, to talk about certain *features* of doghood that are more prominent in a Labrador than in a beagle mix. But this is talk about properties, not existence. And it is in fact what we have been talking about all along. As Chisholm says, '*No* thing has any more or less properties than does any other thing. Every property and every thing is such that either the thing has that property or the thing has the negation of that property.'[35] So the most that can be said is that my beagle has a severe lack of good-making dog-properties. She is no less a dog for a' that—and she is no less real. In the same way, a pain, a feeling, or a consciousness, says Chisholm, is no less real than another pain, feeling, or consciousness because it is less intense or has weaker faculties and powers.

So Chisholm's criticisms of degrees of reality as 'bad metaphysics' are persuasive, and, more to the point, they are right. Where, then, does this leave Kant? In his refutation of Mendelssohn Kant clearly does speak of 'degrees of reality' as an integral part of the notion of intensive magnitude. Can it be that Kant has disregarded his own rejection of existence as a predicate? If so, he has forced on himself a large and glaring inconsistency. Indeed, if Kant accepts the notion of predicative 'degrees of reality', it is not at all clear that his refutation of the Ontological Argument itself still holds water. Briefly, this refutation involves the argument that '"*Being*" is obviously not a real predicate . . . it is not a concept of something which could be added to the concept of a thing' (A598/B626). While this is well demonstrated for existence *per se*, it is not obvious that ascribing 'degrees of reality' to a thing does not 'add to the concept' of the thing. Consider the following statements: '*x* has *n* degree of reality', '*x* has a higher degree of reality than *y*', or even 'At t_i *x* has *n* degree of reality; at t_{i+2} *x* has *n*-2 degree of reality.' Here, degrees of reality can be argued to be predicative, in that they add to the concept of *x*. They make a substantive difference to the way we regard *x*. Indeed, Chisholm, for one, believes that degrees of reality may well involve substantive differences when we talk about, and act in relation to, persons. As he suggests somewhat wryly, the Supreme Court decision on abortion in *Roe* v. *Wade* may have been influenced by a derivative version of Kant's notion of elanguescent persons. And it is also the case that, if we accept Chisholm's reading of the elanguescence passage, we see that the refutation only works on the basis of degrees of reality being in some way predicative. But if 'degrees of reality' are predicative, then it seems that a revised version of the Ontological Argument could easily trade on this fact. One need only consider, say, an invocation to 'conceive a being than which no being has a greater degree of reality' to see how this revision would be framed. That Kant has other shafts in his theological quiver is quite true, but his ruling out existence as predicate is vitiated by his admission of degrees of reality in so far as these degrees are predicates. And predicates they do seem to be.

If for no other reason, this conclusion itself gives us prima facie reason to re-examine Chisholm's reading of Kant. It is not that Kant is incapable of inconsistency but more that he is not prone to *glaring* inconsistency. We need, then, to ask just what Kant is up to when he talks about 'degrees of reality'. In fact, we have much of the answer to this already before us, but this will become clearer after another glance at the real source of Kant's refutation of Mendelssohn: the Anticipations of Perception.

The controversial passage says that 'we . . . cannot deny to (the soul), any more than to any other existence, intensive quantity, that is, a degree of reality in respect of all its faculties, nay, in respect of all that constitutes its existence' (B414). Furthermore, Kant says that 'this degree of reality may diminish'. Looking at the Anticipations of Perception, we see similar statements: 'Every reality in the (field of) appearance has ... intensive magnitude or degree' (a168/b210), 'every reality in the (field of) appearance, however small it may be, has a degree, that is, an intensive magnitude' (a169/b211), 'every reality has ... some specific degree' (a174/b216). So this way of speaking about reality is a commonplace for Kant, and gives Chisholm evidence for saying 'Kant is to be taken literally here.' But I think that in fact Kant is not to be taken literally here, at least not in the way Chisholm suggests.

To see this, it is necessary to consider precisely what Kant is talking about when he discusses reality and sensation. He says that 'what corresponds in empirical intuition to sensation is reality (*realitas phaenomenon*); what corresponds to its absence is negation = o' (a168/b209). So reality is an aspect of intuition, and is opposed to 'negation = o', which Kant says is 'pure intuition'. In the Schematism, Kant says that the concept of reality 'points to being', while negation 'represents not-being' (a143/b182). And in the Analogies of Experience, 'all that is real' is equated with 'all that belongs to the existence of things', and this 'all' has as foundation 'substance' (a182/b225). Reality, then, consists in what is present to us in the 'objects of perception', in the appearances (a182/b225). As such, the real is the *content* of our intuitions, and is opposed by its absence, pure intuition without objective content. Now the real in the appearances also involves sensation. To repeat an earlier passage:

Appearances contain in addition to intuition the matter for some object in general (whereby something existing in space or time is represented); they contain ... the real of sensation as merely subjective representation. (a166/b207)

So appearances involve both the formal structuring (which is part of the intuition) of the sensory manifold and sensation itself, which informs the intuition with 'matter'—with representations of the real. Hence 'the real of sensation': part of an appearance is a sensory encounter with an object, producing a 'subjective representation'. But the real is not exclusively grounded in sensation. It also has objective representation in the intuition, structured and objectified by the forms of intuition.

But, as was explained earlier, it is in terms of sensation that objects have intensive magnitude. And as sensation has degree, or intensive magnitude, so objects of perception (the real) have a corresponding intensive magnitude *qua* the real of sensation, the real as apprehended in sensation. And here, finally, is the key to Kant's expression 'degrees of reality'. In so far as the real is apprehended in sensation, and reflects the intensive magnitude of sensation, the real can be said to have degree. But the crucial point is this: *the real has degree, but not degree of reality*. Kant actually makes this clear in the Anticipations. He says,

Corresponding to this intensity of sensation, an *intensive magnitude*, that is, a degree of influence on the sense (i.e. on the special sense involved) must be ascribed to all objects of perception, in so far as this perception contains sensation. (A166/B208)

The real, then, is an object of perception. To the extent that this perception is informed by sensation, which has intensity, the real ('of sensation') has intensive magnitude, '*a degree of influence on the sense*'. A perceived object will affect the senses with a certain intensity, that is, there will be an intensity of sensation that is due to the influence of the object. In so far as this object is sensible, it is 'the real of sensation', and the degree of its influence on the senses is its intensive magnitude. Thus, 'In all appearances, the real that is an object of sensation has intensive magnitude, that is, a degree' of influence on the senses.

Thus when Kant says that 'Between reality and negation there is a continuity of possible realities and of possible smaller perceptions', he is not talking about degrees of 'realness', but about degrees of intensity in that which is real, and the related degrees of intensity in sensation. He says that

Every sensation, however, is capable of diminution . . . Between reality in the (field of) appearance and negation there is therefore a continuity of many possible intermediate sensations . . . In other words, the real in the (field of) appearance has always a magnitude. (A168/B210)

So it is clear that, since there is a continuous magnitude of possible intensities of sensation, there may be (and is) a similar range of possible intensities of the real. In other words, the real as object of sensation can have any of a continuous range of magnitudes of influence on the senses. It is in this sense alone that 'reality has degrees'. This can be further confirmed by Kant's discussion of the errors of 'natural philosophers' in dealing with the possible emptiness of space. He suggests that 'every reality has, while keeping its quality unchanged, some specific degree (of resistance or weight)...' (A174/B216). Here, as elsewhere, it is clear that the degree involved in reality is not a degree of *reality*, but a degree of intensive magnitude in the real object. This interpretation of degrees of the real is confirmed by textual examples, as we have seen, and gives a coherent reading of Kant's own use of 'degrees of reality'. This, coupled with the inconsistency in Kant's view of existence that is generated by Chisholm's reading, provides confirming evidence, I think, that Kant intended that the only degrees of the real are in fact degrees of intensive magnitude in real objects.

What, then, of Chisholm's reading? His quarrel with Kant, I take it, rests on the notion that things have different degrees of reality, existing in different degrees, with the corollary that persons begin at not-being, ascend to being, and then travel back to not-being. And it was suggested that Chisholm is right to label this view 'bad metaphysics'. But, as we have seen, Kant is not committed to the hypothesis that Chisholm is criticizing. For example, Chisholm argues that there is no sense to the notion that a more intense feeling is more real than a less intense one. Kant, however, will agree with Chisholm here: the real of sensation may have a greater or lesser degree of influence on the senses, and will correspond to a proportionate amount of sensation-intensity. But the real of sensation is real, and that is all we can say about its having reality. Degree for Kant is a matter of intensive qualities (A169/B211). If an object is real and has degree, it has a degree of intensive magnitude that reflects certain qualities of the object as they influence sensation. For Kant, as for Chisholm, that which is real *just is* real, and is no more and no less real than anything else that is real.

IMMORTALITY AND KANT'S AGNOSTICISM

One last reflection on elanguescence, and on the Second Paralogism: Kant argues that the soul, if it is a simple substance, may diminish to nothing, or cease to be, by a gradual diminution of intensive magnitude (or 'degrees of reality'). As we can now see, these degrees of reality are in fact a reference to intensity of magnitude. So when Kant says that the soul has a 'degree of reality in respect of all its faculties', he is suggesting that the intensive magnitude of the soul is in fact a function of that by which we are aware of, affected by, the soul's faculties (in this context the powers of consciousness). Yet he also says that the soul has intensive magnitude with regard to its very existence.[36] The claim is appropriate for Kant, given his position that the real, in so far as we are aware of it, has intensive magnitude, and given Kant's belief that the 'soul' cannot be known in itself but only as it is given to us in its operations. So the essence of Kant's argument is this: a substance to be a substance at all must have intensive magnitude, a capacity to influence the senses. But intensive magnitude is such that it can undergo diminution, loss of degree or intensity, to nothing. So this diminution or loss of powers is a possible outcome for the soul. We do not *know* that this particular intensive magnitude will undergo such a *remissio*, but it is the burden of the holder of 'rational doctrine' to show that it *cannot* so diminish. And consciousness does in fact diminish, particularly self-awareness. So there does seem to be a loss of intensity in the soul even within the bounds of life; as self-awareness and awareness of distinct representations become more obscure, it is proper to say that the intensive magnitude of consciousness (the effect of consciousness on itself, in a way) has diminished. So within the bounds of our experience, it is clear that the soul manifests to some extent the diminution of intensive magnitude. And this is as far as we can go: '(the soul's) permanence during life is, of course, evident *per se*, since the thinking being (as man) is itself likewise an object of the outer senses. But this is very far from satisfying the rational psychologist who undertakes to prove from mere concepts its absolute permanence beyond this life' (B415). The rational psychologist cannot show that such diminution of powers, reflected in a diminution of intensive magnitude, does not occur to negation = o at the cessation of bodily life. And if he cannot do this, then he cannot demonstrate with finality the immortality of the soul.

Interestingly enough, Kant in the Anticipations suggests that the converse is also true: that it cannot be proven that such diminution does occur. He says,

If all reality in perception has a degree, between which and negation there exists an infinite gradation of ever smaller degrees, and if every sense must likewise possess some particular degree of receptivity of sensation, no perception, and consequently no experience, is possible that could prove, either immediately or mediately (no matter how far-ranging the reasoning may be), a complete absence of all reality in the (field of) appearance . . . the complete absence of reality from a sensible intuition can never be itself perceived. (A172/B214)

So while the impossibility of the soul's elanguescence to negation = o cannot be proven, neither is it possible to prove that such diminution to negation = o does in fact occur. Both propositions are beyond the realm of experience. The soul as substance can only be discussed in terms of extensive and intensive magnitudes, which are only known through consciousness. And outside the strictures of our consciousness we can have no knowledge. This is, as was suggested early on, the real moral of Kant's refutation of Mendelssohn: we cannot know that which is beyond the bounds of experience, and the nature of the soul in itself, and beyond its nature as manifested to us, is unknowable.

4

Kant on Self-Identity: The Third Paralogism

KANT's Third Paralogism is, in a number of ways, the most obscure. It is also, perhaps, the Paralogism which has the broadest philosophical interest: here Kant either addresses directly or gives hints of his views on personal identity, on the moral implications of such identity, and on the problem of other minds. The richness of these remarks—and their enigmatic cast—leads, naturally enough, to the temptation to remove them, for purposes of further study, from what is at best a dense and confusing context.[1] This may be a sensible course to follow; before doing so, however, it is worth looking a bit more closely at how the argument may fit into Kant's general account of the paralogistic reasoning of rational psychology. And here again it will become clear that, construed outside the context of this account, Kant's remarks on the Third Paralogism are misleading to the point of unintelligibility.

THE ARGUMENT STRUCTURE OF THE PARALOGISM

The form of the Third Paralogism, as stated in the first edition, is as follows:

> That which is conscious of the numerical identity of itself at different times is in so far a person
>
> Now the soul is conscious, etc.
>
> Therefore it is a person. (A361)

It has been suggested by Ameriks that this argument is 'at least valid'.[2] And this does have a certain plausibility, the argument seeming to be of the undeniably valid form $(x)\,(Cx \rightarrow Px)$, $Ca \vdash Pa$. But is it valid? Kant does not think so: though he does not explicitly state that the Third Paralogism is invalid, he does say that a Paralogism by definition has 'a formally invalid conclusion', and he at least implies that this conclusion is invalid because of the presence of an ambiguous middle term (while he only explicitly makes this latter charge of a *sophisma figurae dictionis* with regard to the First Paralogism, his presentation there indicates that the fallacy of the First Paralogism is exemplary of the others) (A341/B399). If this argument is invalid, then, it is so presumably because of a vitiating ambiguity in the middle term; thus, the ambiguity lies in the predicate 'is conscious of the numerical identity of itself at different times'. But here we meet a serious obstruction: in his own remarks, Kant does not say in what way this predicate is ambiguous. Indeed, given the poverty of Kant's own remarks on the formal structure of the Third Paralogism, it is not obvious what to make of his implicit claim that the argument is invalid. And so—on the face of things—it is not obvious in what way this Paralogism is, in fact, a Paralogism at all.

To see the actual structure of the Third Paralogism, it will be useful to consider again, in some detail, Kant's definition of a transcendental paralogism: 'I conclude from the transcendental concept of the subject, which contains nothing manifold, the absolute unity of the subject itself, of which . . . I possess no concept whatsoever' (A340/B397–8). The Paralogism has 'no empirical premisses' (A339/B397), but purports to draw a synthetic *a priori* conclusion from non-empirical premisses (B410). The major and minor premisses are 'not empirical', however, in different ways. The major premiss is analytic in that it merely offers a definition, presumably of a category, without specifying the means of empirical employment of that category, while the minor premiss affirms the 'transcendental ground' of some concept applied to the subject: it asserts something that is necessarily true of the way the subject is represented. Thus Kant says that to the question 'What is the constitution of a thing which thinks?' only an analytic answer can be given which 'will perhaps explain what is meant by thought' (A398). So the major premiss is not empirical in so far as it is purely definitional, while the minor premiss is not empirical in so far as it asserts a necessary condition of being a thinking subject. Kant's expression 'explain what is meant by thought' is not perspicuous, and would perhaps better make his point were it rephrased as 'explain what the thinking subject necessarily represents as being true of itself'. Given the stipulation, then, that neither premiss is empirical, it becomes difficult to see what Kant means when he says that

Whereas the major premiss, in dealing with the condition, makes a merely transcendental use of the category, the minor premiss and the conclusion, in dealing with the soul which has been subsumed under this condition, use the same category empirically. (A402)

How can the minor premiss both be 'not empirical' and use a category 'empirically'? The answer to this apparent contradiction, once again, underscores the source of what Kant sees as the vitiating ambiguity of the Paralogisms, namely, that the category defined in the major premiss is applied to the subject of the minor premiss *as if* it can be applied empirically; this, says Kant, is 'inadmissible'. The problem lies in our employing the category as predicate of a putative object (in this case the soul) 'without our first having ascertained and established the condition of such employment *in concreto*' (A403). In the second edition, Kant makes this point somewhat more clearly, saying that the major premiss deals with 'a being that can be thought in general, in every relation, and therefore as it may be given in intuition', but the minor premiss deals with a being 'only in so far as it regards itself, as subject, simply in relation to thought' (B411). Thus the major premiss is a statement, roughly speaking, about (in part) objects (given in intuition), while the minor premiss is about thought: in particular, about how the 'I' of the 'I think' must be represented. The source of the paralogistic fallacy lies in treating the minor premiss as if it traffics in objects as well, thus leading to a conclusion about the self as an object. In other words, an illicit shift has occurred from talking about the 'I' transcendentally—and hence not empirically—to talking about the self as it is in itself—and hence not empirically. In effect, the confusion here results from a running-together of two ways in which we can talk non-empirically, the one transcendental, and legitimate, the other noumenal, and inadmissible.

As should now be clear, the minor premiss does not say anything about the subject as an object, but only about the subject as it is thought; the only conclusion legitimately derivable from this premiss properly construed is one which says something about how the subject represents itself to itself. This conclusion is not only likely to be trivial—it is guaranteed to be analytic. And this guarantee removes what Kant called the 'one great stumbling block' to the project of the *Critique*, that is, the purported derivation of synthetic *a priori* truths from a source other than experience, since, as we have seen, if such truths can be derived outside experience, the carefully set limits of what constitutes an epistemically legitimate judgment are removed. We can, in effect, 'run wild' in our judgments: as Kant says in the second edition, 'by such procedure we should have taken a step beyond the world of sense, and have entered into the field of noumena; and no one could then deny our right of advancing yet further in this domain, indeed of settling in it, and . . . of establishing claims to permanent possession' (B409–10).

What, then, is the 'transcendental ground' affirmed in the minor premiss of the Paralogism, which states that 'the soul is conscious of the numerical identity of itself at different times'? One answer lies in the Transcendental Deduction, of course: given the fact that I can synthesize a manifold of experience diachronically as well as synchronically, it follows that there must be one 'I' represented across time as the experiencing subject who performs this synthesis.[3] This kind of synthesis, as we have seen, Kant calls 'the synthesis of reproduction', the synthesis of representations over time. I must be able to remember these experiences and must be able to relate them to my present state. But if I am so to reproduce these experiences, to integrate them into my representing of a course of experience, then I must persist as the experiencing subject across time (or rather, I must represent within my consciousness a perduring subject who has all these experiences). Given a course of experience, it is necessary that this course be held together by a unitary and persistent experiencing subject who brings this data together as his own. To consider another variant on Kant's own example of diachronic unity (that of drawing a line in thought), imagine three chemists, each of whom knows part of an extremely complicated experimental procedure, and knows it to be a part of this procedure, but does not know the details of the procedure itself. None of them can determine exactly at what point in the procedure their part is implemented, and they cannot determine this without knowing the other parts of the procedure. It seems trivially obvious to remark that, given this situation, no one knows the procedure, but the procedure can be known if the three chemists integrate their knowledge. Crucial to this case, of course, is that the chemists must confer, and could not simply perform their own known sub-procedures in sequence to get the desired result. As we know, this is precisely Kant's point against the Humean 'bundle' theory of the self: that a mere sequence of impressions, however orderly in themselves, could not produce so much as the merest impression of a sequence, which would require synthesis by a persisting subject. This trivial observation, then, brings out what Kant takes to be a highly significant fact about experiencing subjects who have experiential histories: if the soul were not 'conscious of the numerical identity of itself at different times', then the synthesis which makes this experiential history a history at all would not in itself be possible.

Given that Kant's doctrine of reproductive synthesis provides a 'transcendental ground' for the premiss that the soul is conscious of its numerical identity over time, it must be pointed out that Kant, somewhat perversely, does not explicitly invoke this doctrine in his discussion of the Third Paralogism. What he does invoke is the thesis, taken from the Transcendental Aesthetic, that time is the form of inner sense. He says that in *determining* the identity of myself over time (though, as will be seen, Kant does not believe that I need to do so) I would have to observe whether or not the subject (= me) persists through its various determinations in time. But to 'observe' myself is possible only through 'inner sense' and time is the *form* of inner sense which structures, among other things, the way I encounter myself (= my thoughts) in introspection. Thus Kant says that 'I refer each and all of my successive determinations to the numerically identical self, and do so throughout time, that is, in the form of the inner intuition of myself' (A362). And so Kant is in fact invoking the transcendental unity of apperception here as well. As he points out in the Transcendental Deduction, 'even the purest and most elementary representations of space and time' depend on the syntheses of apprehension and reproduction (A102). These syntheses in turn depend on the representation of the self as unitary, and so the representation of time itself requires the representation of a diachronically unitary subject. As Kant says, the 'proposition of self-consciousness in time' (= the minor premiss)

really says nothing more than that in the whole time in which I am conscious of myself, I am conscious of this time as belonging to the unity of myself; and it comes to the same whether I say that this whole time is in me, as individual unity, or that I am to be found as numerically identical in all this time. (A362)

This should recall Kant's thesis, in the Transcendental Aesthetic, that 'different times are but parts of one and the same time' and thus, bearing in mind that time is merely a pure form of sensible intuition, 'all this time' is 'one and the same' *as* a form of intuition for a persisting unitary subject (A32). Thus it is no accident that when I supposedly examine myself to determine my 'numerical identity over time', I observe my 'identity throughout the time in which the determinations change'—merely being able to note a change of determinations over time requires that I represent myself to myself as an experiencing subject possessing numerical identity.

If this account of the transcendental ground of the minor premise is right, then, and the Third Paralogism adheres to the form which Kant specifies for the Paralogisms as a whole, then certain things can be concluded regarding the Third Paralogism. First of all, it seems that the major premise should be a definition that specifies 'a being that can be thought in general'. If this is the case, then the definition in the major premise can, presumably, be objective—and thus have criteria underlying its application. The minor premise, as we have seen, considers an aspect of the necessary representation of the soul (at least on its construction as a true premise). Thus, if the Paralogism goes according to form, it will be paralogistic because it trades on the mistake of construing the minor premise to be a specimen of 'object-talk', which it is not, thus leading to a conclusion about the soul as an object about which we can derive synthetic *a priori* truths. Alternatively, however, it should be recalled that the Paralogism does have a valid form if the vitiating ambiguity is avoided, and so if we read both premises correctly (as analytic and not empirical), we validly derive an analytic and trivial conclusion about the way the soul is represented. Kant's own text provides support for this reading of the valid construction of the Paralogism: he says that 'the personality of the soul has to be regarded not as inferred but as a completely identical proposition of self-consciousness in time' (A362). In effect, Kant says that the conclusion is simply equivalent to the minor premise. And the Paralogism makes this equivalence clear: though being represented as a person may be entailed by being represented as numerically identical, this is not in any obvious way inferable from the minor premise by itself; it is eminently inferable from the two premises taken together and read as analytic. Kant effectively emphasizes this alternative and trivially valid reading of the Paralogism when he says that '*In my own consciousness*, therefore, identity of person is unfailingly met with' (emphasis added). All of this being said, then, we can now ask: does the Third Paralogism, perhaps against expectations, go according to form?

TWO QUALMS . . . AND A DISSATISFACTION

If the Third Paralogism did follow the form of the first two, then, as was pointed out, the major premiss would specify the general use of a concept (including its empirical use), and the minor premiss would state something about the representation of the self necessary for experience to be possible. By making an illegitimate *empirical* application of the major premiss to the minor premiss, a putatively synthetic *a priori* conclusion regarding the soul is reached. Kant's refutation of this Paralogism then would involve showing that this empirical application was illicit, and that thus the argument either is invalid or leads to a fairly trivial conclusion, depending on whether or not the major premiss is used in its empirical (schematized) or its 'pure' (unschematized) employment. As was seen, Kant clearly does argue that the conclusion can be read as trivially true on the analytic interpretation of the major premiss. But does he show that the major premiss is subjected to an illegitimate empirical use? At least in the First Paralogism his way of showing this is to make explicit the empirical procedure for determining whether or not an item in experience falls under the concept 'substance'; 'so far from being able to deduce these properties merely from the pure category of substance, we must, on the contrary, take our start from the permanence of an object given in experience as permanent' (A349). He then goes on to show that with regard to the self as soul, this empirical procedure does not work, since the soul is not an object of intuition; in this way is the empirical employment of the major premiss ruled out. And the Third Paralogism at first glance follows this strategy. Immediately following the formal presentation of the Paralogism, Kant says the following:

If I want to know through experience the numerical identity of an external object, I shall pay heed to that permanent element in the appearance to which as subject everything else is related as determination, and note its identity throughout the time in which the determinations change. (A362)

So Kant has given us the rule for the empirical employment of the concept 'numerical identity'; roughly, it is necessary to observe an object and see whether or not it persists through alterations of its state. Kant is here considering an object to have identity over time if it is something which can survive at least some changes in material composition. And Kant can pursue his usual strategy, given this outline of the empirical use of 'identity', by pointing out that the soul is not an object in the first place. But two things should give us pause here.

First of all, this is not what Kant now appears to do. Rather, he seems to show instead that *were* we to follow this procedure with regard to the soul, treating it as object (and it is highly significant that in giving the rule on the use of 'identity', Kant uses the vague blanket-term 'the permanent in appearance' to refer to the 'object' of identity, thereby leaving open, though only for the moment, the possibility that the soul *can* be subject for this employment of the concept), we would have to conclude that the soul *is* permanent since it is integral to all its judgments about determinations in time. Is Kant then saying that the self is subject to an *empirical* employment of this concept? Clearly the 'I' of the transcendental unity of apperception cannot be subject to such an employment, and if the minor premiss points up an aspect of this transcendental unity which constrains us to draw 'a formally invalid conclusion', then it is far from obvious how the minor premiss could be concerned with the other possible mode of self-awareness, empirical apperception. If, though, the consciousness of numerical identity referred to in the minor premiss is in fact a product of inner sense, then Kant's apparent willingness to make an empirical employment of 'numerical identity' in this regard is more explicable. This, however, deviates from the announced form of the Paralogisms, and leaves Kant in an interesting position if he is to refute the conclusion. If the empirical use of the concept of identity does in fact apply in the minor premiss, and thus the premiss reflects a judgment of empirical apperception, then Kant is saying the self of empirical apperception is identical over time, and can be known to be so through use of empirical criteria. And yet Kant makes it fairly clear that any identity noted with regard to the self is the product of the transcendental unity of apperception; furthermore, if Kant were to endorse an identity observed via inner sense, this endorsement would fly in the face of Hume's thought-experiment, in which he does not 'stumble' over the self. After all, in his thought-experiment Hume attempts to follow the very procedure Kant seems to be advocating here—and he doesn't succeed. And part of his error lies in confusing the subject which is integral to all its judgments, that is, the subject which consists in all its determinations, and the subject to which everything else is related as determinations. And as the Transcendental Deduction shows, Kant's treatment of this problem is a good deal more sophisticated than a mere flat denial of Hume. But such a reading is inconsistent with Kant's text even more directly: Kant explicitly says that 'What has necessarily to be represented as numerically identical cannot be thought as such through empirical data', and that 'No fixed and abiding self can present itself in this flux of inner appearances' (A107). The only way the self is known to have 'numerical identity' is as it is represented in the transcendental unity of apperception, but that is not subject to empirical investigation. It seems that the thrust of Kant's counterfactual must be rather that were we to apply criteria of identity to the self of empirical apperception, the self would be taken to be identical over time though its determinations change, solely because of the represented identity over time of the 'I' of the 'I think', that of the transcendental unity. It is interesting that for Hume this spurious identity was the result of habit or custom, while for Kant it is the result of the confusion between the self as encountered empirically and the self of transcendental apperception. The belief that this numerical identity is determined by the application of empirical criteria is an illusion caused by a confusion between the 'I' as revealed in inner sense, the awareness of momentary states, which can for all practical purposes be viewed as a Humean 'bundle of perceptions', and the 'I' of transcendental apperception: it is the latter that provides the notion of the self as having numerical identity over time, and not the former (if Kant is to be consistent). In this light, it is worth noting a remark made by Kant in the *Anthropologie in pragmatischer Hinsicht*:

Can a man be conscious of these changes and still say that he remains the same man (has the same soul)? The question is absurd, since consciousness of such changes is possible only on the supposition that *he* considers *himself* in his different states as one and the same subject. [4]

On this reading, then, Kant is making the expected point that the shift from object-talk in the major premiss to talk about necessary representation in the minor premiss is a shift ignored by the rational psychologist—but his presentation renders this obscure.

The second point which should give us pause when looking at Kant's actual procedure in this Paralogism is related to the first. As was pointed out, Kant's strategy in defusing the Paralogism could be expected to be to show the way in which the major premiss is empirically employed and then show that this employment is illicit with regard to the self. And it appears that this is what Kant does. But strictly speaking, the relevant concept in the major premiss is that of 'a being which is conscious of its numerical identity over time', and it is unclear just what an empirical employment of this concept would be. When Kant makes his stipulation regarding the empirical employment of a concept, it is a stipulation regarding the concept 'numerical identity' as applied to 'external objects'—and since the major premiss is ostensibly about 'being as it is thought in general' (including being as it is thought in intuition and hence empirically), then Kant is implicitly suggesting that it is at least a possibility that beings can be conscious of themselves as having identity over time through intuition, that is, by means of empirical observation of the 'permanent in appearance' where this 'permanent' = themselves as conscious beings. But it is certainly Kant's thesis, in his remarks about inner sense, that *we* do not in fact determine our own identity in this way, and that to think that we do is to fall for an illusion caused by a confusion between empirical and transcendental apperception. It seems that there are three ways to read this implication. The first is that Kant has allowed his passion for systematic presentation of philosophic insights to get in the way of those insights, and that the concept he really wants to explore here is just numerical identity *per se*. Thus by trying to force the remarks about identity into the paralogistic format and strategy we read too many formal complications into what is basically a discussion of criteria of identity—and this has some plausibility. Second, in suggesting that there could be empirical self-consciousness of identity over time, Kant may be making an oblique reference, as he sometimes does, to beings who, unlike ourselves, have a non-sensory intuition: presumably God could have such an unmediated conception of himself. Third, and more fruitful, is the possibility that Kant is in fact not thinking of non-sensory intuition at all, but is at least considering the possibility that, as he says in the Second Paralogism, 'the substance which in relation to our outer sense possesses extension is in itself the possessor of thoughts', in other words, that the thinking self is the same as the corporeal being (A359). Kant rejects this thesis, of course, by saying that we cannot know any such thing to be the case. If the thinking self were the same as the body, and the subject were aware of this, though, then it would indeed be possible to determine one's identity over time by intuition of 'the permanent in appearance', which in this case would be one's body. That Kant says that *we* cannot know this to be true is no obstacle to its being considered to be a possibility for a possible being who knows that he is as a thinking being the same as he is as a corporeal being (it should be noted, though, that such a being would have to have a sort of non-sensory intuition, and so this case is actually a specific variant of the second reading above). In this way there would be a possible empirical employment of the idea of self-consciousness of identity over time. And Kant's stipulation of the rule for empirical application of 'identity' to external objects, and his arguing that we do not actually determine our own identity in this way, suggest that part of what Kant is doing in the Third Paralogism is arguing for an epistemic difference between knowing the identity of external objects and being conscious of one's own identity. If the above reading of the major premiss is correct, then in the background of the project is an implicit consideration, and rejection, of the thesis that bodily criteria are relevant to assertions of one's own personal identity. The significance of this latter point will be considered shortly. But first, a certain dissatisfaction must be registered.

Given the above consideration of the form of the Third Paralogism, the following points emerge: (1) Kant's minor premiss, like those of the first two Paralogisms, draws our attention to an aspect of our necessary conceptualization of the thinking self; (2) the major premiss, if it is to conform to Kant's declared programme, specifies what is the definitive characteristic of a person, and by implication of its generality allows Kant to entertain the possibility that one's own personal identity can be known by empirical observation; and (3) Kant rejects this possibility, saying that in our case it is an illusion resting on a confusion of two modes of self-awareness. It seems reasonable to conclude, then, that in the Third Paralogism Kant is attempting to refute the thesis that self-consciousness of personal identity can be known by empirical observation. The dissatisfaction, however, is this: how would this thesis, which Kant is at pains to refute, be one which would give aid and comfort to the rational psychologist? Given that the programme of the rational psychologist is to derive synthetic *a priori* truths merely from accepted definitions and reflection on the non-empirical datum 'I think', it is not clear how any thesis which invokes *empirical* observation is likely to be relevant to this programme. It appears, then, that something else is afoot in the Third Paralogism.

To see what this something is, we must see what use the rational psychologist can make of this conclusion. Certainly 'The soul is a person' does not obviously appear to have the potential implications of 'The soul is simple' or 'The soul is substantial'. The obscurity of this premiss's implications is increased by the lack of clarity regarding what 'person' even *means* in the context of the Third Paralogism: minimally, it refers to 'an intelligence that is genuinely conscious of its identity over time'—but it may have moral import as well.[5] In this regard, we should consider Kant's remarks about the consequences of the rational psychologist's illegitimate application of schematized categories to the 'thinking substance':

> This substance, merely as object of inner sense, gives the concept of *immateriality*; as simple substance, that of *incorruptibility*; its identity, as intellectual substance, *personality*; all these three together, *spirituality*; while the relation to objects in space . . . leads us to represent the thinking substance as the principle of life in matter, that is, as soul (*anima*) . . . This last, in turn, as limited by spirituality, gives the concept of *immortality*. (A345/B403)

It is clear how the immateriality and incorruptibility of the soul would lend weight to claims for its immortality, but the relevance of its identity over time is not as obvious. From this passage, though, it seems that Kant felt that the personality of the soul—and its self-awareness in this regard—is essential to the rational psychologist if he is to argue that the soul's immortality is at least in part an extension of the mental activity of the thinking subject during its life (this presumably being part of what is meant by 'spirituality': for if the soul were merely immaterial and incorruptible but had no ongoing self-consciousness, it would not be a spiritual substance, a full-blooded continuant of the living person). And this is not an implausible requirement. If the rational psychologist demonstrated that the soul is incorruptible and perdures, yet is not conscious of this perdurance, because its self-consciousness is broken by the corruption of the body, he will have proven less than he wants to prove, as would be evidenced by the fact that our attitude towards the soul's immortality would be radically different than in the case where the soul is taken to be spiritual substance. So it is important that the rational psychologist show that personality, the continuing ability to see one's own course of experience *as* such, is an attribute of the soul. It is noteworthy that on this reading the *personality* of the soul does not lend weight to arguments for the soul's immortality in the way that the soul's immateriality and incorruptibility do. Rather, *given* the earlier proofs of these attributes of the soul which provide the basic support for the argument that the soul is immortal, the proof that the soul is a person provides grounds for arguing that the soul is immortal in a way that could be of more than philosophical interest. Beyond the point that it is important for the rational psychologist that he prove the soul to be the seat of personality, this passage should probably be viewed with a healthy scepticism regarding Kant's architectonic pretensions: he never gives an explicit argument showing why the conclusions of the first three Paralogisms taken together establish the spirituality of the soul, nor, for that matter, does he suggest what 'spirituality' means. That the immortality of the soul is not proven until something called 'animality'—purportedly derived from the Fourth Paralogism—is added to all this, certainly lends credibility to the view that Kant is striving to fit the Fourth Paralogism, and various general conclusions of rationalism, into an overly systematized pattern of argument. [6]

PERMANENCE, IDENTITY, AND THE OUTSIDE OBSERVER

There is, however, another way that personality (as consciousness of self-identity) is perhaps relevant to the rational psychologist's programme, that is, as a way of arguing for the *permanence* of the soul, in that the soul is conscious of its identity over time. But this is not sufficient to prove its permanence in any way useful for the rational psychologist: if the argument is that from the premises that I exist at t_1, and I exist at t_2, it follows that I will exist at all future times, the argument is obviously invalid. But the rational psychologist may, working within what Bennett calls 'the Cartesian basis', have a different argument in mind. If it is the case that in all my experience, which is, from my methodologically solipsistic position, all I have to go on, I exist as numerically identical, then I have the largest possible inductive sample from which to hypothesize that I will continue to exist in future. Obviously this is not the argument of the Third Paralogism itself, and it does leave the rational psychologist rather in the predicament of Russell's chicken, but it is conceivable that some such elision from identity over time to permanence and thence to immortality is what Kant is trying to defuse in his remarks on the Paralogism itself. Clearly Kant addresses himself here to the question of permanence. He says that personality does presuppose permanence, and that if we knew the soul to have permanence of the empirical sort (what Kant in the First Paralogism calls 'permanence of an object'), and thus to be substantial, we could infer 'at least the possibility of a continuing consciousness in an abiding subject'—since we now know that the soul 'abides'—and 'that is already sufficient for personality' (A365). According to Kant, this mere possibility, given an abiding subject, is sufficient for personality whether actualized or not, since 'personality does not itself at once cease because its activity is for a time interrupted' (A365). In other words, a person can lapse into unconsciousness without thereby ceasing to be a person (there is an obvious dissimilarity between the potentially active personality of a sleeping person and the potential personality of an abiding substance *sui generis*, but we can assume that Kant is not interested in providing the argument of the rational psychologist with the rigour it would have to have here). So if we know the self to be permanent and so, empirically speaking, substantial, we can infer the soul's personality. But the only notion of permanence we can attach to the soul is spurious: that which is inferred from the representation of the soul as identical in the transcendental unity of apperception. Thus Kant says that

This permanence . . . is in no way given prior to that numerical identity of our self which we infer from identical apperception, but on the contrary, is inferred first from that numerical identity. (A365)

This 'permanence', as was remarked earlier, is not the 'permanence of an object' which is involved in the empirical use of the term, and hence is not sufficient for establishing that the soul is, empirically speaking, substance—and that, of course, is the moral of the *First* Paralogism. Perhaps, then, one thing Kant is doing is this: in the First Paralogism, he argues that we cannot ascribe substantiality in any significant way to the soul, since a substance in experience is 'an object given in experience as permanent', and the soul is not given as an *object* at all (A349). In the Third Paralogism, Kant takes up the claim that the soul is 'given . . . as permanent', and shows that the only permanence ascribable to the soul is derived from the soul's necessary representation as identical over time.

Does, however, the representation of the soul as having this identity over time entail the soul's actual permanence? Kant straight-forwardly says not, since, reverting again to the First Paralogism, permanence is only properly ascribed to objects. That our aware-ness of the soul is not an awareness of an object renders the application of 'permanent' to the soul as represented to us a cate-gory-mistake; furthermore, that the character of this representation has a binding necessity for us should not obscure the fact that it is not, however binding, known to be an accurate representation of whatever it represents. In this light, we can understand Kant's often commented-upon case of the outside observer. Kant says that

if I regard myself from the standpoint of another (as object of his outer intuition), the outer observer represents me first of all in time, for in apperception time is actually represented only *in me*. Even if he concedes, therefore, the 'I', which accompanies, and indeed with complete identity, all representations at all times in *my* consciousness, he will not conclude from this to the objective permanence of my self. For just as the time in which the observer sets me is not the time met within my own but in his sensibility, so the identity which is necessarily bound up with my consciousness is not on that account bound up with his, that is, with the outer intuition of my subject. (A362–3)

It is clearly part of Kant's thesis that the rational psychologist, in suggesting that the soul is identical over time, is making an empirical use of the notion of permanence where such a notion is illegitimate. To show that this use is illegitimate—as it must be given Kant's position that the soul is not intuited—Kant in using the example of the outside observer underscores the fact that our awareness of the soul is not empirical, or, if it is, that it is completely unlike any other empirical awareness as this is usually understood. Given a dispute over my personal identity as a thinking being, it is not possible on this view to say, as I could in the case of a claim that, say, it is snowing outside, 'look for yourself'—there is no corroboration by outside observers of the permanence I infer from transcendental apper-ception. That my judgment of my identity's remaining the same over time, even though I am *in a way* right in my judgment that I do so persist, is epistemically different from that of any third person is in itself a strong argument against my belief that this judgment is based empirically. Though I am bound to represent myself as identical, others are by no means bound to represent me as such. My own awareness of my personal identity is not based in criteria at all but is a mode of representation which must precede all criterial judgments. The outside observer, on the other hand, is not bound to represent *me* in this way—though he is bound so to represent himself. And if the question of my personal identity arises for him, he will apply criteria to my case (these criteria being for now unspecified) and will make a judgment regarding my personal identity on the basis of these criteria. For the outside observer, the question of my personal identity, if he can answer it at all (and Kant does not say that he can), is answered with an empirical judgment. For me there is no empirical, criterial, answer—and in fact there is no question that is not absurd, for as Kant in effect says in the *Anthropologie*, asking the question is in itself a demonstration that the question is incoherent. But that there is no question, empirical or otherwise, which *I need* ask regarding my personal identity does not rule out *all* questions about my personal identity. That is certainly the main point made by Kant in the example of the outside observer, as should be clear from (1) Kant's emphasis on the non-empirical aspect of apperception, and (2) his emphasis that the Paralogisms rest on illicit empirical applications of concepts to the transcendentally represented unity of the self. Much of the discussion of the case of the outside observer has focused on the question of whether Kant is in fact a sceptic regarding personal identity, whether or not he considers it an unanalysable relation (following Reid and Butler), and what criteria, if any, Kant would say that the outside observer would justifiably apply. Interesting as these questions are (and their interest is compounded by Kant's rare reference to another person in an epistemological context), any such discussion is ancillary to the main point of Kant's example, and I will postpone—for now—detailed discussion of these questions.

It should be stressed that Kant is not only making the point that talking transcendentally about the identity of the 'I' is not equivalent to talking empirically about personal identity; he is also arguing for the sceptical thesis that I cannot know whether or not I *am* identical over time at all. In saying that I am so identical, on the basis of appeals to the transcendental unity of apperception, I make no appeal to empirical evidence—and, for Kant, there is no other evidence on which I can justifiably base such a claim. The most I can *know* is that I am represented to myself as identical, and whether or not I am in fact so is a question which must be noumenally and irrevocably moot. Kant pushes this thesis as well in the case of the outside observer, in the sense that Kant is saying that however convinced I may be of my identity, the grounds of my certainty are not epistemically transferable: 'even if he concedes . . . the "I", which accompanies . . . with complete identity', etc. In a way, the outside observer takes up Kant's own role, granting the function here of transcendental apperception but at the same time pointing out that it is not incoherent to suppose that a non-identical series of subjects are constrained by this transcendental representation and are thereby deluded into thinking it an accurate representation. This is the substance of what Kant is arguing in the footnote to the example of the outside observer, where he suggests the case of a series of elastic balls, each of which transmits its force and position to the next. Analogically, Kant suggests that

If . . . we postulate substances such that one communicates to the other representations together with the consciousness of them, we can conceive a whole series of substances of which the first transmits its state together with its consciousness to the second . . . The last substance would then be conscious of all the states of the previously changed substances, as being its own states, because they would have been transferred to it together with the consciousness of them. And yet it would not have been one and the same person in all these states. (A364n.)

Kant, of course, does not accept that the soul *is* a substance, and so it is reasonable to guess that he is here, as often in the Paralogisms, granting the rational psychologist a generous concession which does not help him against Kant's current attack. It is not clear what Kant means by 'its state together with its consciousness', but basically Kant is arguing that there is no obvious contradiction in the idea that a consciousness could represent itself as unitary over time while being in itself constitutionally diverse. It is worth noting in this regard a remark made by Sellars with reference to this footnote by Kant: 'Compare the materialist who argues that the thoughts which make up the history of an I are states of systems of material particles which are constantly losing old and gaining new constituents.'[7] Kant is certainly not taking the position of the materialist. But he is taking the agnostic position that however unavoidably I represent myself as identical, this representation does not preclude the possibility that what the materialist says is true. Sellars interprets the case of the outside observer to mean that, given this materialist thesis, a 'being with suitable cognitive powers might know me to be such a series'—

and certainly such a being would have good reason to reject my own affirmation that I know myself to be identical over time. But this observer need not be such a being, nor, for that matter, need his thesis be correct for him to have good reason so to reject my affirmation: as was pointed out, he need only be aware of the transcendental ground of my affirmation, and of my lack of empirical justification for it. He does not need to offer any alternative account. We, on the other hand, will do well to look more closely at Kant's own implicit account of personal identity. Before doing so, however, a few general remarks about personal identity need to be made.

THEORIES OF PERSONAL IDENTITY: AN OVERVIEW

In assessing Kant's position, an inventory of available theories of personal identity may be of some help. Within the problematic of personal identity, there are relatively few alternatives to consider, barring variations on standard themes, when determining what constitutes the identity of a person. Roughly, the alternatives are as follows:

Given x at t_1 and y at t_2, x is the same person as y on the condition that
  (1) y could (in some way) remember being x at t_1 (the *memory* condition), or
  (2) y has the same body as x (the *body* condition), or
  (3) x and y are connected by some set of psychological attributes which both x and y possess, and which persists continuously in some (presumably specifiable) way from t_1 to t_2 (the *psychological continuity* condition).

There are two other accounts of personal identity which do not allow stipulation of a necessary condition of personal identity:

Given x at t_1 and y at t_2, no condition can be specified which is such that if it obtains, then x is necessarily the same person as y because
  (4) personal identity is an unanalysable concept, or
  (5) personal identity is illusory, and under no conditions can x at t_1 be the same person as y at t_2.

It seems reasonable to assume that any theory of personal identity could be made out to be an elaboration, or plausible variant, of one of the positions here. I take (1) to be the position held by Locke as he is usually interpreted, and by Quinton and Grice; (2) to be accepted in one way or another by Shoemaker, Strawson, and others; (3) to be the currently prevailing account, held by Lewis, Parfit, Perry, Kitcher, and others; (4) to be the view of Butler and Reid; and (5) to be common to Hume and such 'no-ownership' theorists as Schlick. Obviously there are significant differences among adherents to each of these views; there are also variants within views that threaten neat divisions. For example, Wiggins has argued for psychological continuity as the relevant condition of personal identity, but has also argued that this continuity presupposes embodiment. There are also proponents of the view that not the body *per se* but the *brain* is what must remain the same if personal identity is to obtain. The danger in categorizing such a range of theories is clear, but such categorization does at least provide a rough frame on which to work out the significance of *Kant's* position.

One other general comment about theories of personal identity needs to be made, since it will bear directly on what Kant has to say. Ameriks rightly makes the observation that Kant, unlike most personal-identity theorists, observes a distinction between epistemological and metaphysical contexts (or, to avoid obscuring Kant's own intentions, between phenomenal and noumenal contexts).[8] In effect, the distinction which Kant will deploy is that between what *constitutes* personal identity and what is a *criterion* of personal identity: in other words, between what personal identity is and what we take to be evidence of it, or between the condition of something's *being x* and the condition of my *taking it to be x*. The distinction is not obscure: though the *condition* which must obtain for a new Pope to be elected is that seventy-five cardinals agree on a candidate, the *criterion* by which most observers decide that this condition is fulfilled is white smoke rising from a chimney. The example is particularly appropriate in this context, too, for the criteria of this condition's fulfilment differ depending on whether or not the observer is in St Peter's Square or in Conclave itself—this brings out a distinction which has been fundamental in discussions of personal identity, namely, that regardless of what actually *constitutes* personal identity, the criteria used to determine such identity may well differ depending on whether the 'observer' is, so to speak, 'inside' or 'outside', whether one is considering one's own personal identity or that of another. So in weighing accounts of personal identity, it is essential to distinguish between what personal identity consists in and on what grounds it is (appropriately) ascribed, and also between the grounds on which it is ascribed to others and those on which it is ascribed to oneself. Perry has argued that the conditions for something's being x and our criteria for saying it is x 'are surely related, for in general there is an important connection between our ways of knowing something and what we thereby come to know'.[9] But as the case of papal elections shows, this 'sure' relation may well be far from obvious: our criteria in this case should not lead us to conclude that the election of the pontiff is strictly contingent on the proper functioning of the Vatican flues. That in the matter of personal identity the flues *do* normally function properly (that is, normally those we consider to be persons do retain the same bodies over time, do have coherent sets of memories and psychological dispositions, etc.) merely underscores the importance of keeping in mind the distinction between what personal identity is and how it is ascribed.

To see the importance of this distinction, it is necessary to look no further than certain traditional objections to (2), the body condition for personal identity. It is granted that, as a matter of practice, we do in fact apply bodily criteria to determine the identities of persons: fingerprints and chromosome matching, as well as our most obvious ways of telling with whom we are dealing, make this manifest. So there is certainly a body *criterion* which is applied in normal practice. But this is not to say that the body criterion is itself the definitive test of personal identity, since to point out the use of this *criterion* is not to show that personal identity is itself determined by the body *condition*. Indeed, it has been argued that, though we do in fact use the body criterion for ascriptions of personal identity, the body condition itself is neither a sufficient nor a necessary condition of personal identity. This point dates at least to Locke's case of the prince and the cobbler, where Locke suggests that

should the soul of a prince, carrying with it the consciousness of the prince's past life, enter and inform the body of a cobbler, as soon as deserted by his own soul, every one sees he would be the same person as the prince, accountable only for the prince's actions ... [10]

In other words, though in practice we do correlate bodily criteria with personal identity, we can imagine cases in which these criteria would be overridden, in which other evidence militates against the bodily evidence we have. Locke, at least, takes these cases to show demonstrably that bodily criteria are not conclusive evidence of personal identity. On this account, then, whatever it is that actually *constitutes* personal identity, it is not the body condition in (2) above. In the same vein, it should be noted that more recent arguments which follow the same form have been constructed around the notion of 'Brain State Transfer' (BST) devices, which ostensibly would transfer all of one person's brain activity from one body to another; presumably here our ascriptions of continuing personality would be transferred as well.

Before leaving the body condition for now, it is worth noting one variant of this view of personal identity: that personal identity consists in *brain* identity. Clearly we do not employ brain identity as a criterion of personal identity in a straightforward way, in that we do not—ordinarily—observe the brain as we may observe the body, or hear memory reports, or notice psychological continuities through verbal reports or by studying behavioural consistencies. None the less, it could be argued that though we do not observe the brain's continuity over time directly, we *do* observe what is in effect the brain's *chassis*,[11] that is, the body, and that the continuance of the same body carries with it the presumptive continuity of the same brain. In addition, it is only in cases of 'Brain State Transfer'— or something like it—that we are willing to overlook the bodily criteria that we normally use in determining personal identity. In this case, the brain's being the condition or ground of personal identity would explain the switching of ascriptions which the psychological-continuity theorist would presumably make in 'Cobbler/Prince' and 'BST' cases;[12] it also provides an explanation of our reliance on the bodily criteria we normally use in making ascriptions of personal identity. However attractive such a theory is, though, there is at least one good reason for resisting the idea that brain identity is the ground of personal identity—or at least for resisting this description of this theory. This reason is given by Shoemaker:

It does not seem out of the question that Martians who are not of our species should have the right sort of psychological make-up to count as persons. And it seems conceivable that the Martians might differ from us so much physiologically that they have no single organ that could be called a brain. If it is so much as nomologically possible that there should be such creatures . . . then it seems wrong to say that personal identity consists in brain identity (even if *human* personal identity does consist in this).[13]

Shoemaker's argument as it stands is not completely convincing in that it presupposes (3), the psychological continuity condition: 'the right sort of psychological make-up' is assumed to override the brain condition—and *that* assumption is one which the brain-identity theorist will be disinclined to accept. But Shoemaker's point can be made without this assumption, simply on the grounds that it is not obviously self-contradictory to imagine some being whom (for whatever reason) we would consider a person yet who does not have a nervous system materially constituted like ours. None the less, the point of brain identity as definitive condition of personal identity does not, in all likelihood, rest on the particular *material* configuration of the nervous system but rather on some *functional* characterization of that nervous system, in particular of its brain's operations. So the brain-identity condition is not ruled out by this objection, at least in so far as it does not imply a specific structural brain format, but rather appeals to the brain as a functional *role-player* of sorts. Thus any prudently constructed version of the brain-identity theory would, presumably, deal with Shoemaker's Martian case by saying that the ground of the Martian's personal identity lies in the structural continuity of those organs which are functionally responsible for those roles which the brain plays in us and which make the brain the ground of personal identity. But as Shoemaker says, 'if we make "nervous system" a functional notion, we will have to say what the defining functional role is'.[14] And though that does not leave us *exactly* back where we started, it does leave us with the task of explaining what functions, performed for us by the brain, are definitive of personal identity. Leaving aside this suggestion for the time being, it will be useful to look at (1), the memory condition, as presented by Locke—both because Locke's account of the memory condition is in several ways the beginning of debate on personal identity, and because it arguably provides the basis for Kant's own discussion of this question in the Third Paralogism.

LOCKE (AND REID) ON PERSONAL IDENTITY

Locke's clearest statement of the memory condition is this:

> in this alone consists personal identity, i.e., the sameness of a rational being:
> . . . as far as . . . consciousness can be extended backwards to any past action
> or thought, so far reaches the identity of that person . . .[15]

Thus Locke gives us the boldest and simplest statement of the memory condition, saying that the ground of personal identity is memory, and that a person has identity over time just so far as his memory 'can extend'. Concomitantly, Locke's definition of a person is as follows:

a thinking intelligent being, that has reason and reflection, and can consider itself as itself, the same thinking thing in different times and places; which it does only by that consciousness which is inseparable from thinking, and . . . essential to it . . .[16]

As it stands, Locke's definition of personal identity is remarkably vulnerable to criticism. Thomas Reid, certainly Locke's fiercest critic on the subject of personal identity, presents seven separate objections to Locke's account in the space of roughly four pages. Briefly, these are as follows:

(1) On Locke's account, if consciousness is transferred to others, then many 'intelligent beings may be the same person'.

(2) If one intelligent being regularly loses consciousness of his past, then he may well be many persons.

(3) Given three times in one person's life, A, B, and C, such that at B one remembers A, and at C one remembers B and not A, then the person at C *is* identical to the person at A and is *not* identical to the person at A (the 'Brave Officer Paradox').

(4) Locke's account is such that 'consciousness is confounded with memory'.

(5) 'Personal identity is confounded with the evidence which we have of our personal identity.'

(6) Since consciousness is 'continually changing', it follows that if consciousness is the ground of personal identity, then 'no man is the same person at any two moments of his life'.

(7) Since consciousness ends with sleep, then personal identity, for Locke, must end with sleep. But since the same thing cannot have two beginnings, each time a person awakens he is a different person.[17]

It is not possible here to go into any of these criticisms in any detail, so a few brief remarks must suffice. The first objection, interestingly, seems to be a proto-example of 'fission' problem cases in personal identity, and thus engages the various discussions of person-splitting. And as Reid presents the objection, it is not particularly compelling: if memory is constitutive of personal identity, and this fission occurs, then these intelligent beings will all be the same person *only* at the time of the fission—since after that they will, presumably, have different sets of memories. The second objection is not particularly convincing, since if a person *did* regularly lose all his memories in some irrevocable way, then it is not clear why we would not be justified in saying that he *is* in fact a different person with each obliteration of 'his' past. The fourth objection, in some ways the most significant, will be commented on shortly; the fifth charges Locke with ignoring the very distinction argued for earlier in this chapter, and derives from Reid's belief that memory is a criterion of personal identity but is not its ground.

This leaves objections (3), (6), and (7), all of which bring out aspects of the same weakness in the memory condition: memory is a relatively unstable, and in many ways incoherent, phenomenon, while our notion of a person is a fairly stable and ordered concept. So what leads Locke to endorse memory as the ground of personal identity? It seems that there are several things Locke can mean here. First, it is possible that he is referring merely to one's present conscious memories; though possible, this is clearly absurd, as is brought out in Reid's sixth objection. He is rather more likely to be referring to *potential* memories (note that Locke refers to the range to which consciousness of one's past '*can* be extended'). On this reading, Locke may be including all those memories which could be elicited by the sweeping question 'What do you remember?'; thus a person would be the same as the person who figures as himself in all and only those memories which are included in his presently narrated autobiography. But Reid's 'Brave Officer Paradox' is expressly intended to subvert this kind of condition, and does so convincingly. Locke's notion of potential memories may be broadened in any number of ways, for example, to include all those memories that could, with suitable promptings, be recalled as mine. But even this is not adequate, for it is not clear that any set of promptings, however elaborate and omnisciently constructed, could elicit *all* those memories that are reasonably any given person's. Not to put too fine a point on it, any such dispositionally defined set of memories will exclude a substantial number of short-term memories, which by definition are not retained for extended periods. If this is conceded, however, Locke's broadened account falls prey to an objection not unlike Reid's 'Brave Officer Paradox': though I am appropriately describable as the 'person with ... characteristics who lived in Oxford in October of 1984'—and remember myself as such—and that I am also appropriately describable as a 'person who, while going round Addison's Walk, happened to glance at a rather large magpie'—then even though I did so glance, if this glancing were only stored in my short-term memory, and thus cannot be elicited from me as a genuine memory, then on Locke's view I am not the person who spied magpies in Angel Meadow.

There have been a number of attempts to reinforce a Lockean-type memory-condition, notably by Quinton (and, perhaps, by Grice);[18] to assess the success of these attempts is beyond my present scope. In any case, it seems clear that any theory based upon a memory condition is saddled with the burden of stipulating a range of potential memories, and possibly of a series of related memory-sets, such that this range of memories has a connectedness and stability that is consonant with that of the ordinary concept of a person who endures, whether indefinitely or not, through time. The unlikelihood of success in this attempt is recognized by Reid, who points out that memory is by its nature 'flowing like the water of a river', and as such does not have the 'continued existence' implicit in the concept of a person. And any attempt to 'stabilize' memory, as by the description of consecutive and intersecting sets of potentially elicited memories, whether successful or not, must certainly go well beyond the notion of memory explicitly invoked by Locke.

It is worth asking whether or not this reading of Locke exhausts what he has to say about personal identity. If it does, then it is mildly surprising that Kant, in his treatment of the concept of the person, would take up such a problematic definition of persons and personal identity as this and implicitly endorse it in the premises of the Third Paralogism. It is likely that Kant, even if he had read Reid, was not acquainted with Reid's treatment of Locke's theory of personal identity, which had not been published at the time the *Critique* was written. None the less, it is implausible to think that Kant, who vigorously rejected empiricist attempts to account for the self as a logical construction out of what Kant considered an incoherent 'flux of appearances', would countenance a somewhat similar attempt to posit a more or less fortuitous aggregate of memories as the ground of personal identity. A closer look at Locke's own account, however, shows that the memory condition does not exhaust Locke's theory of personal identity—though Locke himself is not altogether clear about this.

As was noted earlier, Reid's fourth objection to Locke is that, on Locke's account, 'consciousness is confounded with memory'. To see what this means, we should first consider a repetition by Locke of his original statement of the memory condition. Locke says that

as far as any intelligent being can repeat the idea of any past action with the same consciousness it had of it at first, and with the same consciousness it has of any present action; so far it is the same personal self.[19]

In other words, the memory condition is both necessary and sufficient condition of the identity of a 'personal self'. Given that in Locke's earlier definition of personal identity the memory condition is invoked as necessary and sufficient condition, it seems reasonable to conclude that Locke considers 'self' and 'person' to be equivalent. This is confirmed by Locke's remark immediately after the original definition, where he says that in a case where personal identity obtains 'it is the same self (now) as it was then'.[20] The relevance of the equivalence for Locke of 'self' and 'person' does not become clear until later, however, when Locke proceeds to his 'forensic' account and, in doing so, defines 'self'. He says:

Self is that conscious thinking thing ... which is sensible, or conscious of pleasure and pain, capable of happiness or misery, and so is concerned for itself, as far as that consciousness extends.[21]

We can see, now, that 'self' for Locke is not *merely* defined as an intelligent being with duration coextensive with its memories; it is an intelligent being which is not only conscious of itself over time but also has attitudes and desires, aversions and self-concern. And if this enriched account is definitive of the 'self', and the self is equivalent to the person for Locke, then there is at least a tacit assumption in Locke's account of personal identity that not just memory but a full-blooded consciousness, including memory and emotions and self-concern, is definitive of personal identity. In other words, within Locke's arguments for the memory condition is a sometimes complementary, sometimes divergent assumption and development of a psychological-continuity condition of personal identity.

It goes without saying that Locke's explicit, original, definition of personal identity makes it quite clear that for Locke memory is definitive. But much of the chapter 'Of Identity and Diversity' assumes that personal identity is a matter of psychological continuity, and that as such it includes memory as a necessary requisite for self-concern. It has often been noted that Locke makes a 'forensic' appeal to the memory condition when he argues that we do not hold a person responsible for what he does not remember doing. But if Locke uses legal examples to argue for the memory condition, he completely vitiates his argument shortly after by suggesting that drunkards and somnambulists are not exculpated for what they do not remember.[22] In any case, it is noteworthy that when Locke takes up the question of 'forensic' clues to the ground of personal identity, he speaks of these clues with reference to the self and with reference to the person, and in the case of this latter he is explicitly considering personal identity in terms of consciousness rather than merely of memory: 'In this personal identity, is founded all the right and justice of reward and punishment; happiness and misery being that for which everyone is concerned for himself.'[23] Again, Locke says that 'person' is 'a name for this self',[24] and that as such it is a 'forensic term appropriating actions and their merit; and so belongs only to intelligent agents capable of a law, and happiness and misery'.[25] In this last quote Locke confirms quite explicitly that personal identity applies only to beings with a full-blooded consciousness.

It should also be pointed out that Locke's own remarks *about* memory, as opposed to his statement of the memory condition, do not seem to warrant his own supposed confidence in the memory condition. Locke acknowledges 'the forgetfulness men often have of their past actions; and [that] the mind many times recovers the memory of a past consciousness, which it had lost for twenty years together';[26] thus Locke anticipates, in a way, Quinton's case of the senile general who remembers being flogged as a boy but does not remember being a hero as a young officer. Locke also suggests that if we 'suppose any spirit wholly stripped of all its memory . . . as we find our minds always are of a great part of ours, and sometimes of them all',[27] then being either united or separated from this 'spirit' would have no effect on whether or not personal identity obtains. That Locke admits the variable and undependable nature of our access to memories is strong evidence that he does not fully endorse so weak a condition of personal identity as is attacked by Reid. Why, then, does Locke invoke memory as he does? It seems that, to the extent that he does so at all, Locke relies on a simple memory-condition of personal identity precisely because he has tacitly strengthened that condition by importing into it some sort of psychological-continuity condition. And the memory condition itself is subsumed under the psychological-continuity condition fairly consistently in Locke's own application of his definition of personal identity. The force of Locke's forensic considerations, it seems, is not that persons are only responsible for what they attribute to themselves—Locke denies as much—but that the condition of personal identity is revealed by the ongoing self-concern of persons, which presupposes a persisting continuity of at least some psychological properties and an ongoing awareness of oneself as the self-same agent who has these properties; it is this latter concept of oneself that makes legitimate the notions of reward and punishment (and, for that matter, all moral evaluation), which presume a continuant person who acts and is acted upon. For Locke, the crucial notion in a proper account of personal identity is that of a psychologically continuant self with an abiding concern for its own well-being, and, presumably, for the success of its own projects. That this is not entirely clear to *Locke*, however, is the source of Reid's charge that Locke has 'confounded consciousness and memory': in a way, memory confuses the issue, for it is an essential part of that which in practice Locke does take to be the ground of personal identity—yet memory in itself is not sufficient to establish the concept of the person that Locke implicitly endorses.

KANT (AND LOCKE) ON PERSONAL IDENTITY

It should be clear that in the Third Paralogism Kant is working with a notion of 'person' which bears a good deal of similarity to that defined by Locke. Kant, of course, defines 'person' in the major premiss of the Paralogism as 'that which is conscious of the numerical identity of itself' (A361), while Locke, as was seen, defines a person as 'a thinking intelligent being, that . . . can consider itself as itself, the same thinking thing in different times and places'.[28] Presupposing the general interpretation of the Third Paralogism given above, it is worth asking just how far this similarity—in at least the starting-point of both accounts—will take us. To begin, we should recall the distinctions made between the *ground* as opposed to the *criteria* of personal identity, and between the criteria of personal identity which are applied to *oneself* as opposed to those which are applied to *others*. For Locke, it appears that the ground of personal identity is either memory or psychological continuity. Again, though, Locke does not make this absolutely clear: as Reid points out, Locke may not be adequately sensitive to this distinction between ground and criterion. In terms of a third-person criterion of personal identity, Locke offers a remarkably simple-sounding test: ask the party in question whether or not he is the same person. Locke says that 'wherever a man finds what he calls himself, there I think another may say is the same person'.[29] Assuming the honesty of the subject, then, for Locke the subject's own testimony is a conclusive criterion of personal identity. In cases where the subject's veracity can be questioned, Locke suggests that for purely pragmatic reasons it is necessary to rely on bodily criteria, assuming the same man to be the same person, given that 'want of consciousness' cannot be proven. If there is conflict between these two criteria, though, the testimony of the subject, which presumably can include reports from memory, is conclusive for Locke. This suggests what Locke's view of first-person criteria should be as well: if the subject's testimony is indefeasible by others, and if the definition of personal identity is the ability to 'extend' one's consciousness 'backwards to any past action or thought', then it seems that whatever in one's past one takes to be oneself, then that is in fact oneself, to the extent that one remembers the person as oneself. In other words, for Locke there is no first-person criterion of personal identity, because one's own identity is not in question: given a first-person belief about one's identity, that belief on Locke's account is self-warranting. And though Strawson would not endorse the notion of a 'self-warranting' belief, he does make this point: 'When a man ... ascribes a current or directly remembered state of consciousness to himself, no use whatever of any criteria of personal identity is required.'[30]

Strawson, of course, makes this remark in reference to Kant rather than Locke. And in the case of first-person criteria of personal identity, Kant, like Locke, does rule out the existence of such criteria—although he does so for importantly different reasons. For Locke, any judgment made regarding one's own identity is self-warranting, and for this reason does not employ criteria; for Kant, there are simply no criteria available to employ in making such judgments. Kant's reason for this, again, is that the 'I' of the 'I think', the 'I' of transcendental apperception, is part of the logical form which structures all of one's judgments: the fact that I must represent myself to myself as a perduring and unitary being is the source of my judgments with regard to myself. That every experience of mine is represented to me as an experience which is part of an experiential history which is had by a unitary subject ensures that, given any reflection on my experience, I will determine there to be an unchanging self which has these experiences. It is important to remember, however, that I do not empirically observe this to be the case, since the 'I' of transcendental apperception is not a determinate concept but a form or mode of the representation of experience. The only empirical access I have to my self, on Kant's view, is that of inner sense, but that refers only to my awareness of my representations as representations, and yields no determinate object-self either. As Kant says, 'No fixed and abiding self can present itself in this flux of inner appearances' (a107). In this regard, then, Ameriks is mistaken when he says that the identity of a person 'is in a sense empirically determinable (even by the person himself), although . . . ultimately speaking it is not thus empirically knowable'. For Kant, it is not empirically knowable at all, because neither by transcendental apperception nor by means of inner sense are we given an intuition of the self which could be taken as a determinate representation. None the less, due to the form that our experience necessarily takes, it is the case that the 'proposition of self-consciousness in time' is analytic, since at all times when I consider my personal identity, I do so within a cognitive framework which requires the representation of myself as having personal identity. Kant, then, not only agrees with Locke that for the case of oneself there are no criteria of personal identity but goes on to show precisely why this is true; for Locke, if one's consciousness extends back to a certain prior experience, then one is by necessity right in ascribing personal identity to oneself as the subject of both the original experience and the present remembering. Kant, as we have seen, presents an explanation of the ground in experience of this indefeasibility of first-person ascriptions of personal identity.

What, then, is Kant's *third*-person criterion of personal identity? It is far from clear what he takes it to be: in the outside-observer case he does refer to the fact that the observer's representation of me is 'the outer intuition of my subject', which on first glance seems to imply that the outside observer applies a bodily criterion with regard to my personal identity (A363). On the supposition that the Third Paralogism is an attempt to prove the soul's immortality, it could be suggested that since the outside observer determines my continued identity on the basis of bodily evidence, and that since he need have no difficulty in imagining my body's obliteration, then Kant is arguing that the outside observer need not buy into a belief in my immortality to which I must subscribe. But the Third Paralogism does not directly attempt to prove the immortality of the soul, and so the outside-observer case is not in any obvious way being used to blunt such a claim. More significant is the fact that 'the outer intuition of my subject' need not refer to my body *per se*, since any criterion the outside observer applies to resolve the question of my personal identity will by necessity involve some 'outer intuition' which is purportedly of my subject. Thus the criterion applied could be persistence of the same body—but it could also be a set of elicited behavioural responses which in some compelling way establish a suitable degree of psychological continuity, or it could be appropriate verbal reports by me offered in response to questions about what memories I have ('Just what do you remember from the time when you inhabited the body of the prince, cobbler?'). Kant's suggestion that an outside observer applies criteria to 'the outer intuition of my subject' is itself an analytic proposition: it tells us nothing of what criteria are applied, merely that someone else must consider another's identity as that of someone other than himself. And Kant gives us no clues as to what these criteria might be.

None the less, the case of the outside observer does make Kant's point that first-person avowals of personal identity need not be compelling to others, and he does not suggest that there are compelling criteria which others can apply whose satisfaction would be conclusive evidence of personal identity at all. In the *Prolegomena*, Kant does say that the permanence of the soul can, in a circumscribed way, be proven, and it is possible that this may shed light on Kant's criteria of personal identity. He says that

life is the subjective condition of all our possible experience; consequently we can only infer the permanence of the soul in life, for the death of man is the end of all the experience that concerns the soul as an object of experience, except the contrary be proved—which is the very question in hand. The permanence of the soul can therefore only be proved (and no one cares for that) during the life of man. . . .[31]

Clearly Kant is saying that our experience of our own abiding consciousness occurs, at least as far as we know, only and obviously within the bounds of our experience while alive; similarly our experience of another person's abiding consciousness is experience of this consciousness only while the person is alive (leaving open what criteria we use in this latter case). But Kant's remark that 'the permanence of the soul can ... only be proved ... during the life of *man*' (emphasis added) is interesting in that Kant rarely speaks of man at all, but rather of the self, person, or consciousness—and when he does refer to man it is at times an oblique way of invoking a contrast between one's consciousness and one's embodiment. For example, in the Second Paralogism in A, when Kant muses that 'the substance which in relation to our outer sense possesses extension is itself the possessor of thoughts', he says that one result of this musing is that 'we should have to fall back on the common expression that men think' (A359–60). In addition, if Kant's discussion of personal identity is self-consciously Lockean—and it does seem to be so, at least in part—it is relevant that Locke uses 'man' as synonymous with 'human organism', and thus (more or less) with 'body': in the case of the prince and the cobbler, once the prince's soul is in the body of the cobbler, the prince *qua* person is in the body of the cobbler, but the prince *qua* man is not, since the prince *qua* man is presumably now connected with the cobbler *qua* person. If Kant is actually invoking an implicit contrast here between one's embodiment and one's consciousness, then this may imply some bodily criterion of personal identity, suggesting that an observer can know that a person retains identity (during life) on the basis of the body's persistence. But this is not much of a criterion, since, as Kant points out, it is only known to hold in normal cases of a person's continued (and embodied) existence while alive. Kant says nothing one way or the other regarding how this criterion would either fare or function in any of the problem cases of personal identity. It is likely that Kant's use of 'man' is here innocuous, and that his point is just that which he makes in his critique of the Third Paralogism: that within one's experience one experiences oneself as permanent, but this says nothing in answer to the interesting question of how long one keeps on going, or whether and how one is in fact identical over time.

So Kant argues that there are *no* first-person criteria of personal identity, and to the extent that he even mentions the case of one person considering the question of another person's identity, he suggests no criteria which he takes to be compelling. And first-person avowals of personal identity, though they require no criteria, are not thereby conclusive proof of any 'strict and philosophical' personal identity, but are merely the inevitable result of one's cognitive framework, and say nothing about whether one has personal identity aside from the representation of one's identity within this framework. This underscores the fact that Kant's apparent scepticism with regard to conclusive criteria of personal identity is surpassed by his doctrinal scepticism regarding the ultimate ground of personal identity. Of course, within our experience the ground of personal identity is the unity of transcendental apperception. But the very question of what underlies this represented personal identity—whether it is a strictly identical substance, the identity of a series or a system, or something else—is not answerable on Kant's view, since any answer would by definition transcend experience. And the example of the elastic balls should put paid to any doubts regarding the force or character of Kant's fundamental scepticism regarding the ultimate ground of personal identity.

IDENTITY AND 'WHAT MATTERS MOST'

Ameriks asserts that Kant's scepticism about knowledge of personal identity is more fundamental than is generally acknowledged; as we can now see, he is clearly right. But he goes on to say that 'it is this unknown identity (or non-identity) that matters most',[32] and implies that Kant sees this unknown identity as a 'strict and philosophical' identity. It is not entirely clear (*pace* Butler) what a 'strict and philosophical' type of identity is, or how it could differ from other types of identity, or whether or not identity could be 'typed' at all. As has been pointed out, identity just is identity, and it does not seem to come in flavours.[33] So what 'strict' identity, when opposed to 'loose' identity, is meant to signify is presumably something about the kind of *thing* whose identity is in question, and not about the kind of identity that thing purports to have. 'Loose' identity presumably accounts for the identity of evolving organisms and for objects in general which maintain their essential or functional character through incidental changes (thus 'loose' identity is recognizably the identity of Aristotelian substances). What, though, is the sort of thing which can have 'strict' identity? It seems that the kinds of things which could be considered strictly identical (bearing in mind that they are neither more nor less *identical* than any other identical things) would be those things which are *absolutely* unchanging. If the ground of Kant's notion of personal identity is some 'absolutely unchanging' (in some unspecified sense) aspect of the person, then how is it that this aspect is what 'ultimately matters' for Kant?

As Broad has pointed out, 'to say that Mr Smith's ego persists unchanged throughout all Mr Smith's successive experiences is in one sense a tautology and in another sense a synthetic but highly doubtful statement'. It is a tautology, of course, in so far as it says that all Mr Smith's experiences have the character of being Mr Smith's experiences. And it is doubtful if it is

taken to mean that there is at the back of . . . 'the mental history of Mr Smith' a certain timeless or persistent *particular*, for which Mr Smith would use the word 'I' as a proper name . . .[34]

And these two ways of taking this proposition correspond nicely, as Broad intends, to Kant's account of personal identity: the first reflects the necessary representation of a diachronically identical self as owner of all one's experiences; the second reflects Kant's disavowal of any possible awareness of the noumenal substratum of personal identity. Whether this substratum is such that we would ascribe to it 'strict' or 'loose' identity is of course in one sense irrelevant for Kant, since in either case it is unknowable. But Broad's example of the 'timeless or persistent particular' brings out a tendency which is encouraged by talk of 'strict' identity: to assume that if something is strictly identical, it must be absolutely unchanging in a way that is somehow stronger than the way in which, say, a functional characterization of an object is unchanging. And this rather hazy requirement for a stronger kind of unchangeability tends to lead to the idea of an unchanging particular; since arguably our paradigm of particulars is that of material objects, we are left looking for an unchanging material object (or at least something which models on such an object). But this in turn leads to positing either (*a*) *bare* particulars which underlie material objects and do not change, or (*b*) *immaterial* and hence unchanging particulars. And it is a major goal of Kant's critique to expose precisely this kind of categorial shiftiness. Not only does Kant give us no reason to believe he subscribes to 'strict' identity, he gives ample positive reason for us to believe that he would reject this notion on grounds of the illegitimate metaphysics which is its likely—and usual—result.

But this, I think, is to miss, at least partly, the point of what Ameriks is saying about Kant's notion of personal identity. Perhaps the key to Ameriks's point lies in his suggestion that Kant's position is not unlike that of Chisholm, who does argue for a 'strict' personal identity. Chisholm says that a 'loose' sense of identity is one in which we say that '*A* is identical with *B*' and can consistently also say that '*A* has a certain property that *B* does not have', and that the 'loose' sense of identity may refer to those things whose identity is a 'logical construction' from a successive series of changing constituents.[35] Thus in saying that personal identity is 'strict' identity, Chisholm is saying that a person is not a construction of a successive series of what are usually called 'person-stages'. Chisholm argues for this in two ways. First, he argues that no philosopher has adduced compelling reasons to accept 'person-stages' and thus to doubt strict identity; the adequacy of these arguments, though an interesting question, should be forestalled temporarily. Second, he argues that there are cases in which putative 'person-stages' of a (logical construction of a) person, which are separated in terms of consciousness from all other 'person-stages' of that person, and which thus should be of no interest to that person, in fact are of vital importance to him. The value that the person places on these consciously severed person-stages, according to Chisholm, implies that the person at least believes himself to have strict personal identity which persists through these completely fragmented periods—and this belief gives him cause for concern about what happens to the subject who has these experiential episodes, even though these episodes will, properly speaking, never be incorporated into his own experiential history. Now clearly the importance which Chisholm suggests we attach to these fragmented periods is not unproblematic. And the coherence of the notion of a 'person-stage' which is *completely* divorced from the remainder of an experiential history is debatable. But setting aside the thesis that Kant is concerned with strict identity in so far as this implies some absolutely unchanging bare particular or immaterial substratum—as we have seen, Kant admits no use for such a substratum—there is still something Kantian in Chisholm's strategy, in settling questions of personal identity, of appealing to what matters to the person. What matters seems to be deceptively simple: whether or not the person having a certain experience or performing a certain action is *me*. *Contra* Chisholm, it is by no means unintelligible that I can view a future 'person-stage' which is appropriately related to this (my present) 'person-stage' as *me*, but in any case there is at least a sense in which I do not want to know if this future subject is, to use Nozick's expression, the 'closest continuer' of the present subject;[36] what I want to know is whether or not *I* am—in some way that matters to me—this future subject. Setting aside, then, the questionable metaphysics of 'strict' identity, the question becomes: what really matters in personal identity, and in what way or ways is it crucial that *I* continue?

To shift the question from what personal identity is to what matters about personal identity is certainly not an innocuous move. This is somewhat obvious: though what matters about personal identity may well be indicative of what personal identity consists in, still, by shifting to the question of what matters, we at least temporarily relinquish the investigation of the actual constitution of personal identity considered apart from our ordinary ascription practices. From this vantage-point it is not difficult to discard ontological questions of personal identity completely (and a number of proponents of psychological-continuity theories do so). In other words, by shifting the discussion to questions of what matters most, we have tacitly shifted the investigation from the *constitution* of personal identity to the (appropriate, or customary, or intuitively plausible) *criteria* of personal identity—or at least to what we take seriously when we talk about, or act on the basis of our notion of, personal identity. So it is not surprising that Kant, having discussed the impossibility of knowing the ultimate ground or constitution of personal identity, in fact does make this shift—quite properly, for he has clearly argued for a thorough scepticism regarding such ontological questions. Kant in fact explicitly invokes the practical import of the soul's identity throughout time, and thereby makes the shift from questions of what personal identity is to questions of what it is about personal identity that matters to us. He says that 'Taken in this way, the concept is necessary for practical employment and is sufficient for such use' (A365–6). There seem to be two possible ways in which Kant would consider this application of the concept of 'personality' to be necessary for 'practical employment'. The first is that this is simply a reiteration of Kant's thesis that the transcendental unity of apperception is a necessary condition of experience. The second, and here more interesting, is that personality, and its entailed notions of permanence and identity over time, is necessary for 'practical'—in Kant's sense of 'moral'—employment. In turn, there are two ways that this could be made out to be true. First is the point that Locke makes regarding the *practice* of moral judgment, that the very phenomenon of punishment—if it is to be coherent at all—must be 'annexed to personality': that is, punishment implies an abiding person who can both transgress and suffer the consequences of transgression. As Locke says,

The [punishment] shall be justified by the consciousness all persons shall have, that they themselves, in what bodies soever they appear, or what substances soever that consciousness adheres to, are the same that committed those actions, and deserve that punishment for them.[37]

So for the ordinary practices of making rewards and punishments for moral and immoral behaviour, it is necessary that we have a notion of persons who retain the same personal identity through time. Secondly, the idea that persons are continuous not only through the course of their natural lives but through the course of eternity may itself be important, or even essential, as a goal to moral behaviour. Kant makes this point in the Canon of Pure Reason, where he says that belief in the permanence of the soul, in so far as this implies immortality or a 'future life', is a necessary aspect of morality, in that only on the basis of there being a future life is it possible for an individual justifiably to anticipate appropriate rewards and punishments for his actions. Kant says that 'everyone regards the moral laws as commands; and this the moral laws could not be if they did not connect *a priori* suitable consequences with their rules, and thus carry with them *promises* and *threats*' (A811/B839). Of course, for Kant the threat of punishment and hope of reward cannot be the basis of moral behaviour, since acting from such self-interest is clearly not acting from a good will. But Kant goes on to say that though such beliefs cannot produce true moral behaviour, they can at least serve to prevent some immoral behaviour, in that these threats and promises 'may not, indeed, give rise to morality and good sentiments, but may still give rise to an analogon of these, namely, a powerful check upon the outbreak of evil sentiments' (A830/B858).[38] Given the usefulness for morality, then, of the belief in immortality (in so far as this belief holds a promise of ultimate moral accountability) it is clear that the 'permanence' of the soul may have practical (moral) employment.

It should be asked, however, in what way the awareness of the soul's identity as merely a represented identity furthers either Kant's or Locke's practical/moral employments of the concept of a person. In other words, does the fact that the soul is acknowledged to be merely *represented* as identical, rather than identical *in fact*, affect the moral effectiveness of the notion of the soul's personality? On the face of it, Locke's use of the concept (and what is certainly *one* of Kant's uses) is not greatly affected by this awareness: even though it is not *known* that a person remains identical through time, the crucial point here seems to be that his consciousness and his course of experiences are continuous in the relevant ways. But the function of the belief in immortality does not seem to hold up so well when exposed to Kant's transcendental strategy: on the one hand, Kant tells us that belief in the immortality of the thinking self is, in at least some cases, a necessary goad to moral behaviour, and on the other hand, he says that belief in the personality of the soul (for Kant, a precondition of the soul's immortality) is acceptable only if it is acknowledged to be merely a belief that the soul is necessarily represented as something which has personality in the relevant, 'represented', sense. And it is not clear that such a weakened and less robust idea of personality—and hence of immortality—will provide the goad which Kant says is often needed. The possibility remains open that Kant intends this constraint on our knowledge of ourselves to be made clear only to philosophers who try to construct arguments that overstep the bounds of sense, and that this acknowledgement, with its probable effect on the practical employment of the notion of personal identity, is not intended for the great majority.[39] If this is the case, then it seems that Kant, strangely enough, may be tacitly endorsing a sort of 'noble lie'.

Before accusing Kant of such high-minded deception, however, it is worth looking more closely at what the actual function of the concept of the enduring self would be, were it to be 'practically employed' in Kant's sense. It was suggested that one way of looking at this 'practical employment' of personal identity is that it is related to Locke's forensic approach: personal identity is a forensic concept, necessary to the whole enterprise of assessing the moral status of actions and their agents. Since the permanence of the soul is a transcendental illusion, though, is not Kant's commendation of its necessary role in moral valuation somewhat deceptive, a 'noble lie'? And how would advocacy of a deception, however noble, square with Kant's own application of the second formulation of the

Categorical Imperative?[40] Clearly any reading of Kant which leaves him in the position of prescribing general deception for moral ends is tenuous at best, if not completely outrageous, and is almost certain to be based in a mistake. Happily, the mistake which leads to charging Kant with endorsing a 'noble lie' is in this case reasonably straightforward: such an interpretation of Kant misunderstands the way the illusions of the transcendental dialectic function, in that it assumes them to be merely false beliefs of which one can be disabused, and then can relinquish with (more or less) regret. In fact, such illusions are unavoidable, and even when they are exposed as illusions they do not cease to be transcendent *trompe-l'œil*, which cannot be seen aright, though they are known to be illusions. Given that these illusions are unavoidable, though, Kant finds that they can have either a harmful effect, when they are taken to be empirically true, or a good use, when they are given a 'regulative employment' (A642/B670). These regulative ideas, as opposed to constitutive ideas, do not in fact have an empirical basis but function more along the lines of heuristic suppositions. As heuristic devices, these ideas serve to give our interpretation of our experience a systematic unity that it would otherwise lack; thus the use of these ideas is justified by their contribution to our ordering, in perspicuous ways, the empirical knowledge we do have. Kant says that these ideas, which arise as necessary illusions, have

an excellent ... indispensably necessary, regulative employment, namely, that of directing the understanding towards a certain goal upon which the routes marked out by all its rules converge ... a *focus imaginarius* from which ... the concepts of the understanding do not in reality proceed; none the less it serves to give to these concepts the greatest unity combined with the greatest extension. (A644/B672)

These ideas are 'derived, not from the constitution of an object but from the interest of reason in respect of a certain possible perfection of the knowledge of the object' (A666/B694). For Kant, if experience is to be coherently ordered at all, it is necessary that it be seen as conforming to unifying laws. The supposition of regulative ideas, then, does not imply the objective validity of these ideas but merely imposes a hypothetical, and effective, unified framework on our experience. With regard to the illusion of the Third Paralogism, then, Kant says that

In conformity with these ideas as principles we shall . . . under the guidance of inner experience, connect all the appearances, all the actions and receptivity of our mind, *as if* the mind were a simple substance which persists with personal identity (in this life at least), while its states, to which those of the body belong only as outer conditions, are in continual change. (A672/ B700)

Given the transcendental unity of apperception, it is necessary that my experience be had *as by* a single, simple, persisting substance, thus yielding the illusions of rational psychology, which are philosophically dangerous if taken to have *constitutive*, factual, employment. But by the *regulative* employment of these illusions, I unavoidably consider this experience to *be* the experience of a single, simple, persisting substance. The virtues of this regulative endorsement of this concept of the soul are, according to Kant, philosophically prophylactic: by supposing the soul to have this form, one avoids the need to propose 'windy hypotheses of generation, extinction, and palingenesis of souls'; thus this supposition has the virtue of simplicity (A683/B711). But in any case these regulative ideas are not *chosen* but arise from what Kant calls a 'natural predisposition'[41] to being beguiled by the transcendental illusions regarding the self, the world, and God. So the acceptance of the soul's permanence ('in this life at least') which is necessary and sufficient for 'practical employment' of talk about persons is not something which Kant believes *should* be endorsed though known to be untrue; rather, it is something which is accepted on the basis of a natural predisposition to do so, and which in a sense cannot be escaped.

A problem arises, however: the efficacy of the idea of the soul's permanence is said by Kant to consist in its pre-emption of less frugal theories about the soul. But this is far from actually being a *practical* employment of this idea, and at most seems to be a more or less tangential attack against certain philosophical theories. In any case, it does not suggest how the permanence of the soul in this life has a function in enabling us to make moral judgments: and yet this is precisely the function which Kant asserts to be crucial in deploying the concept of the soul's permanence. To see the forensic relevance of this concept, it is necessary to look at a related idea—the belief in the soul's immortality. This belief, according to Kant, is one of three Postulates of Pure Practical Reason, the other two being belief in God and belief in the noumenal freedom of persons. These postulates 'are not theoretical dogmas but presuppositions of necessarily practical import'[42] and as such are postulates which must be believed if one is to be a fully rational and moral agent. Given that the ultimate goal of a good will is the attainment of the highest good, and that it is obvious enough that this highest good is not likely to be obtained in this life, then if there is no prospect of my continued existence (and, perhaps, agency) after death, then my striving is absurd—inasmuch as I am striving to achieve the impossible. Thus it is essential, if I am to be a rational moral agent, that I postulate my own immortality, in order to make room for the possible realization of my goal, which itself must be definitive of moral action. Thus the requirement that I believe in my own immortality 'derives from the practically necessary condition of a duration adequate for the perfect fulfilment of the moral law'.[43] In other words, 'the prospect of the highest good, necessary through respect for the moral law', must be believed to be a real and attainable possibility, or else the agent is placed in the position of being, so to speak, either moral or rational but not both. It is not clear why one must *oneself* attain the highest good, or actually *see* this attainment, since it would conceivably be adequate to know that the highest good would at some point be attained in part through one's own best efforts.[44] But in any case, Kant does argue that belief in one's own immortality is necessary, and on the general grounds that one must see one's projects as potentially subject to completion if one is to attempt them at all—given the extreme unlikelihood of the attainment of the highest good in the here and now, its attainment must be postulated in the hereafter. And that, of course, presupposes the postulation of the hereafter. These points are brought together in Kant's rather uncharacteristically impassioned account, in the Third *Critique*, of the dilemma faced by Spinoza, and by any person who acts out of respect for the moral law but who does not believe in God or an afterlife:

Therefore, let us consider the case of a righteous man (Spinoza, for example) who actively reveres the moral law [but] who remains firmly persuaded that there is no . . . future life: How will he judge his own inner destination to a purpose, [imposed] by the moral law? He does not require that complying with that law should bring him an advantage, either in this world or in another; rather, he is unselfish and wants only to bring about the good to which that sacred law directs all his forces. Yet his effort [encounters] limits: For while he can expect that nature will now and then cooperate contingently with the purpose of his that he feels so obligated and impelled to achieve, he can never expect nature to harmonize with it in a way governed by laws and permanent rules ... Deceit, violence, and envy will always be rife around him, even though he himself is honest, peaceable, and benevolent. Moreover, as concerns the other righteous people he meets: no matter how worthy of happiness they may be, nature, which pays no attention to that, will still subject them to all the evils of deprivation, disease, and untimely death, just like all the other animals on the earth. And they will stay subjected to these evils always, until one vast tomb engulfs them one and all (honest or not, that makes no difference here) and hurls them, who managed to believe they were the final purpose of creation, back into the abyss of the purposeless chaos of matter from which they were taken. And so this well-meaning person would indeed have to give up as impossible the purpose that the moral laws obligated him to have before his eyes. [45]

Does Kant's remark that the concept of the soul's permanence 'is necessary for practical employment and sufficient for such use' imply that the Third Paralogism is ultimately a discussion of Kant's postulate of immortality? It is not straightforwardly so, for this reason: the principle of permanence of the soul, of personal identity, is for Kant a regulative principle based in a transcendental illusion, while the postulate of the soul's immortality is a postulate of pure practical reason. The difference is not merely terminological, since a postulate of pure practical reason *must* be believed to be true, while a regulative idea need not be. Not only need the latter not be believed, but Kant seems to endorse the view that a regulative idea only has a beneficial use if one bears in mind that it is merely a heuristic and systematically useful concept, based in an illusion that cannot be removed—but which at least can be labelled as an illusion. Furthermore, the genesis of the two is different: as was seen, the regulative ideas arise out of a need to systematize one's knowledge, while postulates of pure practical reason are presuppositions of rational moral agency. Also, as has been pointed out, for Kant 'The soul is permanent' simply is not equivalent to 'The soul is immortal', since the former only applies to the soul's persistence in experience. What, then, is the relation between Kant's claim of the necessity of belief in the soul's permanence and his claim of the practical necessity of belief in the soul's immortality?

One thing that is demonstrably true of Kant's notion of immortality is that it requires—if it is to do what Kant considers it must—a full-blooded conception of the immortality of the person. In other

words, it will not do for the person who survives to be merely a
continuing, and strictly passive, consciousness, or a set of memories;
rather, this person needs to have a set of goals and projects (or at
least *one* goal—the attainment of the highest good), and also needs
to have the desire to see these projects completed. Thus for Kant
what matters in the personal identity presupposed in the case of
immortality is, in effect, some fairly strong degree of psychological
continuity of the surviving soul or person. And as was pointed out,
this immortality is only important for us if it implies the continuation
of the experiencing self during and after this life; specifically, it
requires the continuation of this (unspecified) degree of psychological continuity, and the belief that this continuation is part of the
continued experience of the living person. To this can now be added
a stronger claim: if this condition does not obtain in the case of whatever immortality we have, then not only is this immortality of little or
no interest to us but it is incapable of providing a postulate of pure
practical reason which can legitimate rational moral agency. If it is
necessary that we posit immortality for ourselves, then, it follows
that we must posit permanence of the soul during this life as well, and
that this permanence itself be the permanence of a psychologically
continuous self. Of course, Kant maintains that the permanence of
the soul is a regulative idea which is derived, not from the postulate
of immortality but rather from a transcendental illusion. But it seems
plausible that Kant may at least implicitly see not just a connection
from the postulation of immortality to the necessity of permanence
but a less rigorous connection from permanence to immortality: it is
possible that the transcendental illusion of the soul's permanence,
coupled with the regulative tendency to extend any finite series in
appropriate conditions to infinity,[46] itself yields the concept of the
soul as immortal. Though Kant does not say as much, the apparatus
for such an extrapolation from the soul's permanence to the soul's
immortality is certainly available to him, given the apparatus of the
Transcendental Dialectic. If this extrapolation is implicit in Kant's
account, then not only is there a rational constraint on all moral
beings to believe in the soul's immortality, there is a 'natural
predisposition' to do so as well.

In any case, it is clear that—on Kant's view—what is important for
us about immortality, and about the soul's permanence during this
life as well, is the endurance of the person conceived as an intelligent
agent who has an awareness of himself as an agent with an

experiential history, and who has an interest in the attainment of certain goals. In brief, what is important is that *one continues*, with a certain psychological continuity; on the assumption that one is thus psychologically continuous, one is presumed to be the same person. For Kant, the actual ground or constitution of personal identity cannot be known, and yet there are rational and moral constraints which demand the postulation of persons who have identity over time. And the crucial fact about these persons is that they possess enough psychological continuity (and, in particular, self-awareness regarding their own experiential histories) that they can strive for the completion of their projects and can recognize their projects as those of a specific continuant person = themselves. In a way, then, Kant's account—like Locke's—is basically a forensic account, and—like Locke—Kant dismisses questions of underlying substance,[47] though Locke and Kant do have different reasons for not treating seriously the question of underlying substances and strict identity. And Kant's forensic account goes well beyond Locke's in that Kant does not merely argue on the basis of intuitive appeals to the forensic judgments that we do make as a matter of course: Kant goes on to argue the relative necessity of the concept of the person if we are to make these, or any other, moral appraisals at all. Locke, of course, does say that the concept of personal identity is the foundation of 'all the right and justice of reward and punishment', but Kant, in the Postulates of Pure Practical Reason, attempts to demonstrate that this concept is a necessary foundation of morality.

5

Kant and the Mind–Body Problem:
The Fourth Paralogism

THE Fourth Paralogism is, in a sense, something of a stepchild, either passed over in silence or given a minimal treatment in any discussion of the Paralogisms proper. Among recent commentators, Bennett cursorily dismisses the Fourth Paralogism in two quick paragraphs,[1] while Kitcher, in an article entitled 'Kant's Paralogisms', refers to 'all three paralogisms',[2] and does not mention the fourth at all. This is done, of course, not without some justice: the Fourth Paralogism in A is more or less clearly directed toward refuting the thesis that we cannot be sure of the existence of the external world; in B this task is shifted to the Refutation of Idealism, while the Fourth Paralogism in B appears to be reduced to a few remarks on what Sellars has called Kant's *ignorabimus* about the mind–body problem.[3] It is not unreasonable to suggest that almost all the sustained commentaries on the Fourth Paralogism have been undertaken within the context of discussing Kant's position on objectivity and his (putative) phenomenalism, and that *qua* Paralogism the Fourth is usually taken to be merely one of the more awkward of Kant's embarrassingly contrived tetrads. None the less, there is a good deal of philosophical material in this Paralogism that goes beyond that of the Refutation of Idealism and that is directly relevant to Kant's view of the self. Following the strategy of earlier chapters, it will be productive here to examine the two versions of the Fourth Paralogism, beginning with the formal presentation of the syllogism, in order to determine what Kant takes the Fourth Paralogism to be, to suggest likely sources for this Paralogism, and finally, on this basis, to consider in what way the discussion of the Fourth Paralogism contributes to Kant's attack on rational psychology. And again, it will be shown that, though the syllogisms of Kant's Paralogisms often appear to have a forced character, they in fact provide a useful key to the more cryptic remarks in Kant's own commentary.

THE ARGUMENT STRUCTURE OF THE PARALOGISM

The formal presentation of the Paralogism in A is given as follows:

> That, the existence of which can only be inferred as a cause of given perceptions, has a merely doubtful existence.
>
> Now all outer appearances are of such a nature that their existence is not immediately perceived, and that we can only infer them as the cause of given perceptions.
>
> Therefore the existence of all objects of the outer senses is doubtful. (A366-7)

There are a number of questions to ask about this Paralogism, which differs in several respects from the other three. First of all, how is the major premiss an assertion of a categorial truth? Kant waffles on this, at one point saying that the category involved is that of possibility (A344 = B402), and in two other places that it is that of existence (A344n., A404). Kant suggests that the reason the major premiss relates to existence will be 'sufficiently explained and justified' in the discussion of the Paralogism proper, but Kant may well promise too much here (A344n.). Second, the minor premiss does not seem to assert an analytic truth about the 'I' of the 'I think', but rather asserts something that is supposedly true of outer appearances. Given Kant's commentary on the Paralogism, too, it is clear that—at least here—he does not even accept the truth of the premiss: he says that we do in fact immediately perceive outer appearances (A371). But this is inconsistent with Kant's own position, which is that the premisses of the Paralogisms can be read to be true on at least one interpretation. As Walker has pointed out, he 'does rather overstate his case' in saying that outer appearances are 'immediately perceived',[4] and it is not clear in what way Kant in general can be taken to endorse the 'immediacy' of such perceptions. So unless Kant does—in some sense—endorse the truth of the minor premiss, he seems to have contradicted himself with regard to (1) the stated form of the Paralogisms, and (2) the way in which objects are perceived. But it is not obvious in what way Kant would find the minor premiss to be true if he is using 'outer appearance' as he normally does. In any case, the soul itself is notoriously missing from this syllogism, the categorial status of the major premiss is questionable, and it is not clear just what ambiguity is present which provides a sense in which both premises can be read as true propositions, and which invalidates the syllogism itself. Before abandoning the Paralogism as being thoroughly misbegotten, though, it is worth looking to see if an interpretation can be given which brings it into line with the first three (synoptic?) paralogisms.

If we ask what is the ambiguity in the syllogism, Kant does give us at least one answer. He says that 'the expression "outside us" is . . . unavoidably ambiguous in meaning, sometimes signifying what as thing in itself exists apart from us, and sometimes what belongs solely to outer appearance' (A373). In other words, we use 'outside us' (and presumably 'external', 'outer object', etc.) to refer on the one hand to those things that we conjecture to exist but which are not themselves part of our experience, and on the other hand to those things which, within our experience, are represented as being located outside us in space. For Kant, all our representations are represented in time, and those which are *only* so represented are objects of inner sense (including mental states, sensations, etc.) (A371). There are representations which are also represented in space, and these are objects of outer sense, or 'outer appearances': representations of extended beings, of physical objects (construed as broadly as possible) which are represented as being 'outside us'. Apart from these representations, of course, Kant also considers the existence of things in themselves, things which are not phenomenal, part of our experience, but which presumably exist apart from all our possible experience. These 'noumenal' objects are taken to be 'outside' us as well: in practice, Kant takes them to be so in so far as he regularly presumes things in themselves to be a substrate of sorts which underlies outer appearances. Given the rigidity of his phenomenal–noumenal distinction, he has no business doing this, so at best we can say that things in themselves are outside us in that they are inaccessible to us, with no implication of their being spatially outside us (since they are not spatial at all): they are outside us in the sense of being 'beyond the pale'.

How, then, is this ambiguity of 'outside us' applied in the Fourth Paralogism? To see this, we need to note that what is in question is the status of 'outer appearances' whose 'existence can only be inferred as a cause of given perceptions', and whose existence is 'doubtful' on that basis. This, I think, presents us with yet a third referent of the cluster of 'outer object' expressions. Within experience, according to Kant, there are both spatially located objects which we perceive in space as located, having extension, etc., and there are spatially located objects which we do not perceive, but which we infer as the causes of events that take place within our experience.[5] For example, if I look out of my window and see a croquet ball go scooting by on the lawn, then I will likely infer the existence of a croquet mallet nearby, an object which I do not see. The existence of the mallet, of course, is doubtful for me in a way that the existence of the ball is not. Though such objects are not spatially located in the sense that they appear spatially represented within my visual field, they are spatially located in that I infer their existence within the broader (and spatial) world within which I structure my experience. So in fact we have a triple ambiguity in the expression 'outer object'—

(1) within experience, those objects that we perceive within a spatial framework,

(2) things in themselves, which (presumably) exist outside of (apart from) experience,

(3) within experience, those objects we do not perceive, but which we postulate as existing within a spatial framework to explain that which we do perceive within that framework.

The first and third senses of 'outer object' are both experiential, while the second is by definition not. How, then, is this triple ambiguity applied to the Fourth Paralogism?

It was pointed out that, by trading on an ambiguity, each of the premisses in Kant's Paralogisms can ostensibly be made true. And it turns out that this can be done using the triple ambiguity of 'outer object' as follows. The major premiss,

> That, the existence of which can only be inferred as a cause of given perceptions, has a merely doubtful existence,

though not explicitly referring to outer objects at all, is clearly a proposition about what is the case within experience, and is not categorial in the unschematized way of the major premiss in the first three Paralogisms (*vide* 'perceptions'). In fact, it is a description of the epistemic status of the third type of 'outer object' described above, whose existence is, precisely, inferred as a cause of given perceptions. And Kant clearly views this as an accurate account of their epistemic status. The minor premiss,

> Now all outer appearances are of such a nature that their existence is
> not immediately perceived, and that we can only infer them as the cause
> of given perceptions,

cannot be a reference to the third type of outer object, because,
obviously, not all outer objects in experience are unobserved and
inferred. And as was pointed out, in the discussion of this Paralogism
Kant explicitly disallows the thesis that outer appearances are not
immediately perceived, so it is unlikely that he is here referring to
outer objects in the first sense = those objects in experience which
are perceived. So it seems likely that the 'outer appearances' here
referred to are intended to be outer objects in the second sense, or
things in themselves. The use of the expression 'outer appearance' is
an unhappy one, because 'appearances' are precisely what things in
themselves are not, but it is only on this reading that the minor
premiss can be read by Kant to be true. This being the case, perhaps
the incongruity can be laid at the door of loose terminology. And this
reading, it is worth noting, absolves Kant of the two inconsistencies
which were seen to arise from a more straightforward reading of this
premiss. The conclusion, then,

> Therefore the existence of all objects of the outer senses is doubtful,

is true if—and only if—'objects of the outer senses' refers to objects in
the second (noumenal) sense. Again, for Kant things in themselves
are not objects of sense at all, but within the context of the
Paralogism it may well be that Kant is taking the ambiguity which he
imputes to the rational psychologist and is using it within his own,
and more precise, terminology. In other words, for Kant things in
themselves are not objects of sense, but for the transcendental
realist, his opponent in the present context, they are.[6] The transcendental realist/empirical idealist, of course, wants to read the conclusion as referring, in Kant's terminology, to objects in the first, and
possibly the third, senses, and on this reading the conclusion is false.
Given that the empirical idealist wants to render dubious all experience of the external world—*however* 'external' is conceived—he is
committed to casting doubt on objects within experience, and is of
course not committed to that theory within which Kant evaluates the
Paralogism.
  Assigning the meanings above to the cluster of 'outer object'

expressions, then, we get the following picture of the Fourth Paralogism: the rational psychologist, here wearing the mask of the empirical idealist, wants to prove that the existence of all outer objects is doubtful. Within experience, there is a kind of outer object (type three) whose existence is open to doubt (the major premiss), and on this the rational psychologist and Kant can agree—as in the earlier Paralogisms, the major premiss is intentionally not controversial. To get from this fact about some outer objects to a generalization about all outer objects, however, requires an illicit shift to (type two) outer objects which are not experiential at all (the minor premiss). This illicit shift leads (invalidly) to the conclusion that all outer objects have a doubtful existence. But this is only true of type three and type two outer objects, and not of type one. So the conclusion is valid only given a consistent use of one of the three senses of 'outer object', but such a use of any of the three would generate a false premiss. Thus the attempt of the rational psychologist to cast doubt on all outer experience fails *per sophisma figurae dictionis*.

This interpretation is not without its problems, even apart from those mentioned above regarding loose terminology. Among other things, even given appropriate substitutions of senses of 'outer object', we run into problems with the word 'doubtful'. Strictly speaking, only outer objects of type three are doubtful, since their existence is inferred, and in the normal course of events, may be confirmed or denied by a perceptual encounter (I may, after all, see the croquet mallet). And though we can say that type two outer objects have a 'doubtful' existence, this is stretching 'doubtful' farther than it ought to go. If something can be doubted, then our propositional attitudes towards that something have an epistemic status, and it seems that knowledge of its existence can be intelligibly (albeit falsely) asserted. But it is not clear that, for Kant, things in themselves are such that propositional attitudes regarding them have any epistemic status at all. Put differently, we doubt that which occurs within the context of experience, and things in themselves do not so occur—they are not, properly speaking, subject to doubt at all. However, it is not necessary to attribute doubt to type two outer objects in either of the premisses in order to make them true, and is only necessary to make the conclusion true. Though in practice he does provide readings whereby the paralogistic conclusions can be read as both true and innocuous, Kant is certainly not committed to doing so. And it is possible, given his loose approach to things in themselves, that he allows himself the luxury of 'doubting' their existence, where doubt is not an appropriate, since epistemic, term. Kant himself, however, does explicitly suggest that type two outer objects are indeed doubtful. He says that

> if we regard outer appearances as representations produced in us by their objects, and if these objects be things existing in themselves outside us, it is indeed impossible to see how we can come to know the existence of the objects otherwise than by inference from the effect to the cause; and this being so, it must always remain doubtful whether the cause . . . be in us or outside us . . . (A372)

Of course, this doubtfulness is explicitly that required of the transcendental realist, and not that of Kant himself, but it is likely that when Kant, in the Paralogism itself, refers to things in themselves as 'doubtful', he is intentionally speaking from the position of the transcendental realist. With regard to whether or not type one outer objects can be doubted, Kant says nothing directly here. But he does say that

> To avoid . . . deceptive illusion, we have to proceed according to the rule: whatever is connected with a perception according to empirical laws, is actual. (A377)

Here, Kant seems to be responding to the kind of sceptical argument presented by, for example, Descartes in the Sixth Meditation, where he says that

> many experiences little by little destroyed all the faith which I had rested in my senses . . . I from time to time observed that those towers which from afar appeared to me to be round, more closely observed seemed square . . .[7]

In other words, the sceptic's objection is that our senses do deceive us, and that not just inferred outer objects but immediately perceived outer objects may be, in effect, misperceived, and thus their existence is in some way open to doubt. Against this, Kant is implicitly following a well-worn strategy of anti-sceptical argument, pointing out that, though individual perceptual judgments may be mistaken, it does not follow from this that all perceptual judgments are so mistaken. As a corrective to misperception, we rely on those perceptions which, by conforming to 'empirical laws', are judged to be accurate. In brief, Kant's point seems to be that though the veridicality of individual perceptual judgments may be doubted, it is necessary that such judgments be evaluated as part of a coherent system of judgments, the veridicality of which is indubitable. This is not obviously a compelling rebuttal of the sceptic's case, but it does seem that Kant is drawing on just such a strategy, as presented in the Second Analogy, in his defence of our knowledge of the external world in the Fourth Paralogism. So type one outer objects, though possibly subject to doubt in individual cases, are not, taken as a class, to be doubted—at least not on the view presented by Kant in the Fourth Paralogism. But here too it is not necessary that Kant assert that these outer appearances are subject to doubt in order to present true interpretations of the two premisses (and if it were necessary, the game would be up, for the immunity of these outer appearances from doubt is the point of Kant's refutation of empirical idealism).

A more serious objection to this reading is this: as the syllogism is presented, the middle term is not 'outer object' at all, but rather is something like 'is such that its existence is only inferred as a cause'. And this is not obviously ambiguous. Yet it is the middle term, strictly speaking, which renders the argument void through its ambiguity. Consider, though: one objection here that is not valid is that what is being predicated is existence, which Kant disallows as a predicate. In fact, what is predicated is the way in which we are *aware of* the existence of something, and *not* that existence itself. We should then ask, is there an ambiguity reflected in the modes of awareness we have of the different kinds of outer objects which appear in the two premisses of the syllogism? It appears that there is. In the case of type three objects (the major premiss), these objects are inferred, assumed to exist in the external world, due to their explanatory value with regard to observed phenomena, while in the case of type two objects (the minor premiss), they are entities which are not assumed to exist within experience, and which are at best conjectured to exist in some indeterminate way (A384). And, unlike the case of unperceived but inferred objects, conjecture regarding the existence of things in themselves in no way (at least on Kant's official view) leads to knowledge. This conjecture, then, is not an explanatory inference, and has no legitimate purpose. And this ambiguity does provide us with a *sophisma* of the kind Kant requires. However, two points need to be made here. First, this ambiguity only appears in the syllogism given the ambiguous usage of 'outer object' itself—specifically, the ambiguity between types two and three. And the ambiguity of 'outside us' is the one Kant gives as the relevant ambiguity in this argument (A373). Second, the ambiguity of 'inferred' is not really an obvious ambiguity at all, for this reason: it is not clear why things in themselves are more conjectural, less well grounded inferentially, than at least some unseen objects in the realm of appearances which are postulated as explanatory causes of empirical phenomena. In other words, it was suggested that type three objects are entities which are inferred as explanations of existing phenomena, and the question is, in what significant way is this different from the role which could be played by type two objects—specifically, by transcendental objects? Presumably Kant at least would say that type three objects are in principle themselves immediately observable, but this rules out those theoretical entities which are postulated in science and which are fundamentally unobservable, yet which are in the realm of outer objects. Kant may reply that what he is doing is a sophisticated phenomenology, in which such theoretical and unobservable entities have no place, but this falls far short of his avowed intention of circumscribing the limits of knowledge. Any contemporary Kantian must, then, find a way of including such entities within the bounds of knowledge—and it is not clear that he can do so without allowing a theoretical role to things in themselves as well. But this is tangential, and certainly not compelling in determining Kant's intent regarding the ambiguity of 'inferred'. What is clear is that even given this ambiguity (such as it is), the core ambiguity from which it is derived is that of 'outer object', and it is this ambiguity which allows the rational psychologist to run this particular piece of paralogistic machinery.

DESCARTES AND THE FOURTH PARALOGISM

What, though, does all of this have to do with the self, and with rational psychology, as opposed to just the rebuttal of empirical idealism in a fairly abbreviated fashion? Though he does not follow it up, Bennett points out the connection by citing an argument of Descartes, ostensibly put forward in the Second Meditation.[8] Here Descartes says that

I already know for certain that I am, and that it may be that all . . . things that relate to the nature of body are nothing but dreams.[9]

And Bennett draws from this an argument to the effect that 'my own existence is not doubtful, but the existence of physical things is doubtful; therefore I am not a physical thing'.[10] In fact, though, Descartes disclaims this conclusion in the Second Meditation: 'I am not sure about this, I shall not dispute it now,'[11] waiting until the Sixth Meditation to draw the conclusion.[12] The argument, however, is made explicit in the *Discourse*:

> examining attentively that which I was, I saw that I could conceive that I had no body, but yet that I could not for all that conceive that I was not . . . From that I knew that I was a substance the whole essence or nature of which is to think, and that for its existence there is no need of any place, nor does it depend on any material thing; so that . . . the soul . . . is entirely distinct from body.[13]

What Descartes is calling attention to is the difference between the way in which we are aware of our bodies (and of the external world in general), and the way we are aware of our own consciousness. That there is a difference—and one often couched in expressions like 'direct awareness' or 'immediacy'—is doubtless true. Descartes, however, takes the datum of these different modes of awareness and on the basis of this difference argues for a substantive thesis about the nature of the conscious self: that 'thinking beings . . . are conscious of their existence as separate and distinct from all matter' (B409). And this thesis, if true, seems to be an *a priori* judgment which is true of the self, in that it is purportedly derived from nothing more than consideration of the nature of self-consciousness prior to experience (the 'sole text' of rational psychology). If Descartes can derive this thesis about the self in this way, simply from this kind of *a priori* reflection, then this would clearly be an instance of what Kant calls 'the one unanswerable objection . . . to our whole critique' (B409).

Given the importance of this thesis, we should consider Bennett's dismissal of the Fourth Paralogism with certain reservations. Having suggested that Kant may well be considering this (or a related) argument of Descartes, Bennett says that

> even if Kant's attack on 'The existence of physical things is doubtful' is motivated by its role as a premiss in that argument, the attack is still mislocated. For what it implies . . . is that the argument rests upon a mistake about the nature of objectivity-judgments, not that it involves any underlying error about the soul. Elsewhere, Kant . . . associates the fourth (Paralogism)

with the view that 'thinking beings . . . are conscious of their existence as . . . distinct from matter' . . . which is a mistake about matter, not about thinking beings.[14]

Though in a sense correct, Bennett's remarks should be taken *cum grano salis*. It is more or less true that the Paralogism rests on 'a mistake about the nature of objectivity-judgments', in so far as it trades on a confusion between different senses of (outer) object, and that this is a mistake about matter, if matter is taken to be 'mere outer appearance' (A359). And so Bennett is right that, in a sense, the Paralogism does not thereby *involve* 'any underlying error about the soul'. But this particular 'mistake about matter', though it does not *involve* an underlying mistake about the soul's nature, is certainly *relevant to* any number of such mistakes, such as, for example, the postulation of a substantial dualism, or being forced into *ad hoc* hypotheses about pre-ordained harmonies. To say, then, that this Paralogism is not relevant to mistakes about the nature of the soul— in the sense of its conclusion leading to such mistakes—is just wrong, and is not unlike saying that the Third Paralogism rests on a mistake about identity-judgments and so is not relevant to mistaken judgments about the continuance of persons over time. As Descartes's argument shows—and as Kant was aware—what we have to say about the external world is directly relevant to what we can say about the relation of the self to the external world, and specifically to that part of the external world which is the body. If the problem of the relation between mind and body is relevant to theories of the nature of mind, then 'mistakes about matter' are demonstrably relevant to these theories as well, particularly when (1) matter is considered in terms of its relation to ('outside') us, and (2) when the mistakes about matter are used to argue for theses about the nature of mind.

Kant's reason, then, for considering in such detail the question of doubt with regard to the external world is that this very question is the starting-point for Descartes's argument against mind-body identity, an argument which is attempted within the putatively synthetic *a priori* framework of rational psychology. In the Fourth Paralogism in A, Kant begins, in the formal analysis of the Paralogism, by attempting to rebut the postulated doubt which he sees as the ground of this argument. Hence the question of whether or not 'the existence of all outer objects is doubtful': Kant argues that this thesis can only be made good given a confusion between those outer objects that we perceive, those outer objects that we infer, and things in themselves. Kant suggests that 'doubt' only applies to the second of these (and possibly—loosely speaking—the third), but the rational psychologist needs to demonstrate that doubt applies to the first as well. And, as was seen, Kant argues that such doubt (due to 'deceptive illusion') is misplaced, even given the fact that such perceptions of outer objects occur within a framework of 'empirical laws'. Having dealt with the source of the problem through consideration of the epistemic status of outer objects, Kant proceeds to a general consideration of the question, 'How are the mind and body related?' To see how Kant answers this question, it will be useful to look at his statement of the Fourth Paralogism (largely implicit) in the second edition.

In B, Kant does not actually give us a formalized syllogism which he takes to be the Fourth Paralogism, but he does state what seems clearly to be the minor premiss of this syllogism. And it is not the minor premiss of the syllogism as presented in A; rather, he says that 'I distinguish my own existence as thinker from other things outside me' (B409). This is a good deal closer to the form of the minor premisses of the first three Paralogisms in that it is an analytic statement about the 'I' of the 'I think'. If it is the minor premiss of the Paralogism, then, we are given the middle term, and, assuming the standard paralogistic form, we can reconstitute the intended Paralogism as follows:

> That, the existence of which can be distinguished from that of a given other thing, is different from that thing.
>
> I (can) distinguish my own existence as thinker from other things outside me.
>
> Therefore I am different from those things that are outside me.

It should be noted that the major premiss here is a weakened version of Leibniz's Law, giving the necessary condition of identity but not indicating that this is also the sufficient condition as well. Moreover, the major premiss fits the paralogistic formula in so far as it is obviously categorial, but, interestingly, it departs from Kant's architectonic in so far as the category to which it belongs is identity, rather than existence or possibility as in the first edition. Kant, apparently, is aware of this, and attempts to fit it into the appropriate category by use of 'the existence of which can be distinguished'— derived from 'I can distinguish my existence as thinker'. This is exceedingly awkward, and on the face of it again seems to put Kant in the position of asserting existence as property. The relevant property, of course, is not existence *per se* but existence as something, or more perspicuously, as mode of representation— Kant's use of existence in the minor premiss (and thus the major premiss as well) is a case of architectonic garnish, and is otherwise insignificant. In any case, this formulation of the Paralogism gives us a categorial major premiss which is (for Kant at least) presumably both true and uncontroversial, and a minor premiss which is analytically true in so far as it is read as a statement regarding the necessary representation of the 'I'.[15] The minor premiss is false if it is taken to refer to a distinction of the actual properties of the self from those of other (external) things, rather than referring to a distinction between those properties the self is represented as having and those properties had by external objects. Similarly, the conclusion is true if construed as 'I am (necessarily represented as) different from other things', and false if construed as 'I am (in fact) different from other things'. In the second edition, then, Kant is tacitly working with a Paralogism which more closely fits his earlier formulations, and which thereby more explicitly concerns the nature of the thinking self.

The Paralogism is also demonstrably related to Descartes's argument in the *Discourse*. Let us consider, briefly, Descartes's argument. It seems to be of the form

(1) I can conceive that my body does not exist.
(2) I cannot conceive that I do not exist.
(3) Therefore I am distinct from my body.

And taking 'I' here, as Descartes does, to mean 'conscious subject' or 'mind', the conclusion can be taken to mean that the mind is distinct from the body. This is roughly what Hooker has called Descartes's 'Argument from Doubt',[16] and, as Hooker and others have pointed out, it requires a third premiss: a statement of the principle of the indiscernibility of identicals. Given such a premiss, the argument would seem to be valid, since it would attribute a property to the body (= being such that it is conceivable that it does not exist), it would deny that property to the mind, and, since identicals have precisely the same set of properties, it would conclude that mind and body are not identical. As Kenny has noted, though, Leibniz's Law becomes problematic in modal and intentional contexts, and premisses (1) and (2) place the argument squarely in both a modal and an intentional context.[17] Hooker suggests that to make the argument work, Descartes needs to include two such premisses as

> (4) My body has the property of being possibly doubted by me to exist,

and

> (5) I do not have the property of being possibly doubted by me to exist,

thereby removing the modal and intentional contexts, and then applying Leibniz's Law to these two premisses instead of to (1) and (2). But Hooker rightly notes that it is far from clear just how Descartes is to get from (1) and (2) to (4) and (5), 'from *de dicto* propositions to their *de re* counterparts'.[18] In other words, how is Descartes to make the shift from assertions about how I can represent my body and myself as conscious subject to assertions about what is true of my body and myself as conscious subject? And this, of course, is Kant's point against Descartes as well: that he is trading on the distinction between what properties the subject has and what properties it is represented as having. And for Kant, though we can know a good deal about the subject *de dicto*, we are not on that basis alone justified in making any claims about the subject *de re*. Hence Kant's exposure of the Fourth Paralogism in B: conceding the minor premiss, that I do represent myself as a thinking being distinct 'from other things outside me', as analytically true, Kant goes on to say that

> I do not thereby learn whether this consciousness of myself would be even possible apart from things outside me through which representations are given to me, and whether, therefore, I could exist merely as thinking being (i.e. without existing in human form). (B409)

That I represent myself as distinct from external objects—and hence as distinct from my body—does not allow me to infer that I am so distinct. If, then, we set out Descartes's argument as follows:

> (1) I can conceive that my body does not exist.
> (2) I cannot conceive that I do not exist.
> (3) A thing is identical with another thing iff they have exactly the same properties.
> (4) My body has the property of being possibly doubted by me to exist.

(5) I do not have the property of being possibly doubted by me to exist.

(6) My body and I have at least one divergent property.

(7) Therefore I am not identical with my body.

we can see that Kant, in the Fourth Paralogism in A, is refuting Descartes's argument by attacking the first premiss. More accurately, Kant is attacking the (here unstated) premiss which gets Descartes to the first premiss: that all outer objects have a doubtful existence, so even that outer object of which I could presumably be most certain—my body—has a doubtful existence. In the Paralogism in B, Kant is attacking the derivation of the fourth and fifth premisses from the first and second (the shift from *de dicto* to *de re*). In both editions, however, Kant is arguably attempting to refute the same argument for the non-identity of mind and body. That what is required to refute the first premiss is precisely what is required for the Refutation of Idealism—which Kant had independent reasons for presenting—has obscured the role of the Fourth Paralogism in A within the framework of Kant's critique of rational psychology. And this attack on the first premiss does not, as we have seen, fit well within the usual paralogistic pattern. In the second edition, then, Kant moved this attack on idealism to a more prominent and less structurally ambiguous location in the *Critique*, and, turning again to Descartes's argument, refuted it in a manner more consonant with the form of the first three Paralogisms. It is worth noting that Hooker adduces reasons to believe that Descartes did not intend precisely this argument in the *Discourse*.[19] None the less, it is an argument which Descartes has often been taken to have presented, and we now have some reason to believe that Kant was one of those by whom he was so taken. Having seen, then, how Kant deals with Descartes's argument against mind-body identity, it is now possible to appreciate fully how Kant himself deals with the problem of the relationship between mind and body: this will be the project of the remainder of this chapter.

KANT AND THE MIND–BODY PROBLEM: *GEMEINSCHAFT*

In his discussion of the Fourth Paralogism in A, Kant makes the rather startling claim that 'the real goal of rational psychology' is to settle the question of 'the possibility of the communion (*Gemein-*

schaft) of the soul with an organized body . . . of the beginning . . . (and) of the end of this communion' (A384). This claim is suspect, since it seems from Kant's other comments in the Paralogisms that the 'real goal' of rational psychology is to elicit *a priori* truths about the soul, regardless of what is true of the body, and the fact that these truths may have implications about the relation of mind and body is, albeit usefully, incidental. None the less, to dismiss Kant's claim in this way would be jejune: as was pointed out against Bennett above, the relation between mind and body is directly relevant to any theory of the nature of mind; indeed, if Kant is taking as his text Descartes's rational psychology (and we have adduced some evidence that in the Fourth Paralogism at least, this is true), then it is the point of embarkation for the theory at hand. At least in A, then, the mind–body problem presents to Kant a challenge within his dismantling of the rationalist's position. In fact, Kant dismisses the problem—eventually—on an agnostic note, saying that we cannot know the basis of the relation between mind and body. This dismissal is made, it seems, on the basis of Kant's transcendental idealism, and thus is made in what at this point should be a fairly predictable way. But Kant's own comments are far from straightforward, suggesting several possible strategies Kant may be deploying from his transcendental idealist stance: to understand the actual character of Kant's *ignorabimus*, it will be necessary to examine each of these strategies in turn.

First, however, a terminological point needs to be made regarding the word *Gemeinschaft*, which Kemp Smith normally translates as 'communion' or 'association'. *Gemeinschaft* for Kant falls under the category of Relation, and is in the presentation of the Table of Categories referred to as 'reciprocity between agent and patient' (A80/B106). And in the Schematism, Kant says that

The schema of community or reciprocity, the reciprocal causality of substances in respect of their accidents, is the co-existence, according to a universal rule, of the determinations of the one substance with those of the other. (A144/B183)

So 'community' (*Gemeinschaft*) seems clearly to refer to two substances each of which can act upon the other: hence the 'reciprocity between agent and patient' means that both substances are both agent and patient (or can be) with regard to each other. It is worth noting that here Kant seems to take 'community' (*Gemein-*

schaft) and 'reciprocity' (*Wechselwirkung*) to be synonymous. This is confirmed in the Third Analogy as well, where Kant in A presents the 'Principle of Community' as 'All substances, so far as they coexist, stand in thoroughgoing community, that is, in mutual interaction', and in B substitutes 'in thoroughgoing reciprocity' in a text otherwise unchanged in the second edition (A211, B256). But there are problems with the use of 'community', just as there are, according to Kant, with *Gemeinschaft*. Kant says that 'The word community (*Gemeinschaft*) is in German ambiguous. It may mean either *communio* or *commercium*' (A213/B260). Kant illustrates this ambiguity with an example from his own theory of mind:

In our mind, all appearances, since they are contained in a possible experience, must stand in community (*communio*) of apperception . . . If this subjective community . . . is to hold of appearances as substances, the perception of the one (object) must as ground make possible the perception of the other, and reversewise . . . But this is a reciprocal influence, that is, a real community (*commercium*) of substances . . . (A214/B261)

The point is that *Gemeinschaft* can stand for what is essentially an association, a grouping-together or synthesis, as in the synthesis of appearances within one experiential perspective; on the other hand, *Gemeinschaft* can mean an interactive relationship between agents, as in the causal relations between perceived objects, the kind of relationship Kant calls 'a dynamical community' (A213/B260). Kant's cited Latin distinction provides a perfect disambiguation: *communio* means 'mutual participation in' or 'sharing', while *commercium* means specifically 'trade' or 'commerce' or, more generally, 'communication', 'correspondence', or 'negotiation'. The distinction is not in all cases clear, of course, since it is often the case that objects which are in *communio* are also in *commercium*, and vice versa. Essentially, though, the difference is that *commercium* (and that sense of *Gemeinschaft* which is synonymous with *Wechselwirkung*) connotes an active relationship, while *communio* implies no more than a mere grouping or association. It is clear that precisely this ambiguity is inherent in the English 'community' as well. Rather than using Kant's Latin to disambiguate, however, it seems reasonable to use 'association' for the *communio* sense of *Gemeinschaft*, and 'interaction' for the *commercium* sense. (From here on, Kemp Smith's translation of *Gemeinschaft* will be disambiguated accordingly without comment.) Thus *Gemeinschaft* as it will be applied to the mind–body problem is defined in B as follows: 'interaction is the causality of substances reciprocally determining one another'. As schematized category, it refers to causally interacting substances, each capable of affecting (and being affected by) the other. And in the Postulates of Empirical Thought, Kant makes it clear that, for substances to be interactive, they cannot be totally divorced from one another (e.g., spatially): 'interaction is not conceivable as holding between things each of which, through its subsistence, stands in complete isolation' (B293).

This last point is arguably the motivation for the mind–body problem itself, especially in so far as it is viewed as a problem of explaining the interaction between mind and body. As Kant says, 'what appears as matter cannot by its immediate influence be the cause of representations, these being effects which are quite different in kind from matter' (A390). That is, matter appears to be different in kind from mental states, and yet purportedly material changes cause changes in mental states. But if mind and matter are as different as they appear to be, it is not clear just how they can be said to interact at all. As Kant points out in B, 'I distinguish my own existence . . . from other things outside me—among them my body' (B409). And this distinction is not that of similar but distinct objects, but of two entirely different kinds of things, the nature of whose relationship is completely mysterious. Considering again the formal presentation of the Fourth Paralogism, Kant points out there that we represent the experiencing subject and that which is 'outside' this subject in very different ways, such that whatever interaction takes place between mind and body is not obviously like the interaction which takes place between observed physical objects. In the Fourth Paralogism, the fallacy traded on the different ways mind and body are represented, such that the body's existence is considered to be doubtful in a way that the soul's existence is not. The problem of mind–body interaction similarly begins with the observation that the two are (represented as) thoroughly different:

as soon as we hypostatise outer appearances and come to regard them not as representations but as things existing by themselves outside us, with the same quality as that with which they exist in us . . . then the efficient causes outside us assume a character which is irreconcilable with their effects in us. For the cause relates only to outer sense, the effect to inner sense—senses which, although combined in one subject, are extremely unlike each other. (A386)

And this difference between presumed cause and presumed effect gives us the 'difficulty of explaining the origin of our representations from quite heterogeneous efficient causes outside us' (A387). Given some stipulation that causal interactions must take place between entities that are in some sense homogeneous, and the observation that mind and body are not homogeneous in this relevant sense, it becomes clear that causal interaction between mind and body, called by Kant 'physical influence', is not possible (A390). This in turn, according to Kant, has led to two other theories which attempt to account for this relation: 'predetermined harmony', and 'supernatural intervention', each of which, rather obviously, goes beyond what we can surmise about this relation from experience, yet which seem legitimized by the incoherence of the 'common sense' view of causal interaction (A390).

It is, perhaps, interesting to note here an early formulation of this problem by Kant, in the *Dreams of a Spirit-Seer*:

> with a spiritual substance, which must be in combination with matter, as for example the human soul, the difficulty manifests itself that I must think of a reciprocal relation of it with corporeal beings in one whole, and nevertheless must cancel out the only kind of contact which is found between material things.[20]

The context suggests that by 'the only kind of contact' Kant probably means being 'subject to divisibility and to the laws of impact', implying (at least) causal reciprocity. This is confirmed when, in the same text, Kant goes on to say

> how mysterious does the interaction of soul and body become? . . . yet at the same time, how natural is this incomprehensibility, since our concepts of external actions are derived from those of matter, and are always connected with the conditions of pressures or impacts that are not found in this case.[21]

As a tentative solution, Kant offers yet a fourth theory, which is essentially panpsychism, suggesting that matter has a 'spiritual essence', which presumably supplies the requisite homogeneity of composition for there to be causal interaction between mind and matter. It should be pointed out that the mature Kant expressed a wish that works written prior to the *Inaugural Dissertation* (and thus the *Dreams*) be excluded from an edition of his minor works,[22] thus implying—not surprisingly—Kant's rejection of this pre-Critical writing. None the less, it is interesting that here Kant's formulation of the *problem* at least remained essentially the same.

Kant's way of dealing with this problem is confusing, and seems to incorporate several different lines of argument without any indication that Kant was aware that these *are* different lines of argument. But though Kant's solution to this problem is not straightforward, its general strategy is clearly parallel to his strategy in dealing with the Paralogisms in general. He suggests that the problem itself, based on the supposed heterogeneity of mind and body, is the product of a confusion between how mind and body are represented and how they are in themselves. Kant says that 'matter, the interaction of which with the soul arouses so much questioning, is nothing but a mere form . . . of representing an unknown object by means of . . . outer sense' (A385). Matter is merely appearance and not a thing in itself. Thus, being material is merely a way of being represented that is different from the way mental states are represented: 'Matter, therefore, does not mean a kind of substance quite distinct and heterogeneous from . . . (the soul), but only the distinctive nature of those appearances of objects . . . the representations of which we call outer' (A385). Here we can see a solution to the problem suitable for Kant as transcendental idealist: that the body, represented as material substance and as 'outside' the mind, is represented differently from mental states does not alter what Kant takes to be the fact that they are still both representations. As Kant says, 'As long as we take inner and outer appearances together as mere representations in experience, we find nothing absurd and strange in the interaction of the two kinds of senses' (A386). In other words, mind and body are heterogeneous only in so far as they are cognized via different modes of representing—they are homogeneous in so far as they are both representations. From this it would seem that Kant's point would be that in so far as mind and body are homogeneous in the relevant sense, and assuming that their both being representations makes them homogeneous in this sense, then there is no difficulty in explaining their causal interaction.

This point does have a certain plausibility from the standpoint of Kant's idealism, but—perhaps unfortunately—it is not quite the conclusion that he draws. Rather, Kant says that the problem arises from assuming that outer representations are truly outside us, and that their interaction with the mind consists in 'bringing to bear on our thinking subject the activities which they exhibit as appearances in relation to each other', which they cannot do because of the disparity between outer and inner sense (A386). So even though mind and body are both representations, they are such different sorts of representations that it is unintelligible to speak of causal interaction between them: 'For the cause relates only to outer sense, the effect to inner sense—senses which, although combined in one subject, are extremely unlike each other' (A386). This unintelligibility, however, only holds if we take outer objects as transcendentally real, as having in themselves a causal efficacy that is not just operative within the framework of appearances in outer sense, but which is operative across the limits of the representation of outer objects, and which therefore has efficacy with regard to the objects of inner sense: to the self as it is encountered empirically, the self of empirical apperception (and possibly the self of transcendental apperception as well, though Kant does not make this clear). What Kant is pointing out is that talk of causal interaction is appropriate within the framework of outer sense, where all effects are changes of location, or within the framework of inner sense, where all effects are (non-spatial) thoughts, but that it is incoherent to speak of causes within one of these frameworks having effects in the other. (It should be noted, tangentially, that Kant's limitation of material effects to changes of location is a muddle: *vide* a tomato's ripening on the window-sill). Thus Kant does not follow the initially attractive strategy outlined above, since the relevant homogeneity does not obtain between material objects and the representations of inner sense.

In the second edition, Kant offers an alternative, though equally transcendental idealist, solution to the problem. Harking back to the point that both mental states and bodies are only representations, Kant says that

The difficulty peculiar to the problem consists ... in the assumed heterogeneity of the object of inner sense (the soul) and the objects of the outer senses ... But if we consider that the two kinds of objects thus differ from each other, not inwardly but only in so far as one appears outwardly to the other, and that what, as thing in itself, underlies the appearance of matter, perhaps after all may not be so heterogeneous in character, the difficulty vanishes ... (B427)

In other words, even given that as representations mind and body are too heterogeneous to be coherently considered to be causally interactive, it is still possible that whatever underlies both mind and body is homogeneous in a way that would—could we but know it—

adequately explain their interaction. We assume their heterogeneity on the basis of their distinct modes of representation, and this, of course, is the very mistake which is ubiquitous throughout the Paralogisms. And, interestingly, this dismissal of the interaction problem is presented in the first edition as well, but as part of the commentary on the Second Paralogism (within the context of discussing the non-corporeality of the soul). It is worth noting that there Kant says that 'the something which underlies the outer appearances and which so affects our sense that it obtains the representations of space, matter, shape, etc., may yet, when viewed as noumenon (or better, as transcendental object), be at the same time the subject of our thoughts' (A358). So the body may not only be the same *kind* of thing as the mind, it may in fact be (in the best psychophysical-identity kind of way) the *same thing*. Kant goes on to say that

If . . . we compare the thinking 'I' not with matter but with the intelligible that lies at the base of the outer appearance which we call matter, we have no knowledge whatsoever of the intelligible, and therefore are in no position to say that the soul is in any inward respect different from it. (A360)

Thus what is perhaps Kant's most considered, transcendental idealist, view of the interaction problem is that the problem only has purchase within the realm of representations, and that with regard to how mind and body are in themselves, there is no reason to think that there are any differences which would preclude the causal interaction of the two. The usual caveat holds here, of course, namely, that Kant has no right to talk about 'the intelligible that lies at the base of' representations, or indeed about causation outside the realm of perceived objects at all. None the less, Kant's basic point remains—that the interaction problem arises due to an assumed heterogeneity in things in themselves, which is actually only known to be heterogeneity in their representation. If that heterogeneity does not obtain noumenally, then there is no problem, and since we cannot possibly know whether it obtains noumenally or not, there is no problem for us.

To summarize thus far Kant's solutions to the interaction problem: there are three ways in which Kant dismisses this problem from within a transcendental-idealist perspective. First, since both mind and body are homogeneous *qua* both being representations, there is no relevant difference between them which renders their causal interaction tenuous. Kant, though hinting at such a position, does not explicitly draw this conclusion. Second, though causal interaction does occur in inner sense and in outer sense, it does not cut across the boundary between them, and we only imagine there to be causal interaction between mind and body on the basis of mistaking outer objects for things in themselves, with a causal efficacy which could extend to the mind as well as to other (outer) objects. Kant seems to endorse such a position in his discussion of interaction in the Fourth Paralogism in A. Third, the only heterogeneity which calls into question the intelligibility of mind–body interaction is assumed to obtain on the basis of representations which tell us nothing about whether mind and body are in themselves heterogeneous or not; hence we have no relevant data with which to decide the question one way or the other. This is Kant's solution in his discussion of interaction in B; it is also suggested by his remarks about the relation between mind and body which are made in the Second Paralogism in A, and is presumably his most considered solution.

WHAT WE CANNOT KNOW

Having argued in various ways that the problem of mind–body interaction is a pseudo-problem, Kant in both A and B goes on to suggest that there is another, more basic, question which underlies this problem, and which we cannot answer given the limits of our knowledge. But here again Kant is not completely consistent regarding the nature of this question. At one point he says that

> in the end the whole difficulty ... comes to this, how and why the representations of our sensibility are so interconnected that those which we entitle outer intuitions can be represented according to empirical laws as objects outside us—a question which is not in any way bound up with the supposed difficulty (of explaining mind/body interaction) ... (A387)

Here, Kant seems to be saying that the underlying question is how we are able to represent an experience as outside us in the first place; in other words, how it is that experience has the subject/object form which Kant at B409 says is 'analytic'. But this subject/object form applies to inner sense as well, and Kant is here explicitly talking only about outer intuitions. Alternatively, Kant could here be asking 'how and why' we represent outer experience objectively: but Kant would not consider this question unanswerable, since 'how' we represent our experience in this way is presumably a matter to be explained by empirical psychology, and explaining 'why' we do so is half the project of the Transcendental Deduction. And Kant does say that the question 'how in a thinking subject outer intuition . . . is possible . . . is a question which no man can possibly answer' (A393). Kant also suggests in A that

> the question is no longer of the interaction of the soul with other known substances of a different kind outside us, but only of the connection of the representations of inner sense with the modifications of our outer sensibility—as to how these can be so connected with each other according to settled laws that they exhibit the unity of a coherent experience. (A386)

Here, the question is taken to be how our representations of inner sense are ordered together with our representations of outer sense in a way that yields a unified experience: in other words, how is it that sensations and affective states (and, for that matter, intentions) coincide in a coherent and predictable way with those events which I perceive as going on outside me? For example, how is it that pain predictably follows my observation of a brick falling on my foot, or that my decision to throw said brick through a window may reasonably be expected to result in the brick's being thrown? Given that both my mental states and objects outside me are here taken to be representations, then, Kant says that the real question is not how body and mind interact but how two modes of representation are co-ordinated in a way that gives such a representational unity: thus the 'interconnection' of the 'representations of our sensibility'.

What exactly, though, does Kant take to be unanswerable here? It is not *that* our experience is so interconnected, or *why* it is, since Kant has argued extensively that such interconnection is a necessary precondition of experience. Rather, to see what is unanswerable, we should look briefly at Kant's restatement in B of the underlying question, where he says that 'the only question remaining (is) how in general an interaction of substances is possible', which question lies 'outside the field of all human knowledge' (B428). But why does this question lie outside the limits of knowledge? Given that substances are representations within outer experience, and that we represent these substances as interacting in accordance with empirical laws (*vide* the Second Analogy), the interaction of substances itself is something of which we are aware and around which we have formulated a powerful predictive apparatus. So in one sense we can know how the interaction of substances is possible. But note that Kant asks how 'in general' this interaction is possible: this seems to be a question about what underlies our representations of substances and thereby makes possible their interaction. And this, of course, is a question about things in themselves, about which we can know nothing. Presumably, then, what Kant is insisting that we cannot know about the unity of inner and outer experience is not that it obtains or why it obtains, but rather what state of affairs underlying our experience makes possible its unitary character. What is unanswerable, on Kant's view, is the question of what lies behind our representations—in this case the representations which give rise to the interaction problem. Kant says that 'No one . . . can have the right to claim that he knows anything in regard to the transcendental cause of our representations' (A391). (Kant's terminology here is, of course, sloppy: in a sense we can know the *transcendental* cause, that which must necessarily obtain if the effect is to obtain, but we cannot know the *transcendent* cause, that 'cause' which is a thing in itself and is thus unknowable, and is in fact only referred to as a 'cause' analogically.) Thus the question which is the basis of the pseudo-problem of mind–body interaction is itself, on the basis of Kant's transcendental idealism, effectively a pseudo-question in so far as it is unanswerable within the bounds of experience.

Hence we have what Sellars has called Kant's '*ignorabimus*',[23] his shrugging-off from the basis of transcendental idealism the possibility of knowing what outside the bounds of experience makes possible certain aspects of that experience. Kant says that 'I have no general answer to the question' of what the constitution of a subject of experience must be (A398). This is, of course, the same point which Kant makes in the Second Paralogism. And it should be noted that, along with the dismissals of the interaction problem, Kant's *ignorabimus* is multiplex: between the discussions of interaction in A and B, Kant literally makes six different formulations of this avowal of what we cannot know. He says that we cannot legitimately claim to know

(1) how outer and inner experience are interconnected in a unified experience (A386),
(2) how outer intuition is possible (A387, A393),

(3) how interaction between substances is possible (B428),
(4) what is the transcendental (or, more properly, transcendent) cause of our representations (A391),
(5) what is the constitution of a thinking thing (A398, A358),
(6) whether or not I can exist apart from my body (B409).

And as we have seen, (1)–(3) are arguably derivative from (4): in the one sense in which (for Kant) we cannot answer (1)–(3), we cannot do so precisely because we cannot answer (4). And that we cannot know (6) is clearly related to (5), in so far as if we cannot know what constitutes a thinking thing, we cannot know whether or not our bodies are necessary constituents of ourselves as thinking beings. So in effect Kant's *ignorabimus* comes down to two points: that we cannot know the thing in itself which presumably underlies the experiencing subject (5), and that we cannot know that which is the noumenal cause of our experiences. In this way Kant's *ignorabimus* is demonstrably the result of his transcendental idealism.

Kant's response to the problem of mind–body interaction is both relatively brief and, philosophically speaking, rather quick, suggesting that Kant considered it to be a problem not worthy of much consideration. It is worth noting here Erdmann's remark that the 'scanty treatment' of this problem in the second edition 'would seem to indicate . . . that the problem of the interaction of mind and body which so occupied Kant's mind from 1747 to 1770 has meantime almost entirely lost interest for him'.[24] Certainly the second-edition discussion of interaction is brief, but we have seen that essentially all of Kant's transcendental-idealist dismissal of the problem in A is contained, almost intolerably compressed, in B as well. None the less, in both editions (regardless of length of text), it is clear that Kant feels the interaction problem to be a pseudo-problem, one that can be neither answered nor seriously entertained: *vide* Kant's fanciful elaborations of possible theories of the relation of mind and body at A393–4 and at A778/B806. And indeed, in the *Prolegomena* the discussion of the Fourth Paralogism (= Section 49) is a recapitulation of the Refutation of Idealism, with no mention whatsoever of the interaction problem, indicating that by the time the *Prolegomena* was written Kant's interest in the interaction problem had undergone complete elanguescence. That this is so should not, at this point, be terribly surprising: given Kant's adoption of the position of transcendental idealism, the mind–body problem is a problem about the interaction of noumena. And *that* is something about which Kant—at his best—has nothing to say.

Before leaving the Fourth Paralogism entirely, it is necessary to consider, briefly, an idea that has had some currency among recent commentators on Kant: the idea that there is another reason for Kant's diminution of interest in the mind–body problem, namely, that Kant's theory of mind in the first *Critique* provides him with the foundation of a functionalist theory of mental states, and that this newly found proto-functionalism renders questions of mind–body interaction void of interest. The attraction of this reading is understandable: if a Kantian rejection of the problematic of mind–body interaction can be made out which does not depend on Kant's transcendental idealism, it will clearly be a more persuasive argument, at least for those who reject transcendental idealism. Two questions need to be asked here: what is the nature of this incipient functionalism, and can we plausibly attribute this functionalism to Kant?

Discussing the role played in thought by the 'I' of transcendental apperception, Kant says that 'since, in thinking in general, we abstract from all relation of the thought to any object ... the synthesis of the conditions of a thought in general ... is not objective at all' (A397). What Kant is pointing out is that, at its most general level, thought is a matter of logical form, of ways in which thought which is objective can be conceptualized via certain primitive modes of representing. For Kant, of course, these modes are the Categories, and what is significant here is that the Categories are not contentual entities, but are modes of representing. Sellars makes this point:

> Medieval logicians began the process of reinterpreting the categories that culminated in Kant's Critique, by recognizing that certain statements ... which seem to be about queer entities in the world are actually statements that classify constituents of conceptual acts ... Kant not only rediscovered these insights, but extended them in such a way as to connect categories ... with ... the logical powers ... which are essential to a conceptual framework the employment of which generates knowledge of matter of fact.[25]

The categories, in other words, are the most generic logical constraints on the formation of concepts: they impose a unifying structure over our representational system. But in recognizing this, Kant makes a very significant move: he goes from regarding categories as objects (albeit of a rarefied sort) to seeing them as operators, as *entia* that are only characterizable in terms of their function within a system of representations. As Sellars says, 'Kant's revolutionary move was to see the categories as concepts of functional roles in mental activity. Categorial concepts . . . are formed by abstraction, not, however, by reflecting on the self as object, but by reflecting on its conceptual activities.'[26] And it is important to note that for Kant this is true not only of the categories themselves but also of the 'I' of transcendental apperception (cf. A398) and, effectively, of all those concepts which Kant uses to refer to components of the system of mental representations. So these concepts are for Kant defined in terms of their function or role within the representational system. Moreover, they are defined in the language of this system of representational roles, characterized exclusively in terms of their relation to other operators in this system. On this point Kant is in agreement with Putnam, who says that

The functional organization . . . of the human being or machine can be described in terms of the sequences of mental or logical states respectively . . . without reference to the nature of the 'physical realization' of these states.[27]

What seems to be true here is this: if, with regard to a given system, it is true that its constituents are defined solely in terms of their function within the system, then the actual material composition of that system cannot be inferred from the definition of its constituents. Putnam again: 'the important thing is that descriptions of the functional organization of a system are logically different in kind . . . from descriptions of its physico-chemical composition'.[28] And Kant's mental states, being defined in terms of their functions within the system, are such that they are basically different from such composition descriptions.

Hence, again, Kant's *ignorabimus*. If the description of mental representations is logically different from descriptions of composition, then we can infer nothing about the composition underlying these functional states merely from their functional description. Putnam says that 'any physico-chemical system which possesses a "functional organization" which can be represented by a machine table', that is, by a complete functional description of the system, 'is functionally isomorphic to a denumerable infinity (at least) of systems with quite different physical-chemical constitutions'.[29] And this should recall Kant's point in the Second Paralogism, where he says that we do not know whether or not 'the thinking "I"' is different from or the same as the body, considered apart from these entities as functionally described within Kant's system (A360). The mind, in other words, may be compositionally part of the same physical-chemical system as the body, but to say so requires an illicit shift between composition talk and function talk—and the two are not logically contiguous in a way that allows a straightforward transition from one to the other. Hence we find Kant saying that

> If anyone propounds to me the question, 'What is the constitution of a thing which thinks?', I have no *a priori* knowledge wherewith to reply. For the answer has to be synthetic—an analytic answer will perhaps explain what is meant by thought, but beyond this cannot yield any knowledge of that upon which this thought depends for its possibility. (A398)

In other words, within his functionally characterized system, Kant can (and does) give a detailed account of what function is served by the 'I' of the 'I think', but this account is analytic in so far as it is a conceptual analysis of thought in general.[30] To give a synthetic account (here, an account of that which is the compositional basis of the functional 'I') is impossible within the *a priori*, functional, system of representations with which Kant is concerned.[31] If we are given, then, a functional characterization of the mind, nothing follows regarding 'that upon which this thought depends for its possibility', regarding whether or not the body is the compositional basis of the functionally described mind. On this Kant is explicit, saying that I do not know 'whether ... I could exist merely as thinking being (i.e., without existing in human form)' (B409). And from Kant's standpoint I do not know—from the perspective of functional description—whether or not the mind is in fact of a different composition from that of the body. Kant is well aware of the insight which Sellars expresses by saying that 'conceptual acts are transcategorial with respect to the type of logical subject which might engage in them';[32] the logical structure of conceptual representation does not determine the *Beschaffenheit* of the representer. Kant draws precisely the functionalist conclusion when he says that 'I have no general answer' to the question posed above: there *is no* general answer to the question, there being (presumably) an infinity of ways in which the functional system described by Kant could be compositionally instantiated.

If, then, we compare Kant's implicit position with some such definition of a (Turing-machine) functionalism as that given by Dennett, that

(*a*) mental events = physical events in the brain, and (*b*) (*x*) (M*x* = F*x*), where M = 'mental state' and F = 'functional state' such that F is 'physically neutral',[33]

then in a sense, Kant seems to be presenting a precursor to a Turing-machine, type-functional theory. Kant, of course, denies that we can know (*a*) to be true. But he does seem to subscribe to (*b*), endorsing the idea not only that each type of mental state is equivalent to some type of functional state but that types of mental state are definable only in terms of function. And the 'physical neutrality' of type-functionalism, if 'physical' is taken in a Kantian transposition to mean 'noumenal', conforms to Kant's account as well.

What, then, is Kant's 'functionalist' diagnosis of the mind–body problem? It arises, says the functionalist Kant, from a confusion between functional concepts and object concepts: such questions as the mind–body problem generates all 'rest on a mere delusion by which they hypostatise what exists merely in thought, and take it as a real object existing, in the same character, outside the thinking subject' (A384, cf. also A385–6). In other words, the representations of outer sense, which are themselves functional entities within a representational system, are taken to be compositional entities. Given that their (assumed) composition is not that of the mind itself, the problem of interaction arises. Of course, the composition which underlies the mind is completely unknown to us, as is the composition underlying the representations of outer sense. But in the case of the latter, we are disposed to confuse their compositional and functional characterization in one particular way: 'They have . . . this deceptive property that, representing objects in space, they detach themselves as it were from the soul and appear to hover outside it' (A385), and thereby they are taken to be not matter, which is a representation of outer sense, but rather that which underlies matter, which we call the transcendental object and which, being unknown to us, represents 'a gap in our knowledge' (A393). That we can make predicative statements about the objects represented in outer sense leads us into the error of believing these predicates to apply directly to objects in the world. The interaction problem is further fuelled, of course, by the type of function which the 'I' of the 'I think' has (though again it is noteworthy that in discussing interaction Kant speaks of the 'I' both of empirical and of transcendental apperception) in this representational system: it is 'only the formal condition . . . the logical unity of every thought' and is not, unlike outer objects, an intuition (A398). Thus the 'I' itself, not being an intuition, does not, properly speaking, admit predicative statements of the kind that pick out and characterize objects; thus the 'I' is represented differently from the representations of outer sense which are so picked out. As Rosenberg has pointed out, this is one key to the Paralogisms themselves: while intuitable objects collect properties, and thus are the subjects of predicative statements, the 'I' is not an intuitable object, and as such can only be the subject of exclusionary statements.[34] The paralogistic fallacy, on Rosenberg's account, comes about when the exclusionary statements which are true of the 'I' ('The "I" is not represented as material', for example) go through an elision into predicative statements (in this case, 'The "I" is represented as immaterial'), on the basis of which it is concluded that we know the properties of the 'I' *a priori*. This is Kant's point when he says that the Paralogisms confuse 'the possible abstraction from my empirically determined existence with the supposed consciousness of a possible separate existence of my thinking self' (B427). And this mistake can also be construed to derive from a mistaking of the functional character of a mental representation: this time wrongly assuming the 'I' to function in one respect (being intuitable, a proper subject of predicative statements) like the objects of outer sense, which it does not. The functional role played by the 'I' of transcendental apperception is radically different from that played by these objects, and if it is not recognized that both are functional entities, and as a result they are hypostatized into real (compositional) objects, then their functional difference is likely to be taken to be a heterogeneity of real properties—and thus explaining their interaction becomes problematic. Putnam says that 'If discussions in the philosophy of mind are often curiously unsatisfying . . . it is because . . . the notion of functional organization . . . has been overlooked or confused with notions of entirely different kinds.'[35] This insight is the basis of Putnam's dismissal of the problematic of interaction: though Kant's grasp of the point is not precise nor his presentation of it—in the Fourth Paralogism—pellucid, this insight looks remarkably Kantian as well.

It should be asked, though, in what sense is Kant's purportedly 'functionalist' solution separable from his transcendental idealism? Certainly Kant's idealism provides him with a sufficient reason to dismiss questions about the mind–body problem—at least in so far as these are questions about things in themselves. And each time Kant dismisses questions about composition, it is possible to read this dismissal as being motivated by Kant's idealism rather than by an incipient functionalism about which Kant himself is admittedly not completely clear.[36] None the less, it is demonstrably true that Kant's dismissal of the mind–body problem does at least tacitly acknowledge the (functionalist) insight that function does not determine composition, and that his account of mind does elucidate aspects of the mental by locating these aspects within a system of mental representation. And to this extent, perhaps, Kant can in some sense be considered, albeit laboriously, a 'functionalist'. But what must be borne in mind is this: those aspects of Kant's strategic dismissal of the mind–body problem which could be construed to indicate a Kantian functionalism in fact arise from two constraints imposed by Kant's systematic philosophy—his commitment to transcendental idealism and to methodological solipsism. By subscribing to transcendental idealism, Kant is committed to the view that questions about the underlying composition of mental states are unanswerable. This in turn leads, naturally enough, to a concentration on the description of the phenomenology of mental states, which more or less inevitably becomes a description of what role they play within a representational system. And by describing these mental states from the standpoint of methodological solipsism, Kant is led to restrict his analysis to all and only those mental states which occur within *one* representational system. Taking these two constraints together, Kant is left with what is in effect a characterization of the functional components of one representational system such that each component is characterizable only in terms of the system itself. In this regard, Kant's theory of mind conforms essentially to Armstrong's functionalist dictum that 'the corresponding concepts must be introduced together or not at all', where 'corresponding concepts' are those which, in Kantian terms, pertain to appearances which presumably correspond to a noumenal substrate.[37] So, again, there are at least these similarities between Kant's account of mind and that of a functionalist account: (1) Kant, like the functionalist, is aware of the function–composition dichotomy, and (2) Kant, like the functionalist, elucidates aspects of the mental only in terms of their role within a representational system, avoiding any attempt to achieve a 'view from outside'. But, as we háve seen, the first similarity is—at least for Kant—inextricably related to the doctrine of transcendental idealism, and the second similarity is demonstrably an incidental result of Kant's methodological solipsism.

What, then, of Kitcher's claim that Kant 'seems genuinely surprised and impressed by his discovery', ostensibly in the Subjective Deduction, that analysis of the conditions of experience tells us nothing about the constitution of the experience?[38] It should be borne in mind that Kant's 'surprise' is presented rhetorically, and probably should not be taken at face value ('Suspicion is thus thrown on the view, which at first seemed to me so plausible, that we can form judgments about the nature of the thinking being, and can do so from concepts alone') (A399), especially since Kant was arguably suspicious of this 'view' as early as the *Träume*. But if it is correct to say that Kant's 'functionalism' is the somewhat incidental result of other aspects of Kant's Critical commitments, it is also plausible to say that Kant's extension of the insights of the Terminist logicians (cited by Sellars above) is itself the result of Kant's analysing mental states within these constraints, the one being epistemological, the other methodological. And it is also plausible to suggest that rather than merely saying that 'it was Kant's own attempts to characterize the necessary properties of a thinking self that led him to this recognition [of the function–composition dichotomy]',[39] we can now say that it was Kant's own attempts to characterize these necessary properties of a thinking self, undertaken within the framework of transcendental idealism and from that methodological perspective which Bennett has called 'the Cartesian basis', which led him to this recognition. To say, then, that Kant is a functionalist does highlight certain important threads woven into the fabric of his theory; at the same time, by being both anachronistic and—much more importantly—insensitive to the sources of Kant's 'functionalist' claims, this assertion obscures much, if not all, of the weaver's intent.

6

Kant and the First Person

From the preceding account, it should be clear that Kant's theory of self-consciousness is largely—though not completely—a negative one: the focus of his position is certainly to disabuse us of the illusion that we know that which, he thinks, we cannot know about the self. Does Kant's position, though, point us toward useful, and in some sense positive, perspectives on the problematic of self-consciousness? In what follows, I want to canvass one aspect of this problematic as it has surfaced in recent years, and to read through, with an explicitly Kantian eye, certain contemporary perspectives on self-consciousness. It should be stressed at the outset that this is somewhat anachronistic, given Kant's distance from linguistic analysis; none the less, it is worth demonstrating that Kant's ways of dealing with the elusive self not only provide a background for, but are capable of extending, our own forays into the problem of capturing the more revealing philosophical nuances of talking about 'the I . . . which thinks'.

In recent years, a good deal of literature has developed around the location of a philosophical/linguistic datum: that the first-person pronoun is completely immune from reference failure.[1] In fact, this datum is actually two, since there are two ways of failing to achieve a reference that are not ways that one can fail when using the expression 'I'. The first kind of reference failure, which I will call R-failure(1), is the referential equivalent of shooting at one's shadow: the attempted reference fails precisely because no referent exists. As an example of this, consider 'the sixth Marx brother' or 'the Unitarian bishop of Budapest', neither of which refers to any actual person, though each is clearly capable of being an attempted referring. The second kind of reference failure, which I will call R-failure(2), is more a matter of shooting an innocent bystander: the attempted reference actually does refer, but to the wrong referent. If, in speaking of the author of *Pudd'nhead Wilson*, I refer to him as 'William Dean Howells', then I have committed R-failure(2), since the intended referent was Samuel Clemens, not the man who was Clemens's editor and the author of *The Rise of Silas Lapham*. Given this distinction between two kinds of reference failure, we can note that our philosophical/linguistic datum still obtains: a speaker who uses the first-person pronoun cannot fail, either by committing R-failure(1) or R-failure(2).[2] On the face of it, both of these immunities certainly seem to hold; if a speaker uses 'I', this is ostensibly a reference to himself, and by necessity could only be so used if the relevant user (himself) were available for referential service. Similarly, though a speaker can make false attributions to himself (as in 'I am the King of Prussia', said by C. T. Powell), these attributions are still attributed by him to himself via the use of the first-person pronoun. There is simply no sense in the idea of attempting to refer to oneself and then not succeeding, at least in so far as this attempt is made using the expression 'I'. Is this peculiar feature of the grammar of self-reference significant, then, for the formulation of a theory of self-consciousness? And does Kant's theory of self-consciousness shed any light on this feature? To explore these questions, we should begin by considering a position taken by Anscombe, in her now classic paper, 'The First Person'.

ANSCOMBE AND THE CARTESIAN EGO

Anscombe maintains that if 'I' is a referring expression, it must refer to a Cartesian Ego, since the only plausible alternative explanations of its referential character are ultimately untenable. To show this, she considers the alternative that 'I' is a sort of proper name with two salient characteristics: (1) it refers to an embodied person, and (2) each and every person uses it only to refer to himself. And Anscombe argues that this alternative is nonsensical on the basis of a hypothetical case in which each person, while having a 'public' proper name, also has a name 'A' which has these two characteristics. The 'public' name is inscribed on each person in appropriately 'public' places, while 'A' is inscribed on the inside of the wrist (presumably to ensure its privacy, and thus to fulfil the second condition). In making third-person reports, each person uses the public names of others, read off from their public inscriptions. But 'reports on one's own actions, which one gives straight off from observation', are made using the name on the wrist.[3] There are, says Anscombe, two problems with this idea of a private proper name for oneself. First, this name does not provide for 'self-consciousness on the part of the people who use the name "A"'; rather, self-consciousness is 'something manifested by the use of "I" as opposed to "A"'.[4] Second, the use of 'A', unlike that of 'I', requires a reidentification of its object.[5] As has been pointed out by Strawson and others, the use of 'I' does not require empirical reidentification of the self with each use.[6] The use of 'A', on the other hand, does require a reidentifying of the referent with each use. This re-identification is presumably parallel to the identification of others, accomplished by consulting their 'public' proper names—which are similarly inscribed, and which differ from the 'private' proper names in their availability to more than one person.

Now, says Anscombe, it is clear that if 'I' refers at all, the second condition above holds with regard to 'I': it is used by each and every person only to refer to himself. But the first condition does not hold for 'I', and it is this, along with the provenance of 'I' for self-consciousness, that distinguishes 'I' from 'A'. If 'I' referred to an embodied person as 'A' does, then it would be possible to commit an R-failure(2), a referring to the wrong thing. Anscombe says that 'a man B may sometimes make a mistake through seeing the name "A" on the wrist of another'.[7] As an example, we can imagine B waking up in the gutter after a night's carousing and, upon seeing before him a wrist on which are emblazoned both the letter 'A' and a particularly tasteless tattoo, exclaiming (ungrammatically) 'A have defaced my wrist!' The fact is, however, that the wrist belongs to one of his less judicious cronies, C, also lying in the gutter, and whose wrist is, as the result of a drunken impulse, inscribed with the letter 'A'. So 'the "A"-user would not be immune from mistaken identification of someone else as "A"', while it is 'absurd' to say that the 'I'-user would not be so immune.[8] Anscombe concedes that the 'A'-user would be immune from R-failure(1), since by identifying an object of reference (on which is inscribed an 'A') there is no possibility of failing to refer to something, even if it turns out to be the wrong something (C's 'A' instead of A's 'A'). But she says that

It seems clear that if 'I' is 'a referring expression' at all, it has both kinds of guaranteed reference ... The bishop may take the lady's knee for his, but could he take the lady herself to be himself?[9]

Thus, since the correlate of 'I' as a private proper name, 'A', is not immune from R-failure(2), then 'I' does not refer to a person in the ways that a purely private proper name would do. Anscombe's point is this: if 'I' refers, it refers to something, and specifically to something which would guarantee the immunity of the use of 'I' from R-failures(1) and (2).

What would have to be true of this something to which 'I' putatively refers for the use of 'I' actually to have this R-failure immunity? Anscombe says that 'this reference could only be sure-fire if the referent of "I" were both freshly defined with each use . . . and also remained in view so long as something was being taken to be I'.[10] Presumably the redefining of the referent with each use ensures against R-failure(2), while the referent's remaining in view throughout the referring ensures against R-failure(1). If these conditions are necessary for the requisite immunity to obtain, then it is clear that the object of reference could not be the person's body at all. As Anscombe points out, a person in a state of complete sensory deprivation who says 'I won't let this happen again!' is obviously referring to himself (if, of course, 'I' refers at all) —yet his body is not 'remaining in view' in the way required to preserve the reference from the possibility of R-failure(2).[11] And, says Anscombe, 'like considerations will operate for other suggestions'.[12] So we are left with the only object to which 'I' could refer which can meet both immunity conditions: 'Nothing but a Cartesian Ego will serve. Or rather, a stretch of one.'[13] Since the Cartesian Ego is nothing but 'the thinking that thinks this thought', it is 'freshly defined' with each use, with each 'I-thought'.[14] And the thought is 'in view' so long as it is 'being taken to be I'. This Ego, then, is the only object of reference that could possibly meet the requisite conditions of being the object referred to by the first-person pronoun.

Anscombe rejects the possibility of such a Cartesian Ego, however, for reasons that are borrowed from Hume and Kant: how can we identify 'the same referent in different I-thoughts'; how do we know that there is 'just one thinking which is this thinking of this thought . . . not ten thinkers thinking in unison'; what is it that we are aware of when we are aware of this Cartesian 'I'?[15] Thus Anscombe suggests that her argument has actually been a *reductio ad absurdum* of the assumption that 'I' refers at all. She says that

If 'I' were a name, it would have to be a name for something (that is connected to the body as would be a Cartesian Ego), not an extra-ordinary name for this body. Not a name for this body because sensory deprivation . . . is not loss of

I ... But 'I' is not a name: these I-thoughts are examples of reflective consciousness of states, actions, motions, etc., of this object here, about which I can find out ... that it is E. A. About which I did learn that it is a human being.[16]

So 'I' refers to nothing at all, unlike 'E. A.', which refers to that human being who is Wittgenstein's literary executrix. Rather, E. A.'s thoughts which include 'I' are merely 'unmediated conceptions' of aspects of the person E. A. In this case, 'I' does not refer to the embodied E. A., because this object of reference would not guarantee the immunities which 'I' would have to possess, were it a referring expression. To insist that 'I' is a referring expression—on Anscombe's view—requires the postulation of a Cartesian Ego, which is incoherent, and stems from 'the (deeply rooted) grammatical illusion of a subject' where there is no subject referred to at all.[17]

REIDENTIFICATION AND REFERENCE-FAILURE IMMUNITY

There is much that is attractive in Anscombe's account, not least the implicit affinity with Kant's own views. For Kant, of course, 'the I or he or it (the thing) which thinks' (A346/B404) is not an intuition, that is, it is not an object which can be perceived. Rather, the 'I' of the 'I think', as we know, designates a necessary mode of consciousness, in which experience is structured as being had by a unitary subject. And, as we know, though this 'I' is merely a function of conceptualized experience, it involves a necessary hypostasis of this function into the concept of a self *qua* subject, which leads to the illusion of this self as substantial, and thus to the illusion that the self is an object which can be picked out and characterized as an object among objects. And, significantly in terms of Anscombe's account, this illusion is the source of the paralogistic science of rational psychology, which trades on the hypostasis of the 'I' into an object of immediate awareness. Similarly, Anscombe argues that 'Getting hold of the wrong object is excluded, and that makes us think that getting hold of the right object is guaranteed. But the reason is that there is no getting hold of an object at all.'[18] And this illusion of 'getting hold of' the 'I' as object is a reflection of what Kant calls '*apperceptionis substantiatae*', the nominalization of an activity (= thinking). Anscombe makes this point a linguistic one: 'With names, or denoting expressions . . . there are two things to grasp: the kind of use, and what to apply them to . . . With "I" there is only the use.'[19] Anscombe is surely correct in pointing out that the elusiveness of the self has generated philosophical muddles from Descartes to Hume—and, as we now know, these muddles are effectively dealt with by Kant, both in the Paralogisms and the Transcendental Deduction. In a sense, Anscombe's position is a strongly Kantian one.[20] Before bringing Kant back into this picture, though, it is necessary to evaluate Anscombe's denial of the referring function of 'I'.

In her dismissal of 'I' as a private proper name, Anscombe says first that 'A' does not 'provide for' or 'manifest' self-consciousness as does 'I'. But she does not argue for this, and it is not clear precisely in what way 'A' precludes self-consciousness. We are given a clue in Anscombe's comment that 'I-thoughts . . . are unmediated conceptions . . . of states, motions, etc.', but in what way are these conceptions unmediated, and in what sense does this lack of mediation provide for—or at least flag—the presence of self-consciousness? It seems that we can take 'unmediated' to mean that these conceptions are in some way 'self-presenting'. The notion of a self-presenting mental state is one developed by Chisholm, and is used to describe those mental states which are such that if I have them, I know them to be my states and know them to be states of a given kind. And in saying that I know them to be my states (of a given kind), Chisholm stresses that this knowledge is indefeasible.[21] But if these states as unmediated are self-presenting, I do not have to identify them as mine: I am self-conscious, that is, I automatically ascribe certain states to myself, of which I clearly have an abiding concept. And this is, in fact, the second objection which Anscombe raises against 'A': to say something about myself, given the ordinary use of 'I', requires no reidentification of myself, whereas to say something about myself where I can only do so using a private proper name does require reidentification. Given no more elaborate justification of Anscombe's self-consciousness objection, it seems merely to be a rather vague prefiguration of the second, 'reidentification', objection.

What of this second objection, that 'A' requires reidentification prior to its use while 'I' does not? On a mildly carping note, it is not obvious that 'A' need be reidentified with each use, since the subject's memory of himself as 'A' would certainly obviate regular and repetitive wrist consultations. To circumvent this objection, of course, Anscombe need only stipulate a more complex inscription than 'A'—say, a long series of numbers—that would not be memorable in the way 'A' would be. And this criticism really does miss the point of Anscombe's insistence that 'A' must be reidentified with each 'A'-thought. Recalling her characterization of names or (Russellian) denoting expressions as having both a use and a kind of thing to which they are applied: one must be capable of picking out the things(s) denoted by the name. Thus the use of a proper name implies the ability to identify that which is named, and to reidentify it with each use if necessary. (Of course, one can use a name and not be able to perform such an identification. But one's referring would be suspect on this basis.) The key here is precisely that one must be able to reidentify the referent if necessary—though there is an implicit identification of the object in the use of the name itself, this implicit identification rests on the possibility of an explicit identification. But this explicit identification (often a definite description, often not) need not be performed with each use of the name: if one uses the name 'Samuel Clemens', it is assumed that one can in some sense pick out the referent of this referring expression—but the use of the expression 'Samuel Clemens' does not in itself stipulate how this referent is to be picked out. So to this extent the 'A' paradigm of a private proper name is misleading, not in terms of its privacy conditions but in terms of the severe kind of reidentification which it requires of proper names in general. To refer to Clemens does not require the explicit reidentification of Clemens that Anscombe requires of both 'A'-references and 'B'-references. So the requirement that 'A' be reidentified with each use is not only not a requirement for the use of 'I', it is not a requirement for the use of ordinary proper names in general. Clearly, then, if 'I' is not a name, it is not a name for some other reason than *merely* that it does not require an explicit empirical reidentification with its referent prior to each use.

But there is a point to be made regarding the reidentification of referents: it is reasonable to assume that for any name or denoting expression one uses, there may arise occasions in which one is in fact called explicitly to identify the referent of the expression, i.e. to exhibit one's grasp of the concept of what kind of thing the name is applied to. And these occasions would arise, presumably, when either the speaker's or the hearer's grasp of the concept, or application of the concept, is in doubt—when the proper application of the expression is unclear. But in the case of 'I', it is not at all obvious what these occasions would be like: there is no reasonable way of doubting that a speaker who uses 'I' is referring to himself, and it is nonsensical to ask him to check up on himself and make sure he's latched on to the right referent. Of course, if I say 'I am the King of Prussia', the appropriate challenge is 'Are you *sure* you are the King?', but this is a challenge to the way I choose to characterize myself; there is no question that I *have* referred to myself, regardless of the absurdity of the characterization I make of this referent. So Anscombe's point may be amended slightly to say, rather than that 'I' does not require explicit empirical reidentification before each use, that 'I' is not vulnerable to demands for such referent identifications, as are, presumably, other referring expressions. But this, of course, is just to say that 'I' is immune from challenges regarding the success of its reference; in practice we take any use of 'I' to be a successful referring. This is not obviously true of the use of any (other) proper names. So the result which emerges from Anscombe's 'A' argument is this: the distinctions made by Anscombe between 'I' and 'A' on the basis of 'manifesting self-consciousness' and 'requiring empirical reidentification' are reducible to Anscombe's other claim, offered more or less *en passant*, that 'I' is immune from R-failure in a way that ordinary proper names are not. And one question this raises is in what way susceptibility to R-failure is a definitive criterion of being a referring term at all. The 'A'-argument, then, is superfluous to her argument against 'I' as a referring expression, which hangs on the R-failure immunity of 'I': it does not establish this immunity to hold, and if this immunity is accepted (which on the face of it seems reasonable), it adds no substance to her argument. What, then, can be said about the R-failure immunity of 'I'?

First of all, it should be noted that a successful reference involves what Anscombe calls a 'latching onto' an object by a concept. In referring to an x, something is picked out as an x that is in fact an x (if the reference is successful). When Hemingway mistakenly refers to the passing Aleister Crowley as Hilaire Belloc, he has made an (extraordinarily) unsuccessful reference, since he has picked out as Belloc someone who is most certainly not Belloc (hence a case of R-failure(2)).[22] Had he referred to Crowley as 'the author of *The Bad Child's Book of Beasts*, Aleister Crowley', he would have made a successful reference, along with a completely false characterization of that referent. And this is consonant with Anscombe's account of successful reference. But what Anscombe does not point out is the essentially public character of reference: that there is referential success for both speaker and hearer. Consider again Hemingway, once he is corrected by his friend regarding Crowley's identity: if Hemingway—mistakenly—hears his friend say, 'the wickedest man in the world, a man from Cowley', then what we can call the *hearer's reference* of the expression is not successful. Similarly, the reference would also fail if Hemingway knew an Aleister Crowley other than the practitioner of magic to whom his friend referred, and took his friend to be referring to this other Crowley. Both are cases of an R-failure(2) on the part of the hearer. And if Hemingway's friend had not actually said what Hemingway had taken him to say, and were instead bored by their conversation and merely muttering obscure verse (e.g., 'All eyes stir Cowley'), then Hemingway will have taken there to be a reference where there is none—and though in this case he has hit on a referent for this imagined reference by the speaker, there is obviously no necessity that he will do so. Thus the hearer can commit a kind of R-failure(1) as well. It is clear, then, that there are two kinds of R-failure for the hearer as well as for the speaker, and that the two kinds for the hearer parallel those for the speaker. For brevity, I will call the hearer's R-failure which occurs when the hearer takes the reference to refer to the wrong referent (H)R-failure(2). To avoid ambiguity, it will be well to call the speaker's parallel failures (S)R-failure(1) and (S)R-failure(2).

Given these distinctions, it is possible to expand a bit on the R-failure immunity of 'I'. It has been conceded that 'I' is immune from (S)R-failures of both kinds. But is it immune from either (H)R-failure? Clearly it is not immune from (H)R-failure(2). If I ask two friends if they take cream in their coffee and they respond simultaneously, with Boris saying 'I do' and Morris saying 'I do not', then I may very well take the 'I' in the utterance 'I do' to refer to Morris and vice versa, so that each 'I' is taken by me to refer to the wrong referent (Boris and Morris, of course, each seem to have referred successfully to themselves). But is 'I' immune from (H)R-failure(1)? That is, is it possible to hear 'I' used as it normally is used and take there to be a referent where there is none? It would seem that this is not possible, since 'I' when used properly refers (ostensibly) to the speaker, so that if it is used, it does have a referent of some sort, and thus if I hear it used and take it that there is a referent, I must be right. Though I can confuse the referents of Boris's and Morris's 'I' utterances, I cannot mistakenly assume there to be some referent for these expressions used in the normal way. But the situation is a bit more complex than this. Consider the case of a parrot who has been taught to say 'I am the King of Prussia', and imagine a hearer who for whatever reason takes there to be an 'I' referred to where there is none (assuming, of course, that the parrot does *not* take himself to be the King of Prussia). Such cases, and others which readily come to mind, rest on an illusion that 'I' is actually used by some speaker familiar with ordinary linguistic practices. The expression 'I' is not used at all in such cases, but is at best mentioned; in the case of the parrot it is not even that, but is rather a mimicked sound which the hearer takes to be an utterance of 'I'. None the less, there are occasions where a hearer may consider an 'I'-reference to have been made when there is in fact no speaker—and thus no referent—at all. So, in this rather extended sort of case, 'I' is susceptible to (H)R-failure(1). And though this kind of case is extended from ordinary linguistic practices, it also extends back to these practices. Indeed, it is part of the structure of these practices: consider such a reasonable question as 'Did I really hear someone say "I am thy father's spirit, Doom'd for a certain term to walk the night"?' The fact that we are misled into hearing 'I'-references where there are no genuine linguistic utterances at all does lead to challenges, requests for an identification of the 'I' putatively referred to. So the expression 'I', while being immune from (S)R-failures of both kinds, is susceptible to (H)R-failure(2) in a straightforward way and to (H)R-failure(1) in a way extended from, but affecting, ordinary linguistic practices.

This does not answer the question Anscombe led us to: whether or not susceptibility to R-failure is a necessary condition of being referential. But it does offer a provisional response to Anscombe's conclusion which led to this question, that 'I' is immune from reference failure. We can see now that, considered in terms of its actual use, 'I' is not so immune. It is granted that the speaker of 'I' cannot fail in his reference, but what Anscombe does not consider is that reference is public, and requires both a speaker and a hearer, and that the hearer of an utterance of 'I' can fail to make the proper reference or can make a reference on the basis of the heard utterance when in fact there is no referent at all. The key here is that there is no sense in the idea of a purely private reference, and only as a purely private reference is 'I' immune from reference failure. But this is not the way 'I' is used, and its R-failure immunity collapses when its actual use within a linguistic community is considered. And it is worth noting that in this context, broader than that considered by Anscombe, the speaker who uses 'I' can be challenged to provide an identification of the referent of 'I': if in a dark room I say 'Is anyone there?' (feeling sure there is not) and I faintly hear the response 'I am', I may well respond 'Who are you?' And if I am unsure that I really heard anything, I may add, 'if anyone at all'. So though it is the case that my successful referential use of 'I' does not require that I be able to further identify myself (*vide* Strawson's 'Whoever I am, I feel terrible'),[23] my use of 'I' can occasion a request for further identification by a hearer who requires such identification to ensure his having made a successful hearer's reference. So the use of 'I' by a linguistic community does indeed imply that for successful hearer's reference, an identification of the referent must be possible, and can be demanded of the putative 'I'-user.[24]

None the less, it could be objected that this talk of speaker's and hearer's reference merely obscures the basic point of Anscombe's argument, which is that 'I' is unique in its R-failure immunity in some way which does militate against classing 'I' with referring expressions at all. It may be granted that 'I' is susceptible to (H)R-failure of both kinds, and that 'I' cannot be considered as an expression independent of its use within a linguistic community of both speakers and hearers. Still, 'I' is immune from (S)R-failures, and this presents a prima-facie case for suspecting 'I' to be unlike any other referring expression, since it is true that, at least in the case of proper names, there do not seem to be any which are similarly immune. It seems possible that 'I' is referential for the hearer but not for the speaker; indeed, this may be what Chisholm is getting at when he says that 'I' has no 'speaker's meaning'.[25] How, then, do we account for this immunity of 'I' which is apparently unique—and potentially disqualifying—among candidates for the class of referring expressions?

Before accepting the uniqueness of 'I' in this regard too readily, we should consider one other kind of referring expression besides proper names, since in addition to proper names there are other referring expressions which may be more closely matched to 'I' in their (S)R-failure immunity. Specifically, does 'I' function as a demonstrative expression, the other major type of expression used for making singular references? And do demonstratives more closely match the (S)R-failure immunity of 'I'? The notion that 'I' functions as a demonstrative is attacked by Anscombe: she says that demonstratives are, in fact, susceptible to R-failure(1), to lacking any referent at all. As an example, she suggests the following:

> Someone comes with a box and says 'This is all that is left of poor Jones'. The answer to 'This what?' is 'this parcel of ashes'; but unknown to the speaker the box is empty.[26]

So Anscombe's objection to 'I' being a demonstrative is that demonstratives can attempt a reference when there is no referent to which they can 'latch on'. In other words, demonstratives are susceptible to (S)R-failure(1), and thus are unlike 'I', which is not so susceptible. Whether or not demonstratives are susceptible to (S)R-failure(2) Anscombe does not consider, since for her purposes it is only necessary to show some categorical difference in (S)R-failure immunity. And on the basis of having putatively shown that demonstratives are not suitably immune in at least this one regard, Anscombe takes it that the claim that 'I' functions as a demonstrative is rendered implausible: were it a demonstrative, it would be one that unerringly has a referent, and this property is for Anscombe atypical of demonstrative expressions.

Is Anscombe right, then, that not only all proper names but also all demonstratives are susceptible to (S)R-failure? It is certainly plausible that all demonstratives are susceptible to (H)R-failure of both kinds; to see this we need only recall Wittgenstein's arguments against the epistemically privileged status of ostensive definitions.[27] But such arguments do not also establish that the user of a demonstrative may fail in latching on to his demonstrative's intended referent; this claim requires argument of its own. Anscombe attempts to provide such an argument with her example of 'This is all that is left of poor Jones', where the ostensible referent of 'this' is 'a parcel of ashes', which is in fact not a parcel of ashes. In this case, then, Anscombe finds reason to charge an (S)R-failure(1), since 'this' is meant to refer to a referent which does not exist. But this example will not do. The question that must be asked is, does 'this' refer to a parcel, to some ashes, or to some third thing?—for both the parcel and the ashes have some claim to be the referent. If 'this' refers to the ashes themselves, then there is no referent—since the parcel is empty. But here the demonstrative would be remarkably oblique: one is not gesturing at the ashes themselves but at the parcel which, supposedly, holds the ashes, since the ashes are not such that one can at the moment gesture at them at all. It is reasonable, then, that one cannot use 'this' to refer directly to the ashes, since the ashes *per se* are not presently available as a 'this'. We are left, then, with the choice of referring to the ashes obliquely via referring to a parcel (presumably *of ashes*), or to the parcel itself. If the latter, then 'this' certainly has a referent (the parcel), but one that is rather unlikely to be the actual remains of poor Jones, and unlikely to be referred to as such. If the former, then saying 'This is all that is left of poor Jones' is merely a *façon de parler*, in this case an abbreviated and dramatic way of saying 'This (parcel) contains all that is left of poor Jones.' But here again, 'this' has a referent, and again it is the parcel itself. What is predicated of the parcel is false, of course, but that is a different matter from the parcel itself not being present: it is merely not present *as described* (as a parcel of ashes). But that description is not part of the demonstrative reference, and to say that 'this' refers to 'a parcel of ashes' is itself a bit quick, since 'a parcel of ashes' implies that a certain description of that which is gestured at is part of the demonstrative reference itself—and demonstrative reference is not descriptive reference. I do not gesture at 'a box such that it contains ashes'; I gesture at a box. It does seem, though, that we should be able to make a direct demonstrative reference to the ashes which are presumed to be in the box, and we can do so: by using 'here', as in 'Here is all that remains of poor Jones'. In this case the reference of 'here' is a location, and what I am saying is that what is in that location (inside the box) is what's left of Jones. That nothing is in the box renders my assertion false—but it does not imply (S)R-failure(1), since the location referred to was there all along. So Anscombe's example, at least, should not persuade us of the susceptibility of demonstratives to (S)R-failure(1). Even were Anscombe's argument sound—which it is not—it would only have established the susceptibility to reference failure of one demonstrative, and more than this is required to show that all demonstratives are similarly susceptible, which is the conclusion Anscombe must establish if she is to argue that 'I' is categorically different from demonstratives in terms of R-failure immunity.

There are, in any case, certain demonstratives that do seem to be immune to (S)R-failure(1): 'here' and 'now' are prime examples. In our ordinary usage, when a speaker uses the demonstrative expressions 'here' and 'now', they do necessarily have a referent = the location of the speaker in space and time. Since speakers, at least in our linguistic community, are spatio-temporally located, their use of 'here' and 'now' guarantees the existence of a referent for these expressions with each use. It is quite impossible coherently to imagine a speaker uttering a sentence that could not be prefaced by a successful demonstrative reference to the time and place of the utterance (e.g., 'Now I believe x', 'I stand here speaking before you'). So these demonstratives, and possibly others, are immune to (S)R-failure(1). Are they similarly immune to (S)R-failure(2)? On the face of it, perhaps not: one can say 'Here is the place I told you about' and find that the place is somewhere else; one can say 'Now is the time that the clock strikes' and the clock may remain silent for another five minutes. In these cases, it seems as though one has latched on to the wrong referent, thus committing an (S)R-failure(2). But in fact there is no wrong referent, only a mistaken characterization of the intended referent. In the first case 'here' is meant to refer to the present location of the speaker—which it does. The sentence characterizes this present location as 'the place I told you about'—which it is not. But as in the case of the parcel of ashes, this is merely a false predication, and says nothing about the success or failure of the reference itself. And the second case is similar: 'now' was intended to refer to the time of the speaker's utterance, which it did. That this time was not the time for the clock to strike is again merely a false characterization, and not a failed reference. It is possible to construct cases in which these demonstratives refer to something which is given a faulty characterization, but it is not at all obvious, given the use of 'here' and 'now', what would count as an unsuccessful (S)-reference of either kind by a speaker who used these referential expressions.

It is true, of course, that 'here' and 'now' (and even more so 'this' and 'that') have a fairly vague referential scope. That is, though they refer to particular locations and times fixed on the basis of the spatio-temporal location of the speaker, the outer limits, or generality of scope, of these locations and times is not clearly specified. Thus if a friend says 'Meet me here tomorrow' and we are on the beach at Venice, it is not necessarily clear to me (though context may make it so) whether I am to meet him (1) in Venice, as opposed to Turin, (2) on the Lido, as opposed to the Piazza San Marco, or (3) at the third blue umbrella west of the deck chairs. Similarly, if one says 'Things are not so good for me now', it is not necessarily clear how long one's prospects have been in decline. And this vagueness of demonstrative referential scope obviously contributes to much, if not most, (H)R-failure(2) with regard to demonstratives. But recalling again Wittgenstein's remarks on ostensive definition, we should not expect any referring expression, however 'immediate', to be completely immune from (H)R-failure(2). And the relevant point here is that at least some demonstratives are immune to precisely those kinds of reference failure that 'I' is, and it is precisely these characteristics of 'I' that led Anscombe to reject its referential function. It would be possible, of course, to argue that these demonstratives are not referring expressions themselves. But unless some other reason for this could be adduced beyond the simple fact that they have (S)R-failure immunity of both kinds, then the question is begged rather severely.[28]

A brief summing-up: Anscombe's reasons for saying that 'I' does not refer (specifically, that 'I' does not function as a proper name) are all derivative from the datum that 'I' is immune from reference failure—and the 'A'-argument does not expand on this datum at all. Anscombe does not consider the essential publicity of reference: that reference failure occurs within a linguistic community of speakers and hearers, and that 'I' is susceptible to hearer's, though not to speaker's, R-failure. Thus 'I' is not in actual practice immune from all R-failure, and is subject to identification challenges. Even given these considerations, however, Anscombe may argue for the rejection of 'I' as a referring expression on the grounds that it is unlike any referring expression in so far as it possesses (S)R-failure immunity, even if it does not possess (H)R-failure immunity. But in fact 'I' is not even unique in having this immunity, which is also possessed by certain demonstrative expressions, including 'here' and 'now'. Anscombe's argument that demonstratives are all susceptible to (S)R-failure(1) failed because it imported an illicit descriptive element into the demonstrative reference. Thus Anscombe's reasons for rejecting 'I' as a referring expression are not compelling in that (1) 'I' is not immune from reference failure when considered in terms of its actual use, and is subject to public identification challenges like any other referring expression, and (2) 'I' is not even unique in that immunity from reference failure which it does possess.

None the less, it is far too facile to say that the speaker's reference-failure immunity of 'I' is not significant in itself. Though Anscombe is wrong in arguing that this immunity is unique to 'I', it is still the case that those other referring expressions which possess a similar immunity are themselves indexical expressions, and thus are dependent, for their truth or falsity, on the situation of their speaker. And the ground of this dependence in turn seems to be that their referent is itself always relative to the speaker's situation. So in a sense it could be argued that the (S)R-failure immunity of such demonstratives is itself due to their being parasitical in some way on the implicit correlative use of the expression 'I', with its correlative (S)R-failure immunity. Thus it would be maintained that any use of 'here' ('Come over here') itself implies a use of the first person pronoun ('Come over to where I am'), and that it is this implied use which gives 'here' its reference-failure immunity. In any case, it does appear to be true that, for any demonstrative expression which has (S)R-failure immunity, that demonstrative is used in a way that is closely related to some use of 'I' which itself carries with it guaranteed referential success. Thus there is some room for doubting that these other cases of (S)R-failure immunity are independent of the immunity of 'I' in a way that genuinely indicates that (S)R-failure immunity is not an atypical feature of referring expressions. Moreover, it would be disingenuous to deny that 'I' does seem to work differently from most referring expressions, which do not have the kind of R-failure immunity which 'I' seems to have, and which do appear to 'latch on to' objects in a way that 'I' does not. As was pointed out, it is just this difference between 'I' and (other) referential expressions which is a key source of Kant's *apperceptionis substantiatae*: by taking 'I' to refer to an object, and by noting that this 'object' is not apprehended as other objects are, we are led—paralogistically—to make illicit characterizations of 'I' as an 'object'. Yet on the other hand, there are uses of 'I' which do in fact latch on to an object in much the same way as is typical of referring expressions in general: those uses of 'I' in which 'I' is used, in Anscombe's terms, to refer to 'the person E. A.'. What sense can be made of these seemingly conflicting uses of 'I'?

MACKIE AND THE SENSES OF 'I'

It is worth considering one attempt, made by Mackie, of sorting out these potentially conflicting uses. Mackie accepts the prima-facie immunity of 'I' from both kinds of (S)R-failure but rejects

Anscombe's conclusion that 'I' does not refer. Conceding that 'I' is different from 'A' in that it does not admit of (S)R-failure(2), Mackie says that this only shows 'that the sense of "I" differs from that of "A"': it could be that 'I' and 'A' have the same referent but that the sense of 'I' somehow always ensures its referring to the right referent, while the sense of 'A' does not.[29] But what sense of 'I' could guarantee this immunity, and how could it also guarantee immunity from (S)R-failure(1), from failing to refer at all? Mackie says that our use of 'I' is actually subject to two linguistic rules. The first of these he derives from Locke's observation of a 'basic fact', that is, 'the occurrence (in each of us) ... of co-conscious experiences ... awareness of feelings, bodily positions, intentional movements, and so on. These, as they occur, joining on to a pre-existing co-conscious system ... are ascribed to a single supposed subject.' From this 'basic fact' arises a 'linguistic rule for the use of "I"': each item that enters this co-conscious system (is) I-ascribed'.[30] Given this linguistic rule, there is a sense in which 'it is ... guaranteed that whatever I take as "I" in this way is I; but the reality on which this linguistic procedure is based is just the serial co-consciousness of experiences and thoughts'.[31] The second linguistic rule for 'I' says that 'if someone says to *x* "You are ...", *x* can agree by saying "Yes, I am ..." or disagree by saying "No, I'm not ..."'.[32] This rule classes 'I' with, and as a counterpart to, 'you', 'he', 'she', and other pronouns which refer to human beings. Thus, says Mackie, the expression 'I' is subject to 'at least two meaning rules: one which makes it refer to whatever it is whose self-consciousness it expresses, which is at best factually and contingently this human being, and one which binds it directly, linguistically, as Anscombe's "A" is bound, to the human being who uses it'.[33]

How do these two meaning rules account for the R-failure immunity of 'I'? Mackie gives a straightforward account: the first rule ensures against (S)R-failure(2), while the second rule ensures against (S)R-failure(1). In other words, it is not possible to mistake one of my co-conscious experiences for one of someone else's (or vice versa), given that the first linguistic rule stipulates that 'I' is used to refer to the subject of all and only those experiences that are those of the being who is doing the referring. And since the second rule binds 'I' to a referent (a human being) on every occasion of its use, there is no possibility of 'I' being used without referring to something. Given that our ordinary use of 'I' is subject to both of these rules, it follows that 'I' is immune from both kinds of (S)R-failure, though each rule only renders it immune from one of the two kinds. Mackie admits that the applicability of these two rules creates 'an over-determination of meaning',[34] and this at least appears to be true. In effect, the two rules provide two senses of 'I' rather than just one: the first sense of 'I' is, broadly speaking, that of an experiencing subject, and the second is that of a human being. Mackie says, however, that 'since the rules contingently converge in the end' this is not a problem—at least not for us.[35] In other words, the two rules provide conventions for using 'I' to talk about what is in fact one person considered in two ways. Mackie, in a sense echoing Kant in the Paralogisms, points out that in those cases where the two senses diverge, such as disembodiment or 'feats of transference', and which thus seem to argue for the (separate) existence of a Cartesian Ego, the intelligibility of these cases rests on 'some vagueness or equivocation about the scope of a definite description' of 'I'.[36] That is, such problem cases advance from talk about the experiencing subject *simpliciter* (the 'I' of the first rule) to talk about the person (fixed as referent of 'I' by the second rule); at the same time, these cases are coherent only on the minimal, first, description, and trade on the overdetermination of meaning with regard to 'I' by only using that determination which renders them coherent.

Mackie summarizes his rebuttal of the thesis that 'I' is not a referring expression by saying that Anscombe fails

to disprove what indeed seems to be the case, that 'I' not only is regularly a referring term, but also regularly refers to the human being who uses it. But this reference is secured by two different rules which constitute different senses for 'I'. One rule links it, like Anscombe's 'A', directly to this human being. The other rule links it directly only to the subject, whatever it may be, of these experiences, and therefore only indirectly and contingently to this human being.[37]

Thus Mackie is in the position, with regard to the Cartesian Ego, of saying that the expression 'I' is used part of the time to introduce something which seems quite a bit like a Cartesian Ego: an experiencing subject, contingently linked to a body. On the other hand, he says that this use of 'I' refers 'to something which is introduced in the style of a Cartesian Ego': it is not obviously true that the experiencing subject *exists* as a Cartesian Ego, even though it may be *thought* as one—a point which should now seem quite familiar.[38] None the less, Mackie says that we do in part use 'I' as having the sense of a Cartesian Ego, given our ability to perform 'feats of transference': imagining myself and/or others at the Battle of Cannae, for example. So 'the ordinary concept of the "I"' is in part 'itself Cartesian', or at least seems to be so in so far as it refers to what Kant would call a 'bare form of consciousness', a mere experiencing subject.[39] But to the extent that 'I' refers only to the experiencing subject *qua* Cartesian Ego, 'it always fails of reference. For the arguments which suggest that our ordinary concept is (partly) that of a Cartesian Ego have no tendency to show that there are really any such things.'[40] In any case, Mackie argues that though this Cartesian Ego sense of 'I' is one sense which we do in fact deploy, it is grounded in a successful reference only in so far as 'I' also has the sense of 'an actual persisting thing', in our case a human being among others like it.[41] It is presumably this human being which is—albeit contingently—the referent of 'the transcendental "I"', the experiencing subject.

In a reply to Mackie, Strawson rejects the significance of the datum which exercises both Mackie and Anscombe. He says that

the immunity of 'I' from reference-failure (of either kind) in the thought, or speech, of any human user of it, whatever his condition, is guaranteed by the role of the expression in the ordinary practice, well established among human beings, of reference to themselves and each other. . . . it follows that no case for the existence of any use of 'I' other than its use in reference to a human being (a thinking and corporeal language-user) is established simply by the fact of this feature.[42]

On Strawson's view, then, the (S)R-failure immunity of 'I' is merely a result of the practice of personal reference: 'it is a rule of that practice that the first person pronoun refers to whoever uses it'.[43] Given this rule, it is clear that (S)R-failure(1) cannot occur, since the very use of 'I' implies some user, and some user is by practical definition the referent of 'I' when used. Similarly, (S)R-failure(2) is (quite literally) ruled out, and on like grounds: 'I', when used, refers not just to some user but to the user of 'I' in that instance of its use. And 'user' here should be construed as referring to the 'thinking and corporeal language-user', the person as language-practitioner. 'I', then, refers to the person, and though it may be argued that there are other referents and/or senses of the first person pronoun, they are not legitimized or made necessary by the datum of (S)R-failure immunity. This datum is completely accounted for within the framework of 'I' as an expression which refers to persons, to whom we ascribe, on Strawson's view, both mental and physical predicates. To the extent that Mackie's (and Anscombe's) views on 'I' depend on the idea that the datum of (S)R-failure immunity requires an explanation more complicated than this, then, according to Strawson, they are simply going beyond what the datum itself requires.

If Strawson is right in his account of the datum we have been considering, then Mackie's 'two-sense' theory of 'I' is otiose as a defence of 'I' as a referring expression. In arguing that 'I' can and does refer perfectly well to a person, Strawson in effect refutes Anscombe by showing that, in arguing that 'I' either refers to a Cartesian Ego or does not refer at all, Anscombe has created a false dilemma. None the less, Strawson does go on to consider the merits of Mackie's 'two-sense' theory in its own right—and finds it wanting. According to Strawson, this theory implies that 'I' has not merely two senses but three, since we use 'I' as (1) the subject of mental predicates, e.g., 'I am thinking of a tree', (2) 'what we take our Cartesian Ego to take to be "his" body, as in "I am bald"', and (3) the person who is in some sense the concatenated product of (1) and (2). This third sense is necessary since, as Strawson says, '"I am writing" (is) an activity which cannot be credited to either Ego or body alone.'[44] So Strawson's first objection to Mackie's 'two-sense' theory is that it seems to be at least a three-sense theory. And the second objection stems from this whole project of multiplying senses of 'I'. Strawson says that

This view of our ordinary concept(s) of ourselves, or of what we ordinarily mean by 'I', seems to me quite implausible. When we say such things as 'I closed my eyes and (I) thought of you . . .' we do not, I suggest, for a moment suppose that we are switching the reference of 'I' between its first occurrence in each sentence and its second. We are ordinarily content to operate with a concept of ourselves and other people as beings who are both corporeal and conscious; and it is to such beings that we ordinarily employ the personal pronouns to refer.[45]

There is, on this view, a serious implausibility in the notion, which Strawson considers integral to the 'two-sense' theory, that we regularly juggle between at least two and possibly three referents for 'I' in the practice of ordinary discourse. And on the face of it, there is a certain implausibility in this sort of 'sense-switching'. In addition, the fact that one of the juggled referents (the Cartesian Ego) does not exist at all does not help the plausibility of this theory. And Strawson objects to the suggestion that the Cartesian Ego is 'part of our "ordinary concept" of the referent of "I"', though Strawson concedes that it 'has figured prominently in our Western culture' and is 'a natural enough illusion'.[46] Mackie's arguments about 'feats of transference' and about the datum of (S)R-failure immunity were presumably intended to bridge the gap between the Cartesian Ego as a 'natural' and prevalent illusion and this Ego as part of the ordinary concept of 'I'; but this, Strawson argues, Mackie has not done.

Can we dismiss reference-failure immunity as being explicable entirely in terms of the role of 'I' in ordinary linguistic practice? It would seem that we can, given reflection on the disparity between Anscombe's assumptions about reference and our actual referring practice, with its successes and failures. In a way, then, it is not necessary to dwell on the 'two-sense' theory of 'I', for, as was pointed out, if Strawson is right about 'I' there is no need for such a theory at all—and it should be clear that the explanation of the (S)R-failure immunity of 'I' does not require such a theory to establish that 'I' does refer. None the less, Mackie's theory is of interest in its own right, not least because it has a certain intuitive appeal: it is a very 'natural . . . illusion' to have the concept of ourselves as Cartesian Egos; indeed, and as we have seen, if Kant is right, it is not only natural but quite necessary. And it is not obvious that such a theory is in any way inconsistent with what else has been said here about the referring function of 'I', since Mackie would agree that 'I' after all does refer to a person. In a manner of speaking, the 'two-sense' theory could be said merely to point out an additional richness in the modes we use in referring to persons: it has been argued that we ordinarily refer to persons demonstratively, descriptively, and in a subjective and reflexive mode, so it is not implausible to argue that within this subjective mode of personal reference there is more than one way of referring to 'I'. Just how implausible, then, is the 'two-sense' theory?

SENSE-SWITCHING

If the 'two-sense' theorist is committed to the thesis that as a matter of course we switch back and forth between two, and possibly three senses of 'I' in ordinary discourse, then the burden is on him to show that this is plausible linguistic behaviour. It certainly does not seem to be *impossible* linguistic behaviour: imagine that I am very close to a great painter with whom I am forbidden to discuss his art, and that I am also an art historian specializing in this painter's work (let us call him Monet). Clearly I will refer with some regularity to Monet the friend, e.g., 'Monet and I cooked asparagus for lunch'; I will also regularly refer to Monet the painter, e.g., 'Monet's Giverny work displays bold experimentation with light.' And, of course, I am perfectly well aware that each reference to Monet is to the same person. But the two contexts of reference impart strikingly different senses to 'Monet'. If I find myself in two somewhat fragmented conversations at once, in one of which I am arguing the merits of the artist Monet and in the other I am recounting what Monet and I did yesterday, then I will switch senses while maintaining the same referent—and given a preoccupation with both Monet the painter and Monet the friend, I will probably perform this kind of sense-switching with some frequency. But this is not completely unlike the kind of switch I would perform with regard to 'I' on Mackie's theory.

It is also worth considering that on Mackie's view it may not necessarily be the case that we ordinarily operate with two (or three) senses of 'I'. Granted, Mackie himself seems to argue that we do (though, as Strawson points out, he is not completely consistent in this): our doing so is the basis of our being able to achieve our observed dexterity at feats of transference. Now the whole question of such feats is well beyond my present scope. But if we regularly refer to the self as a Cartesian Ego, then at least this use of 'I' seems to be a perennial (S)R-failure(1), since there presumably are no Cartesian Egos to which we can refer—or it may be argued to be an (S)R-failure(2), since we are implicitly referring to something else as a Cartesian Ego. In either case, of course, we would have a refutation of Anscombe's claim that 'I' does not refer since it is immune to R-failure. But the price we would pay for this refutation would be positing an (S)R-failure of a particular type as part of the ordinary practice of using 'I' to refer; in any case, the price need not be paid, since Anscombe has already been refuted. The question we do need to ask is whether or not the 'two-sense' theory itself commits us to the claim that we ordinarily operate with multiple senses of 'I'.

It may, of course, be possible to construe Mackie's two senses as, in his own words (used in a different context), having 'a causal, historical sense' rather than being 'contemporaneous linguistic constraint(s)'.[47] In other words, if the two linguistic rules which give rise to these two putative senses of 'I' are merely reflections of the ways in which our 'I'-concept is developed, there is no obvious implausibility in the theory. Our ordinary sense of 'I' is more or less the third sense Strawson finds in Mackie's theory: that which refers to a thinking and corporeal individual, and it is reasonable to assume that the two senses posited refer to these two aspects of this individual. The 'linguistic rules' which determine these 'senses' do not in fact stipulate two senses of 'I' as it is used but reflect those learned linguistic behaviours which have served to inform our ordinary 'I'-concept, one that incorporates both these aspects. That we occasionally stray from this third, full-blooded, sense of 'I' is explained by the fact that this 'I'-concept is developed out of quite disparate linguistic representations, so that an unwarranted focus on only one kind of linguistic behaviour relevant to 'I'-reference can lead to the positing of, for example, disembodied selves. Again, the point is evocative of Kant's own diagnosis of the sources of such illicit positings, and considerations of the scope and taxonomy of 'I'-reference certainly point to such an explanation.

Part of the problem, of course, is that it is not clear, on the 'two-sense' theory, whether or not it is merely *senses* of 'I' that are being switched. Mackie does say that his second sense of 'I' refers to the person, that human being fixed by the rule as the 'I'-referent.[48] But in the case of the first sense of 'I', Mackie says that 'I' in this case refers 'to something which is introduced in the style of a Cartesian Ego';[49] in other words, it refers to the experiencing subject *simpliciter*, abstracted from the person referred to by the second sense of 'I'. This seems clearly to imply that not merely the sense but also the *referent* of 'I' is switched between the two uses. And Mackie in a way corroborates this later, when he suggests that it may be the case that in this first sense, 'I' is subject to a perennial reference-failure. He does say, however, that this reference failure only occurs in cases where the reference to this Cartesian Ego-like 'something' is not 'grounded' in a reference to the human being.[50] What I take Mackie to be getting at is something like this: the person E. A. may use 'I' with the sense implied by the first linguistic rule, that is, 'I' construed as the experiencing subject. Moreover, the person E. A. may use 'I' in this way such that 'I' actually does refer to the experiencing subject. But this is a successful reference only so long as the experiencing subject is in fact identical with the person E. A.—so long as the two senses of 'I' continue to 'converge' on the same referent (which, so far as we know, must be the person rather than a Cartesian Ego that may or may not exist). It follows, then, that the 'something' which is 'introduced in the style of a Cartesian Ego' must itself be the person—if the 'I'-reference to this something is to be successful. So if thoughts are, by Mackie's first linguistic rule, ascribed to an 'I', and reference to this 'I' is to be successful, then these thoughts are ascribed to the person. But it is important to note that they are, on this view, ascribed to the person who is here introduced not as a person but as something like a Cartesian Ego.

KANT AND THE FIRST PERSON

Why, though, need we go to the lengths of positing, in our ordinary language, such common—and even, perhaps, universal—references to Cartesian Egos? To see what is going on here, we need to consider again Locke's 'basic fact', which leads to the first linguistic rule of 'I'-reference. As Mackie puts it, Locke observes that co-conscious experiences are such that 'these, as they occur, joining on to a pre-existing co-conscious system . . . are ascribed to a single supposed subject', and that from this fact we derive the linguistic rule that 'each item that enters this co-conscious system (is) I-ascribed'.[51] Consider again Bennett's reading of Kant's 'doctrine' of the necessary unity of consciousness: Bennett says that all this term signifies, on the most generous interpretation, is that in the case of any thought p which I have, I can also have the (true) thought 'I think that p'.[52] Mackie, of course, does not mention Kant at all in this context. None the less, it would seem that Mackie is thinking of something along Bennett's lines when he suggests that this linguistic rule, which derives from the formation of a co-conscious system, specifies that each member of this system is 'I-ascribed'. If so, Mackie commits the very mistake which Bennett—rightly—points out that Kant does not: it is simply not true that each thought I have I in fact ascribe to myself; after all, I do not as a matter of course ascribe all of my thoughts in the first place. And, as we now know, to read *Kant* as saying this completely obscures his real point, which is—briefly—that one condition of having coherent experience is that this experience be structured as if it is the experience of one ongoing subject—a single subject which has all these experiences. It is this posited subject which Mackie, most appropriately, characterizes as 'a single supposed subject'; in effect, it is a subject introduced as a Cartesian Ego, in so far as we take a Cartesian Ego to be a single, simple experiencing subject persisting over time. It is the necessary representation of this subject that Kant argues for in the Transcendental Deduction, and it is its necessary characterization as just such a Cartesian Ego that he elaborates in the Paralogisms.[53]

If we accept that Kant is right that the apperceptive 'I' must be represented as such a subject, then we can deal, at least tentatively, with two of Strawson's criticisms of the 'two-sense' theory. The implicit criticism suggested above, that on this theory one of the uses of 'I' involves a perennial R-failure, can be conceded: if in using 'I' to refer to the experiencing subject as described by Kant—and this is the most persuasive account of the 'subject of consciousness' that we have—then it is indeed a failure of reference in so far as it is assumed to refer to an actual entity: in this case, a Cartesian Ego. That is *precisely* Kant's point about this Ego, namely, that it is a necessary illusion, an entity which we posit, and presumably refer to, that we do not know to exist. Second, regarding Strawson's objection that the Cartesian Ego is not part of the 'ordinary concept' of the referent of 'I', or more generally, that such an Ego is part of our ordinary way of looking at ourselves: it is important to ask what work is being done here by the expression 'ordinary concept'. Strawson says that the idea of a Cartesian Ego has played a significant role in Western culture, and that it is 'a natural enough illusion'. If both of these are true, then it is hard to see how it could be a more ordinary concept. Of course, it is not true that as a matter of course we think of ourselves as disembodied minds, but that is a stronger claim than Mackie—or Kant—need make: the point is rather that we do, as a matter of course, structure our experiences as if they are had by a Cartesian Ego. And again, as Kant has taken pains to show, this is not merely a natural illusion but a necessary one.

It is worth noting that, if we have drawn out the appropriate consequences of the 'two-sense' theory, we have stood our original datum upon its head. Rather than it being the case that 'I' is immune from R-failure, there is one use of 'I'—related to Kant's apperceptive 'I'—which, if it is a referring expression at all, is either such that it (1) is subject to perennial (presumed) R-failure, since it refers to a Cartesian Ego, or (2) is actually a somewhat veiled reference to the person or human being who is—contingently—the 'subject of consciousness'. But neither of these courses is in any obvious way satisfactory. In the former case, the question should be asked, what sense does it make to talk about referring expressions that never actually refer? In the latter case, it is highly suppositious merely to assume that the apperceptive 'I' refers to the human being, incidentally or not. If this 'I' does refer to the human being, as Mackie apparently would have it do, it does so quite obliquely, especially given the necessary characterization of the 'I' as an entity which has a number of properties that the human being does not (simplicity, to take one example). If the apperceptive 'I' refers at all, it seems to refer to a necessary fiction. And this does not conform to that account of reference (following Russell) whereby referring expressions pick out objects as referents. Though referents clearly need not be physical objects, they do need to be such that they can be picked out in a way that we cannot pick out the experiencing subject. But this, too, we learned from Kant, who points out that the 'I' of the 'I think' is a thought and not an intuition: it is that which in effect does the picking out, but is not itself pickable.

There is at least some reason, then, for suggesting that the 'I' of apperception is, after all, *not* a referring expression. This point has been well made by Rosenberg, who says that

The moral of Hume's *Gedankenexperiment* and Kant's Paralogisms is that what is represented in apperceptive encounter is not oneself in relation to one's representings but merely one's representings (as representings). The point of Kant's Paralogisms is that the Cartesian form I think that-*p* lacks the putative implications of its surface grammar. Properly understood, 'I' here is a dummy substantive and 'think' a dummy verb. What we should rather say is that 'I think that-' functions here logically as a unit, to bracket the representing which follows it and thereby represents it as a representing. It is, in other words, to put it rather bluntly, nothing more than a form of quoting . . .[54]

The 'I'-ascription cited by Mackie is, then, not actually an 'I'-ascription at all. To assume that statements of the form 'I think that-*p*' are ascriptions of thoughts to an object, represented by 'I', is to be misled by the similarity between this grammatical form and that of an ordinary self-ascription. Rather, 'I think that-*p*' is a *meta*-representing of the representation *p*: it represents *p* as one representation within a system of representations. Taking { } to mean 'is a member of S', on this view we find that, in effect,

I think that-p

actually has as its logical form

$\{p\}$

Again, it is not the case that all members of S are in fact represented as being within S. Still, any member of S can be so represented, and 'I think that-p' is the grammatical form used for this purpose.[55] The basic point here again is that made by Kant: that the 'I' of the 'I think' does not refer to an entity which stands in some relation to its properties, but rather is a logical operator which serves to group members of a co-conscious system as such. But if the apperceptive 'I' is no more than this, it is not an object of reference at all; in this Rosenberg seems to be in agreement with Anscombe.

Where, though, does the experiencing subject fit into this account of the 'I' of apperception? Though we acknowledge there to be good reasons to deny a referring role to this use of 'I', it seems that to say that the 'I' of the 'I think' is merely a logical operator which brackets thoughts and represents them as such leaves out the full breadth of the Kantian insight that this system of representations must be unified by a 'supposed single subject'. The key, I suspect, is that in bracketing representations as such, they are represented not merely as members of a co-conscious system but as members of one particular system. In other words, when I say

I think that-p

this, as was suggested, brackets the thought p as a member of a system of thoughts:

$\{p\}$

but this, in turn, says that

p is a representation within this system

But what system are we gesturing at when we refer to 'this' system? Here we see Hume's old problem surface: if his thoughts are merely a series of impressions and ideas, how is it that he knows that they are his thoughts in the first place? Hence Kant's point that experience requires a subject, and—less truistically—it requires awareness of oneself as such a subject. So 'this system' must itself stand in for

p is one of *my* representations

and this, of course, leads us to

I think that-*p*

It would seem, then, that we are being led in a fairly pointless circle, since the notion of 'my' representations brings us back to the 'I' of apperception. But perhaps not: it is worth considering that the apperceptive 'I' may well be merely a logical operator, a quoting device, but that *its use demands an awareness of oneself as the subject whose representations these are*.[56] In other words, though the apperceptive 'I' is not itself a referring term, it can only be used in such a way that its use carries an implicit acknowledgement of, *and reference to*, that being who is the experiencing subject (in our case the person). Thus the 'I' in that 'I think that-*p*' with which we began is the apperceptive 'I', which does not itself refer, and which merely represents thoughts as such; but the 'I' in the second 'I think that-*p*' implicitly acknowledges the experiencing subject. And this implicit reference to the experiencing subject is also, at least for us, an implicit reference to the full-blooded person as well.

On this view, the use of the apperceptive 'I' is not itself referential, but it implies a referential use of 'I'—that use in which 'I' refers to Strawson's 'person'—as a condition of its use. Such a view would account for the supposed perennial R-failure of 'I' when used in Mackie's first 'sense': it is, in a way, true that the apperceptive 'I' consistently fails to refer to anything, since it is not a referring term at all. But this does not drive us to Anscombe's conclusion that 'I' is not a referring term, since the use of that 'I' which is not referential itself acknowledges a use of 'I' which is. Anscombe's conclusion is derived using an appeal to the immunity of 'I' from R-failure. But this immunity can be explained as follows: as 'I'-users we are protected from R-failure(1) by something not unlike Mackie's second rule, that when we use 'I' as a referring term the term is bound to the speaker who uses it. And as 'I'-users we are also protected from R-failure(2), from failing to find a referent at all: since the correct use of 'I' presupposes its reference to the user, it is guaranteed that it will have a referent (this is precisely what ensures against R-failure(1) as well). But it is also worth considering that, if one does (mistakenly) take the apperceptive 'I' to be a referring term, then both kinds of R-failure will be accounted for on precisely the basis suggested by Anscombe, that 'getting hold of the wrong object is excluded, and this makes us think that getting hold of the right object is guaranteed', where there is, in fact, no object at all but merely a logical operator. And this insight, as was remarked before, is one that is not only Kantian, it is—given certain justifiable transpositions of terms—Kant's own.

Are there then two senses of 'I'? It would seem not. Rather, there are two *uses* of 'I': the one in which 'I' is a referring term, and in which it refers to the person who uses it, and the other in which 'I' is not a referring term but is rather a quoting operator within a representational system. None the less, it should be emphasized that there is also a use of 'I' within which 'I' refers—or attempts to refer—to something like a Cartesian Ego; this use appears to derive from precisely the kind of confusion over the apperceptive 'I' to which Anscombe draws attention. And it is not entirely certain that this 'I' is without a function beyond that served by the quoting operator itself—Kant, as we know, thought it a necessary illusion, not merely on the grounds of providing an abiding experiencing subject but on grounds of providing a justification of morality as well. As such, the 'I' clearly does have a referring function, albeit one which arguably refers to a useful—for Kant a necessary—fabrication. But it is important to note (with Kant, in a way) that this sense is derivative of a use of 'I' which is itself non-referential, and that, founded in a mistake in surface grammar, it seems itself either to be subject to that perennial R-failure suggested by Mackie or to be non-referential.

Finally, it should be pointed out that on this account there is no problem with 'sense-switching', since there is only one correct sense which 'I' can have: that of a person. But is there a problem with use-switching? To take Strawson's case, when I say 'I closed my eyes and I thought of you', do I switch from (1) 'I' as a referring expression to (2) that quoting operator which we style the apperceptive 'I'? First, if we do so switch, that in itself is not a particularly strong objection, since, as was argued in the Monet case, we are in fact fairly dextrous at switching senses, and are arguably equally dextrous when having to switch uses of a word. And though the second use of 'I' here does seem to be that of a quoting operator (it does, after all, represent a thought as being a thought of mine), this non-referential use is, to use Mackie's term, 'grounded in' a reference to the person who is in this case the subject who does the thinking. More precisely, this non-referential use of 'I' to meta-represent thoughts as members of a set of mental representings presupposes the existence of the owner of that set of representings. And that owner is, clearly, the person who is doing the representing. Here again, perhaps, we are not that far from Kant. Consider a curiously prescient passage in the *Dreams of a Spirit-Seer*:

Suppose . . . that it had been proved that the soul of man is a spirit . . . then the next question which might be raised is—where is the place of this human soul in the corporeal world? I would answer, the one body the changes of which are *my* changes, is *my* body, and its place is, at the same time, *my* place. If the question be continued, where then is your place (the soul) in this body? then I might suspect that this is a loaded question. For it is easily observed that it presupposes something which is not known by experience, but rests, perhaps, in imaginary conclusions; namely, that my thinking I (*mein denkender Ich*) is in a place which differs from the places of other parts of the one body which belongs to myself. Nobody, however, is immediately conscious of occupying a separate place in his body, but only of that place which he occupies as man in regard to the world around him. I would, therefore, keep to common experience, and would say, provisionally, where I sense, there *I am*. I am just as immediately in the tips of my fingers, as in my head. It is myself who suffers in the heel and whose heart beats in affection. When my corn torments me, I feel a painful impression, not in a cerebral nerve, but at the end of my toes. No experience teaches me to believe some parts of my sensation to be removed from myself, my I to be shut up in a microscopically small place in my brain from whence it may move the levers of my body-machine and cause me to be thereby affected. . . . *my soul is as a whole in my whole body, and wholly in each part.*[57]

The point should be underscored, for it is a thoroughly Kantian one: the mere fact that I can use the first-person pronoun as a quoting device, a way of representing my thoughts as such, in no way implies that I am a mysterious concatenation of a physical body and a somehow ineffable soul, self, or 'I'. If we look again at Strawson's example, 'I closed my eyes and I thought of you', it becomes clear that 'I' in the first case refers directly to the person who closes his eyes, and that 'I' in the second case is a quoting device, used, in effect, to assert that {these thoughts of you} are members of a system of thinkings. But what is important here is that, as we have seen, to represent these thoughts as members of a representational system is—necessarily—to represent these thoughts as thoughts had by an experiencing subject. And that experiencing subject is, after all is said and done, the person who, in Strawson's case, both closes his eyes and thinks.

Notes

INTRODUCTION

1. For reasons that will become apparent in my discussion of the Paralogisms, I will use the expression 'experiencing subject' rather than the
more common 'subject of experience', the latter expression having a
good deal of potential for ontological infelicity.
2. René Descartes, *Discourse On Method*, Part IV.
3. Gottfried Leibniz, *New Essays Concerning Human Understanding*, 469.
4. Ibid. 469.
5. Ibid. 11.
6. Leibniz, *Monadology*, 30.
7. Leibniz, *Correspondence With Arnauld*, 126.
8. Leibniz, *Monadology*, 17.
9. Ibid. 24.
10. Benedictus Spinoza, *Ethics*, Proposition xiii.
11. Ibid. Proposition xxiii.
12. George Berkeley, *Principles of Human Knowledge*, 25.
13. Ibid. 27.
14. Ibid. 27.
15. This characterization of the Cartesian tradition, of course, implicitly
assumes that Descartes takes the *Cogito* to be an assertion of his
immediate awareness of the 'I' rather than an inferring of the existence of
the 'I' from certain data of which we *are* immediately aware. This
assumption is contentious: cf., for example, Jaako Hintikka's '*Cogito,
Ergo Sum*: Inference or Performance?' and Chapter 2 of Margaret
Wilson's *Descartes*. In any case, rather than settle the question here, I
will merely suggest that *Hume* engages the intuitive, rather than the
inferential, Descartes.
16. David Hume, *A Treatise On Human Nature*, 252.
17. Ibid.
18. Gilbert Ryle, *The Concept of Mind*, 186.
19. A. A. Milne, *When We Were Very Young*, 83.
20. Cf. Patricia Kitcher, 'Kant On Self-Identity', *Philosophical Review*, 91
(1982), and Wilfrid Sellars, '. . . this I or he or it (the thing) which thinks
. . .', *Proceedings of the American Philosophical Association*, 44 (1970–
1), reprinted in *Essays in Philosophy and its History*.

CHAPTER I

1. Hume, 252.
2. In what follows, I will not presume to give a systematic, much less an exhaustive, exegesis of the Transcendental Deduction itself. None the less, a reading of the Deduction does underlie what I have to say in this chapter, and some exegesis is by necessity attempted. To borrow a recommendation from Kripke, I suggest that the reader reread the Transcendental Deduction 'in the light of the present exegesis and see whether it illuminates the text'. Cf. Saul Kripke, *Wittgenstein On Rules and Private Language*, 2n.
3. Cf. Robert Paul Wolff, 'Kant's Debt to Hume via Beattie', *Journal of the History of Ideas*, 21 (1960), 117–23; Kitcher's 'Kant on Self-Identity', 41 ff.; and Manfred Kuehn, *Scottish Common Sense in Germany, 1768–1800*.
4. Patricia Kitcher, 'Kant's Paralogisms', *Philosophical Review*, 91 (1982), 524.
5. Ibid. 524–5.
6. Ibid. 525.
7. Kitcher, 'Kant On Self-Identity', 49–50.
8. Ibid. 53.
9. Ibid.
10. Ibid. 53–4.
11. Ibid. 54.
12. Ibid.
13. Ibid. 55.
14. Ibid. 56. A *possibly* minor quibble here: it is fairly clear that though the distinction of these two senses of 'synthesis' is coherent and useful, they are not '*Kant's* two senses', given no textual support for Kant drawing the distinction. At any rate, given Kant's notorious 'methodological solipsism', it would be somewhat startling if he *did* draw this distinction.
15. Kitcher, 'Kant On Self-Identity', 56.
16. Ibid. 57.
17. Ibid. 58.
18. Ibid. 59–60.
19. Ibid. 61.
20. Ibid.
21. Ibid. 63.
22. Ibid. 64.
23. This interpretation of Kant as a kind of functionalist will be discussed in some detail in my account of the Fourth Paralogism.
24. Kitcher, 'Kant On Self-Identity', 63.

25. Richard Rorty, 'Verificationism and Transcendental Arguments', *Nous* (1971), 3–15.

26. Kitcher, 'Kant On Self-Identity', 55.

27. Ibid. 57. Cf. also B161 and B275.

28. Ibid. 63.

29. Cf. Wilfrid Sellars, 'Metaphysics and the Concept of a Person', in *Essays in Philosophy and its History*, 236–8.

30. Kitcher, 'Kant On Self-Identity', 55.

31. P. F. Strawson, *Individuals*, 96–7.

32. Kitcher, 'Kant On Self-Identity', 72.

33. My objection to Kitcher's account of synthesis is, again, that an adequate description of relation R cannot be given which does not at least implicitly appeal to an unanalysed notion of the self which it is intended to define. It is worth noting that Sydney Shoemaker, in commenting on Kitcher's later paper, 'Kant's Real Self', makes a related point: 'it is one thing to judge that a state belongs to some self or other, and quite another to judge that it belongs to me—I am not, after all, the only self in the world. So how do I get to the judgment that I have the state in question—that it belongs to my own "I that thinks"? Kitcher's answer is: "because I am aware of the state by inner sense, I attribute it to my own I that thinks." But this had better not mean that I get to this self-attribution by a deduction having as a premise that I am aware of the state by inner sense—for that would assume that I have the very sort of self-knowledge we are trying to explain.' Shoemaker, 'Commentary: Self-Consciousness and Synthesis', in Allen W. Wood, *Self and Nature in Kant's Philosophy*, 153.

34. Cf. A123, A122, B134–6.

35. Kant uses reproduction as an example at A102, A103, B138, and B154.

36. Kant's example of several subjects each having parts of a complex representation and yet not representing the complex representation itself will be discussed in more detail in my account of the Second Paralogism.

37. W. H. Walsh, *Kant's Criticism of Metaphysics*, 89.

38. Using (with modifications) a model used by Jay Rosenberg. Cf. Jay F. Rosenberg, '"I Think": Some Reflections on Kant's Paralogisms', *Midwest Studies in Philosophy*, vol. X.

39. Ibid. 507.

40. Strawson, *The Bounds of Sense*, 88.

41. Cf. Rorty, 'Strawson's Objectivity Argument', *Review of Metaphysics*, 24 (1970); Leslie Stevenson, 'Wittgenstein's Transcendental Deduction and Kant's Private Language Argument', *Kant-Studien*, 73 (1982); and J. L. Mackie, *The Cement of the Universe*, 88–116.

42. Stevenson, 323–4.

43. Sellars, 'Some Remarks on Kant's Theory of Experience', *Journal of Philosophy*, 64 (1967), 636.
44. Cf. also A320/B376, A79/B105.
45. Bennett, for one, has resisted this reading of intuitions as conceptual. He argues against this Sellarsian reading, though, by citing Kant's remark at A111 that 'intuition without thought' is 'not knowledge; and consequently would be for us as good as nothing'. But this is a case of reading Kant out of context: at A111 Kant is talking about a different kind of intuition from those which we have. He is considering what it would be like to have intuitions which are *not* conceptual, and, given that we do not experience bare particulars, such 'intuitions' would indeed 'be for us as good as nothing'. Cf. Rosenberg, '"I Think": Some Reflections on Kant's Paralogisms', n. 2, 528, for further discussion of Bennett's error.
46. Sellars, 'Some Remarks on Kant's Theory of Experience', 636.
47. It is significant that an *Anschauung* is a 'view' = a perspectival seeing, or, to import a bit of Wittgenstein's terminology, a 'seeing-*as*'.
48. Stevenson, 324.
49. Ibid. 324.
50. Ibid.
51. Mackie, *The Cement of the Universe*, 99.
52. Stevenson, 325.
53. Ibid.
54. This example will be used to different, but related, purpose in my account of the Second Paralogism.
55. Cf. Plato's *Meno*, 97a5–98b6.
56. This is not, in fact, what Strawson is actually doing in this part of the argument. None the less, consideration of this objection will be useful in making clear what *is* at stake in the argument.
57. Stevenson, 325.
58. Ibid.
59. Ibid. 325–6.
60. Strawson, *The Bounds of Sense*, 99.
61. Ibid. 100.
62. Ibid. 101.
63. Ibid.
64. Mackie, *The Cement of the Universe*, 100.
65. Since Stevenson's presentation is clearer than that of Rorty, and more perspicuously makes the same mistake, I will confine my discussion to Stevenson's reading.
66. Stevenson, 324.
67. Ibid. 322; Strawson, *The Bounds of Sense*, 24.
68. J. L. Austin, *Sense and Sensibilia*, 112–15.
69. Stevenson, 326.

70. Strawson, *The Bounds of Sense*, 108.
71. Or, in keeping with Kant's disavowal of rational psychology, he is preserving the possibility of the literal truth of 'the common expression that men think' (A359). As will be argued, however, this particular quote must be treated with caution and in context.
72. Allison, *Kant's Transcendental Idealism*: *An Interpretation and Defense*, 3–4.
73. Cf. H. E. Matthews, 'Strawson on Transcendental Idealism', in R. C. S. Walker (ed.), *Kant on Pure Reason*, 134.
74. Allison, 242.
75. Matthews, 136.
76. Strawson, *The Bounds of Sense*, 173. On the incoherence of this 'tangential point of contact', see also R. C. S. Walker, *Kant*, 133–4.
77. Cf. A364, A364n.
78. Strawson, *The Bounds of Sense*, 108.
79. Ibid. 107.
80. Ibid. 31–2.
81. Ibid. 32.
82. Walker, *Kant*, 83–4. On Tetens's psychology, see J. N. Tetens, *Philosophische Versuche über die menschliche Natur und ihre Entwicklung*. For a recent account of Tetens's philosophy, see Jeffrey Barnouw, 'Psychologie Empirique et Epistémologie dans le "Philosophische Versuche" de Tetens', *Archives de Philosophie*, 46 (1983). For an account of Tetens's relation to Kant, see Lewis White Beck, *Early German Philosophy*, 412–25.
83. The point should be underscored that Strawson is no longer willing to discount the role of synthesis in Kant's account of experience: he has suggested recently that Kant's analysis of synthesis in the first edition may well be analogous to current research into cognitive psychology. Cf. also Strawson, 'Imagination and Perception', in R. C. S. Walker (ed.), *Kant On Pure Reason*.
84. And though considerably less important, it is worth noting that it may not be possible to distinguish adequately Kant's terminology in general, much less his sometimes oracular distinctions of the various ways these terms are to be deployed, without understanding his theory of synthesis.
85. Kant, *Prolegomena to Any Future Metaphysics*, *Ak.* IV, 304.
86. Rorty, 'Strawson's Objectivity Argument', *Review of Metaphysics*, 24 (1970), 218.
87. Strawson, 'Imagination and Perception', 97.
88. Strawson, *The Bounds of Sense*, 117.
89. One exegetical possibility to which this reading may point is an explanation of Kant's cryptic remark in the *Metaphysical Foundations of Natural Science* that the Transcendental Deduction 'can be carried out

almost in a single step from the precisely specified definition of a *judgment* in general' (*Ak*. XX, 271, quoted in Walker, *Kant*, 77).

90. Finally, there is one remaining criticism of objectivity arguments in general that has not been touched on at all: that the necessary seems–is distinction may only require a network of properly ordered *events* to provide the regularities needed for an operative concept of mistakes, and thus of corrigibility (suggested by Walker in *Kant*, 119–20). This objection deserves more attention than it will receive here.

CHAPTER 2

1. This is most obviously true in the case of the arguments which are developed in Kant's discussion of the Second Paralogism: cf. B. L. Mijuskovic, *The Achilles of Rationalist Arguments*, *passim*. And it is important to bear in mind Walsh's observation that 'When Kant wrote (the Paralogisms) his immediate attention was directed on Wolff and Baumgarten, but he clearly had more formidable opponents in mind as well. The very fact that he makes free use of the Cartesian expression "I think" shows as much.' W. H. Walsh, *Kant's Criticism of Metaphysics* (Edinburgh, 1975), 177.

2. Kant, *Logic: A Handbook for Lectures*, General Doctrine of Elements, Section 90. *Ak*. IX, 138 (my trans.).

3. Interestingly, in the Paralogisms themselves Kant does occasionally refer to a given paralogism as a *sophisma*, apparently without the intention of charging intentional deception, thereby blurring the distinction he makes in the lectures on logic. It is worth noting that in the original Greek, 'paralogism' seems to derive from the verb παρα-λογίζομαι, meaning 'to reckon fraudulently' (in keeping accounts), or 'to defraud', referring specifically to the actions of a dishonest accountant, who 'cooks the books'. For Aristotle, as for Kant, however, the sense of intentional fraud has disappeared from the notion of a paralogism, which is merely a fallacious (deductive) argument.

4. Cf., for example, *Topics* 101a5–17, *Sophistical Refutations* 165a15, *Physics* 186a10.

5. *Ak*. IX, 139.

6. *Sophistical Refutations*, 169a22–5. I follow Ross in reading τήν ὁμωνυμίαν here as 'ambiguity'.

7. Norman Kemp Smith, *A Commentary on Kant's Critique of Pure Reason*, 470.

8. Jonathan Bennett, *Kant's Dialectic*, 40–81.

9. Ibid. 72.

10. Ibid. 73.

11. Ibid.
12. Ibid. 74.
13. Ibid. 73.
14. Ibid. 66.
15. Whatever plausibility this second interpretation might have depends on accepting the rather loaded claim—which Bennett does—that Kant is a phenomenalist. Cf. Ch. 1, n. 41 above.
16. Bennett, *Kant's Dialectic*, 74.
17. Ibid. 74.
18. Ibid. 75.
19. Ibid.
20. Specifically, in his Reply to the Third Objection. Quoted by Bennett, 75–6.
21. Ibid. 77.
22. Ibid.
23. Ibid. 78.
24. Ibid.
25. Ibid. 81.
26. Goethe's 'argument' is, however, strikingly reminiscent of Wittgenstein's remarks about solipsism in the *Tractatus* (5. 62–5. 641). In *Insight and Illusion*, P. M. S. Hacker presents an interesting discussion of this part of the *Tractatus* which, somewhat incidentally, relates Wittgenstein's remarks to Kant's theory of apperceptive consciousness. Unfortunately, however, Hacker conflates the self of the transcendental unity of apperception and the self of empirical apperception. The relation between the solipsistic self of the *Tractatus* and the self of the transcendental unity of apperception would be a fascinating topic for the historian of ideas—but it is a topic which goes beyond the scope of this investigation.
27. Cf. A364, A364n., A684/B712.
28. Bennett, *Kant's Dialectic*, 74.
29. Cf., for example, Kant's refutation of Mendelssohn's proof, B414–17.
30. Bennett, *Kant's Dialectic*, 81.
31. Ibid. 79.
32. Leibniz, *Nouveaux Essais sur l'entendement humain*, 92. Leibniz continues, interestingly, by saying that 'Or l'âme renferme l'être, la substance, l'un, le même, la cause, la perception, le raisonnement, et quantité d'autres notions, que les sens ne sauraient donner.'
33. Thomas Hobbes, *Leviathan*, 44.

CHAPTER 3

1. Bennett, 'The Simplicity of the Soul', *Journal of Philosophy*, 64 (1967), 648; C. D. Broad, *Kant: An Introduction*, 255–7; Kemp Smith, *A Commentary on Kant's Critique of Pure Reason*, 458–61.
2. In paragraph 2; cf. also paragraphs 5 and 6. Given the confusing and somewhat fragmentary nature of Kant's discussion of the Second Paralogism in A, I have followed Kemp Smith's (and Karl Ameriks's) salutary practice of numbering Kant's paragraphs, beginning immediately after the Paralogism's formal presentation at A351.
3. In paragraphs 3 and 4.
4. In paragraphs 7–9.
5. In paragraphs 10–18; cf. also paragraphs 5 and 6.
6. As we will see, Kant endorses a good deal—but not all—of the rational psychologist's response to the anti-rationalist.
7. Since Kant presents the anti-rationalist's own argument as the beginning of this *reductio* by the rational psychologist, I have kept the numbering of the premisses continuous from the anti-rationalist's argument to the response by *reductio* of his opponent.
8. Broad, 256–7.
9. William James, *The Principles of Psychology*, i, 160 (cited by Kemp Smith, 459).
10. Broad, 257.
11. Curiously, Broad goes on to say that premiss (6) 'even leaves it possible that [the soul] is a compound composed of egos interrelated in a very different way from that in which the egos associated with different human bodies are interrelated' (257). But the lesson of this premiss, as we have seen, is that the simplicity of the ego has a logical, rather than a merely physical warrant: it is unlikely that Broad can tell a story which interrelates egos in any way whatsoever such that, so interrelated, they can generate a complex thought and yet not then be one ego rather than several. In any case, it is not clear just what Broad would be claiming were he to insist that in such a case there were several egos interacting.
12. Thomas Nagel, 'What Is It Like To Be A Bat?', in *Mortal Questions*, 165–80. I am indebted to Paul Ziff for suggesting this criticism of Nagel.
13. Bennett, 'The Simplicity of the Soul', 648.
14. Here, it is worth noting an important ambiguity in the paragraph above: though I can, as a central-state materialist, view my composite nervous system as 'the *source* of all my thinkings' from the objective standpoint, I cannot, from the subjective standpoint, so view this composite as the subject, or source, which has these thoughts. The expression 'source' of thought can be taken, in Kantian terms, to mean in the first instance the

substrate of the 'I' of the 'I think', and in the second instance the *representation* of this 'I', which serves to order my thoughts as those of a unitary subject. And Kant's point is, of course, that though the substrate of the 'I' may be composite, the 'I' 'which can accompany all my thoughts' cannot, given its logical function, be represented as a composite.

15. Strawson, *The Bounds of Sense*, 166.

16. A similar logical slippage from '*A* is not represented as *X*' to '*A* is represented as not-*X*' is described by Sellars, '. . . this I or he or it (the thing) which thinks. . .', 236–8, and also by Rosenberg, 'I Think'': Some Reflections on the Paralogisms', n. 12, 530.

17. Cf. A80/B106, A344 = B402, B419.

18. Plato, *Phaedo* 78b5–c4, Gallop translation amended (I have used 'dissolution' rather than 'dispersal' here).

19. It is important to realize that for Kant 'actual' simplicity refers to a property of a phenomenal but non-composite representation, and not to that simplicity which would be a property of a thing in itself.

20. It should be noted that Kant does *not* say that, even in this sense, we *know* that the soul is non-corporeal. All he says is that, since all our experience of souls (here, Humean 'bundles') is non-corporeal, we are *justified*, presumably on the basis of induction, in saying that souls are non-corporeal. This seems to leave open the possibility of additional soul-sampling leading to a refuting instance = a corporeal soul. As we have seen in considering Kant's earlier remarks about other minds, however, it should be clear that Kant need not be so parsimonious: he can say that—in this attenuated sense—we do in fact know that we cannot represent another soul via outer sense, and that any such refuting instance is a logical impossibility.

21. It is unlikely, of course, that the rational psychologist will derive much comfort from being told that the self of empirical apperception is non-corporeal, since what is, in effect, a bundle of perceptions is an unlikely foundation on which to build an *a priori* 'science of the self': among other things, even if it is non-corporeal, it is clearly composite. And, as we shall see, there is little comfort indeed in Kant's concession.

22. Kant is speaking loosely here: what is the case is that the *noumenal substrate* of matter may be simple.

23. This is, of course, reminiscent of Strawson's account of persons, who, rather than being reducible to minds and bodies, are ontologically prior to both, and have both M-predicates and P-predicates. Cf. Strawson, *Individuals*, Chapter Three, especially 101–8.

24. That we need not grant this will be argued shortly.

25. Moses Mendelssohn, *Moses Mendelssohn: Selections from His Writings*, ed. and trans. Eva Jospe, 189–90.

26. Mendelssohn, 191.

27. Ibid.
28. Ibid. 192–3.
29. This objection to Mendelssohn's argument (and others) is also presented in Franz Brentano's *The Theory of Categories*, 75. As will become apparent, however, I am quite sceptical of Brentano's claim that 'Kant fails to notice these errors.'
30. Chisholm, 'Coming into Being and Passing Away: Can the Metaphysician Help?', reprinted in John Donnelly (ed.), *Language, Metaphysics, and Death*, 19.
31. Ibid.
32. Ibid.
33. Ibid.
34. Ibid. 20.
35. Ibid.
36. This is, of course, true for all substances that have intensive magnitude, which is an intrinsic, and not merely relational, attribute of the substance. It is true that the degree of influence on the senses is relational, as in those cases in which an intrinsically loud sound is far away and does not exert its full influence on us. But a case in which an intrinsically loud sound diminishes in intensity because of our relation to it (due, for example, to our travelling away from the source) provides us with a useful paradigm of those cases in which a sound intrinsically diminishes, or, in Kant's term, undergoes elanguescence. That this distinction of relational and intrinsic continua is implicit in Kant's account can be seen in his contrast of an 'intensity of sensation', or degree of actual influence in a specific apprehension, and 'intensive magnitude' in the object of sensation itself, which is the intrinsic capacity of the object to influence the senses. (A166/B208)

CHAPTER 4

1. This is what a number of Kant's most acute commentators have done. Cf. Bennett, *Kant's Dialectic*, 93–6; Broad, 257; Karl Ameriks, *Kant's Theory of Mind*, 130–1.
2. Ameriks, 130.
3. Cf. A102: 'When I seek to draw a line in thought . . .'
4. Kant, *Anthropologie in pragmatischer Hinsicht*, *Ak*. VII, 134n. Cf. Mary J. Gregor's translation, *Anthropology from a Practical Point of View*, 15n. (emphasis added).
5. Ameriks, 129. That 'person' in the Third Paralogism may not be completely without moral significance will be considered in due course.
6. None the less, and as will become clear in my reading of the Fourth

Paralogism, I am not convinced that Kant gerrymanders this argument quite as much as is usually assumed.

7. Sellars, '. . . this I or he or it (the thing) which thinks . . .', 70.
8. Ameriks, 166.
9. John Perry, 'The Problem of Personal Identity', in Perry (ed.), *Personal Identity*, 12.
10. John Locke, *An Essay Concerning Human Understanding*, Bk. II, Ch. 27.
11. I am indebted to Jay Rosenberg for this felicitous expression. Cf. *Thinking Clearly About Death*, 48–9.
12. The brain-identity advocate would presumably argue that cases like Locke's are only *coherent* on a 'brain-switch' interpretation.
13. Shoemaker, 'Personal Identity: A Materialist's Account', in S. Shoemaker and R. Swinburne (eds.), *Personal Identity*, 127.
14. Ibid. 128.
15. Locke, 333.
16. Ibid.
17. Thomas Reid, 'Of Mr. Locke's Account of Our Personal Identity', in Perry, 113–17.
18. Cf. Anthony Quinton, 'The Soul', and H. P. Grice, 'Personal Identity', both in Perry.
19. Locke, 334.
20. Ibid. 333.
21. Ibid. 340.
22. Though he does suggest this to be only due to the pragmatic grounds that 'want of consciousness' cannot be proven. Ibid. 342–3.
23. Ibid. 340.
24. Ibid. 346.
25. Ibid.
26. Ibid. 344.
27. Ibid. 345.
28. Ibid. 333.
29. Ibid. 346.
30. Strawson, *The Bounds of Sense*, 165.
31. Kant, *Prolegomena to Any Future Metaphysics*, Section 335.
32. Ameriks, 149.
33. I am intentionally ignoring here the contemporary discussions of 'strict' as opposed to 'relative' identity, which do not appear to be relevant to Kant's—or Ameriks's—account. Cf. David Wiggins, *Sameness and Substance*, Ch. 1; P. T. Geach, *Reference and Generality*, Sections 31–4; and Perry, 'The Same F', *Philosophical Review*, 79 (1970).
34. Broad, 258.
35. Chisholm, *Person and Object*, 89–113 *passim*.

36. Robert Nozick, *Philosophical Explanations*, 29–37.

37. Locke, Bk. II, Ch. 27.

38. It really is not obvious why such self-interested motives could not lead to moral behaviour, much as Pascal's gambler is—it is hoped—led to genuine piety through enough insincere practice. This is precisely the point Kant makes with regard to the development of one's moral stance (*Gesinnung*): though a person may present a righteous *Gesinnung* for the sake of others' esteem, it is possible that by force of habit the assumed moral stance will become genuine. On the other hand, such hypocrisy may eventually 'poison the heart'—cf. A748/B776. I am indebted to Rick Varcoe for calling my attention to Kant's fascinating use of the notion of a 'moral stance'—a notion which calls for considerably more attention than I have given it here.

39. Kant, after all, believes that ordinary mankind—as opposed to philosophers—for the most part see the world aright through 'the common reason of men' (B424).

40. Specifically, that in deceiving a rational being you are not treating him as an end but rather as a means. Cf. Kant, *Groundwork of the Metaphysic of Morals, Ak.* IV, 429–30.

41. Kant, *Prolegomena*, Section 363.

42. Kant, *Critique of Practical Reason*, 137.

43. Ibid. I am indebted to Ralph Walker for this point.

44. In this regard, Lucien Goldmann has raised the very interesting question of why Kant argues that belief in one's own immortality is necessary, and of why he posits in general a theology rather than a (presumably Marxist) philosophy of history with an historical evolution toward the highest good. Cf. Goldmann, *Immanuel Kant*.

45. Kant, *Critique of Judgment, Ak.* V, 452. I have followed Werner Pluhar's translation here. It is worth observing in passing that Kant, in this context, says that with regard to, on the one hand, denying God's existence and, on the other hand, denying the existence of an afterlife for oneself and other persons, 'as far as [achieving] the object of morality is concerned, the consequence is the same' (cf. 452 *passim.*). Kant is playing fast and loose here with the possible range of consequences for morality that could ensue as the result either of the existence of God or of our own immortality. After all, one could well imagine (*a*) an afterlife which is itself so bleak and defeating of the projects of moral agents that it offers no solace of the kind that Kant's righteous mortal lacks, or (*b*) a God who is malevolent, or capricious, or thoroughly ineffectual, and hence whose existence in no way validates the moral ends of persons in the way Kant presumes it would.

46. This tendency, of course, is considered in detail in Kant's comments on the Antinomies.

47. This conclusion may represent a disagreement with Ameriks's reading of the Third Paralogism, a reading which is in a number of other ways congenial to my interpretation. Ameriks says that even though personal identity for Kant is not 'certainly knowable', Kant 'still would reject Locke's notion that personality is a mere forensic term and that we can be satisfied with detaching it from debatable issues of substance' (cf. Ameriks, 128).

CHAPTER 5

1. Bennett, *Kant's Dialectic*, 71–2.
2. Kitcher, 'Kant's Paralogisms', 519.
3. Sellars, '. . . this I or he or it (the thing) which thinks . . .', 68.
4. Walker, *Kant*, 110.
5. See the Second Analogy, *passim*, especially A194/B239, A201–2/B246–7; also the Postulates of Empirical Thought, A221/B268, A225/B272.
6. Cf. A369, A371.
7. Haldane and Ross (eds.), *The Philosophical Works of Descartes*, i, 189.
8. Bennett, *Kant's Dialectic*, 72.
9. Haldane and Ross, 152.
10. Bennett, *Kant's Dialectic*, 72.
11. Haldane and Ross, 152.
12. Ibid. 190.
13. Ibid. 101.
14. Bennett, *Kant's Dialectic*, 72.
15. Perhaps the most interesting question here is *why* this premiss is analytic.
16. Michael Hooker, 'Descartes's Denial of Mind-Body Identity', in M. Hooker (ed.), *Descartes: Critical and Interpretative Essays*, 171–4.
17. Anthony Kenny, *Descartes: A Study of His Philosophy*, cited in Hooker, 173.
18. Hooker, 173.
19. Ibid. 174.
20. Kant, *Dreams of a Spirit-Seer*, Ak. II, 321.
21. Ibid. 327.
22. Kant, *Werke*, Edition Hartenstein: viii, 812.
23. Sellars, '. . . this I or he or it (the thing) which thinks . . .', 68.
24. Quoted by Kemp Smith, *A Commentary on Kant's Critique of Pure Reason*, 471.
25. Sellars, 'Some Remarks On Kant's Theory of Experience', 53.
26. Sellars, '. . . this I or he or it (the thing) which thinks . . .', 68.
27. Hilary Putnam, 'Minds and Machines', in *Mind, Language, and Reality*, 373.

28. Putnam, 'The Mental Life of Some Machines', 424.
29. Ibid. 428.
30. Though for Kant, of course, this account is really in large measure synthetic *a priori*.
31. It should be noted that 'constitution' in German is *Beschaffenheit*, which in its primary sense has a connotation of physical composition.
32. Sellars, 'Metaphysics and the Concept of a Person', 237.
33. Daniel C. Dennett, *Brainstorms*, Introduction.
34. Rosenberg, '"I Think": Some Reflections on Kant's Paralogisms', 524.
35. Putnam, 'The Mental Life of Some Machines', 424.
36. Kitcher has suggested that Kant lacks the notions 'theoretical term' and 'functional description', and that this obscures his functionalist insight. Though I think Kant has working *notions* of both, he clearly does not have explicit *terms* to bring to bear here with which to use these notions effectively. In any case, whether or not Kant does have these notions, it is not obviously true that he deploys them in the kind of functionalist strategy suggested here. Cf. Kitcher, 'Kant's Paralogisms', 545.
37. D. M. Armstrong, *A Materialist Theory of the Mind*, 88.
38. Kitcher, 'Kant's Paralogisms', 531.
39. Ibid.

CHAPTER 6

1. In what follows, I do not intend to canvass exhaustively all of the recent work on the problem of self-reference. Rather, I hope to show the relevance of Kant's—or a Kantian—position to understanding one particular dialectic within this (now burgeoning) literature.
2. As Anscombe says, 'The object an "I"-user means by it must exist so long as he is using "I", nor can he take the wrong object to be what he means by "I"'. Cf. Elizabeth Anscombe, 'The First Person', 30.
3. Ibid. 24.
4. Ibid. 24–5.
5. Ibid. 27.
6. Strawson, *The Bounds of Sense*, 164–5.
7. Anscombe, 24.
8. Ibid. 30.
9. Ibid.
10. Ibid. 30–1.
11. Ibid. 31.
12. Ibid.
13. Ibid.
14. Ibid. 34.

15. Ibid. 31–2.
16. Ibid. 34.
17. Ibid. 36.
18. Ibid. 32.
19. Ibid.
20. None the less, there are serious divergences between Kant and Anscombe: for example, it is not at all clear that Kant would countenance Anscombe's talk of 'unmediated' states of consciousness.
21. Chisholm, *The First Person*, 79–83.
22. 'A great friend of mine who rarely came to the Lilas came over to the table and sat down, and just then as my friend was ordering a drink from Emile the gaunt man in the cape with the tall woman passed us on the sidewalk. His glance drifted toward the table and then away.

    "That's Hilaire Belloc," I said to my friend. "Ford was here this afternoon and cut him dead."

    "Don't be a silly ass," my friend said. "That's Aleister Crowley, the diabolist. He's supposed to be the wickedest man in the world."

    "Sorry," I said.'

    Reported by Hemingway in 'Ford Madox Ford and the Devil's Disciple', *A Movable Feast*, 88.
23. Strawson, 'Reply to Mackie and Hide Ishiguro', in Zak van Straaten (ed.), *Philosophical Subjects: Essays Presented to P. F. Strawson*, 267.
24. It is important, however, to underscore the fact that, even if I cannot produce such an identification, my use of 'I' is not flawed *qua* reference.
25. Chisholm, *The First Person*, 86.
26. Anscombe, 28.
27. Wittgenstein, *Philosophical Investigations*, Section 28 ff.
28. I now find that Gareth Evans has also pointed out that 'I' is not unique in terms of 'immunity to error through misidentification', and on similar grounds. Evans, however, seems more sanguine than I am that this immunity is a characteristic of all demonstrative identification. Though the point is worth developing, it cannot reasonably be developed here. Cf. Gareth Evans, *The Varieties of Reference*, ed. J. McDowell (Oxford, 1982), 217–18.
29. Mackie, 'The Transcendental "I"', in *Philosophical Subjects: Essays Presented to P. F. Strawson*, 52.
30. Van Straaten, 52.
31. Ibid. 52–3.
32. Ibid. 53.
33. Ibid.
34. Ibid.
35. Ibid.

36. Ibid. 56.
37. Ibid.
38. Ibid. 60.
39. Ibid.
40. Ibid. 61.
41. Ibid. 60.
42. Ibid. 267.
43. Ibid. 266–7.
44. Ibid. 268.
45. Ibid. 268–9.
46. Ibid. 271.
47. Ibid. 59.
48. Ibid. 260.
49. Ibid. 61.
50. Ibid.
51. Ibid. 52.
52. Bennett, *Kant's Dialectic*, 74.
53. Mackie's account of co-consciousness may be more sophisticated than is here implied, as evidenced by his use of 'single supposed subject', 'introduced in the style of a Cartesian Ego'. But his failure to note the necessity of this represented subject renders his account ambiguous in this regard.
54. Rosenberg, *One World and Our Knowledge of It*, 77.
55. It is worth noting that though not all members of S are represented as being members of S, no member of S is represented as not being a member of S. This is true in so far as we discount such cases as that of Mrs Gradgrind, noted by Terence Wilkerson: '"I think there's a pain somewhere in the room," said Mrs. Gradgrind, "but I couldn't positively say that I have got it."' (Dickens, *Hard Times*, Bk. II, Ch. 9). Cf. Wilkerson's 'Kant on Self-Consciousness', *Philosophical Quarterly*, 30 (1980), 56.
56. And, conversely, awareness of oneself as an experiencing subject certainly implies that one is the kind of subject which has (a system of) representings, and hence which is able to deploy a synthetic operator such as is designated for Kant by the 'I' which thinks.
57. Kant, *Dreams of a Spirit-Seer*, Ak. II, 324–5 (emphasis added).

Bibliography

ALLISON, H., *Kant's Transcendental Idealism*: *An Interpretation and Defense* (New Haven, 1983).

AMERIKS, K., *Kant's Theory of Mind*: *An Analysis of the Paralogisms of Pure Reason* (Oxford, 1982).

ANSCOMBE, E., 'The First Person', in S. Guttenplan (ed.), *Mind and Language* (Oxford, 1975).

ARISTOTLE, *The Complete Works of Aristotle*, i, ed. J. Barnes (Princeton, NJ, 1984).

ARMSTRONG, D. M., 'The Causal Theory of the Mind', *Neue Hefte für Philosophie*, 11 (1977), 82–95.

—— *A Materialist Theory of the Mind* (London, 1968).

AUSTIN, J. L., *Sense and Sensibilia* (Oxford, 1962).

BARNOUW, J., 'Psychologie Empirique et Epistémologie dans le "Philosophische Versuche" de Tetens', *Archives de Philosophie*, 46 (1983).

BECK, L. W., *Early German Philosophy*: *Kant and his Predecessors* (Cambridge, Mass., 1969).

BENNETT, J., *Kant's Dialectic* (Cambridge, 1974).

—— 'The Simplicity of the Soul', *Journal of Philosophy*, 64 (1967).

—— *Kant's Analytic* (Cambridge, 1966).

BERKELEY, G., *Two Dialogues Between Hylas and Philonous*, ed. R. M. Adams (Indianapolis, 1979).

—— *The Principles of Human Knowledge*, ed. G. J. Warnock (London, 1962).

BIRD, G., *Kant's Theory of Knowledge* (London, 1962).

BRENTANO, F., *The Theory of Categories* (The Hague, 1981).

BROAD, C. D., *Kant: An Introduction*, ed. C. Lewy (Cambridge, 1978).

CHISHOLM, R., *The First Person*: *An Essay on Reference and Intentionality* (Minneapolis, 1981).

—— 'Coming into Being and Passing Away: Can the Metaphysician Help?', in J. Donnelly (ed.), *Language, Metaphysics, and Death*, (New York, 1978).

—— *Person and Object* (London, 1976).

DENNETT, D. C., *Brainstorms*: *Philosophical Essays on Mind and Psychology* (Montgomery, Vt., 1978).

—— *Content and Consciousness* (New York, 1969).

DESCARTES, R., *The Philosophical Works of Descartes*, trans. E. S. Haldane and G. R. T. Ross (Cambridge, 1931–4).

EVANS, G., *The Varieties of Reference*, ed. J. McDowell (Oxford, 1982).

GEACH, P. T., *Reference and Generality* (Ithaca, 1962).

GOLDMANN, L., *Immanuel Kant* (London, 1971).

GRICE, H. P., 'Personal Identity', *Mind*, 50 (1941), reprinted in J. Perry (ed.), *Personal Identity* (Berkeley, 1975).

HACKER, P. M. S., *Insight and Illusion* (Oxford, 1972).

HEMINGWAY, E., *A Movable Feast* (New York, 1964).

HENRICH, D., 'The Proof Structure of Kant's Transcendental Deduction', in R. C. S. Walker (ed.), *Kant On Pure Reason* (Oxford, 1982).

HINTIKKA, J., '*Cogito, Ergo Sum*: Inference or Performance?', in W. Doney (ed.), *Descartes: A Collection of Critical Essays* (Garden City, NY, 1967), 108–39.

HOBBES, T., *Leviathan: or the Matter, Forme and Power of a Commonwealth Ecclesiasticall and Civil*, ed. M. Oakeshott (New York, 1962).

HOOKER, M. (ed.), *Descartes: Critical and Interpretative Essays* (Baltimore, 1978).

HUME, D., *A Treatise of Human Nature*, ed. L. A. Selby-Bigge, 2nd edn., rev. P. H. Nidditch (New York, 1978).

JAMES, W., *The Principles of Psychology* (New York, 1950).

KANT, *Critique of Judgment*, trans. W. Pluhar (Indianapolis, 1987).

—— *Metaphysical Foundations of Natural Science*, trans. J. W. Ellington, in J. W. Ellington (ed.), *Philosophy of Material Nature* (Indianapolis, 1985).

—— *Prolegomena to Any Future Metaphysics*, trans. P. Carus, rev. J. W. Ellington (Indianapolis, 1977).

—— *Anthropology from a Pragmatic Point of View*, trans. M. Gregor (The Hague, 1974).

—— *Logic*, trans. R. S. Hartman and W. Schwarz (Indianapolis, 1974).

—— *Kant's Introduction to Logic, and his Essay on the Mistaken Subtilty of the Four Figures*, trans. T. K. Abbott (New York, 1963).

—— *Critique of Practical Reason*, trans. L. W. Beck (Indianapolis, 1956).

—— *Kritik der reinen Vernunft* (Hamburg, 1956).

—— *The Critique of Pure Reason*, trans. N. Kemp Smith (London, 1929).

—— *Gesammelte Schriften*, ed. Königlichen-Preussischen Akademie der Wissenschaften (Berlin, 1902–).

—— *Dreams of a Spirit-Seer*, trans. E. F. Goerwitz (London, 1900).

—— *Sämtliche Werke in chronologischer Reihenfolge*, ed. G. Hartenstein (Leipzig, 1867).

KEMP SMITH, N., *A Commentary to Kant's Critique of Pure Reason* (London, 1923).

KENNY, A., *Descartes: A Study of his Philosophy* (New York, 1968).

KERFERD, G. B. and WALFORD, D. L. (trans.), *Kant: Selected Pre-Critical Writings* (Manchester, 1968).

KITCHER, P., 'Kant's Real Self', in A. W. Wood (ed.), *Self and Nature in Kant's Philosophy* (Ithaca, 1984).

—— 'Kant On Self-Identity', *Philosophical Review*, 91 (1982).

—— 'Kant's Paralogisms', *Philosophical Review*, 91 (1982).

—— 'The Crucial Relation in Personal Identity', *Canadian Journal of Philosophy*, 8 (1978).

KRIPKE, S., *Wittgenstein on Rules and Private Language* (Oxford, 1982).

KUEHN, M., *Scottish Common Sense in Germany, 1768–1800* (Kingston and Montreal, 1987).

LEIBNIZ, G., *New Essays on Human Understanding*, trans. P. Remnant and J. Bennett (Cambridge, 1981).

—— *Discourse on Metaphysics/Correspondence with Arnauld/Monadology*, trans. G. R. Montgomery (La Salle, Ill., 1973).

—— *Nouveaux Essais sur l'entendement humain* (Paris, 1966).

LOCKE, J., *An Essay Concerning Human Understanding*, ed. A. C. Fraser (New York, 1959).

LONG, D. C., 'The Bodies of Persons', *Journal of Philosophy*, 71 (1974), 291–301.

MACKIE, J. L., 'The Transcendental "I"', in Z. van Straaten (ed.), *Philosophical Subjects: Essays Presented to P. F. Strawson* (Oxford, 1980), 48–61.

—— *The Cement of the Universe* (Oxford, 1974).

MARTIN, G. (ed.), *Sachindex zu Kants Kritik der reinen Vernunft* (Berlin, 1967).

MATTHEWS, H. E., 'Strawson on Transcendental Idealism', in R. C. S. Walker (ed.), *Kant on Pure Reason* (Oxford, 1982), 132–49.

MENDELSSOHN, M., *Moses Mendelssohn: Selections from His Writings*, ed. and trans. E. Jospe (New York, 1975).

MIJUSKOVIC, B. L., *The Achilles of Rationalist Arguments* (The Hague, 1974).

MILNE, A. A., *When We Were Very Young* (New York, 1924).

NAGEL, T., 'What Is It Like to Be a Bat?', in *Mortal Questions* (Cambridge, 1979), 165–80.

NOZICK, R., *Philosophical Explanations* (Cambridge, Mass., 1981).

PARFIT, D., *Reasons and Persons* (Oxford, 1984).

PERRY, J., 'The Problem of Personal Identity', in J. Perry (ed.), *Personal Identity* (Berkeley, 1975), 3–30.

—— 'The Same F', *Philosophical Review*, 79 (1970), 181–200.

PLATO, *Phaedo*, trans. D. Gallop (Oxford, 1975).

—— *Meno*, trans. W. R. M. Lamb (Cambridge, Mass., 1967).

POWELL, C. T., 'Kant's Fourth Paralogism', *Philosophy and Phenomenological Research*, 48 (1988), 389–414.

—— 'Kant, Elanguescence, and Degrees of Reality', *Philosophy and Phenomenological Research*, 46 (1985), 199–217.

PUTNAM, H., 'The Mental Life of Some Machines', in *Mind, Language, and Reality: Philosophical Papers*, 2 (Cambridge, 1975), 408–28.

—— 'Minds and Machines', in *Mind, Language, and Reality: Philosophical Papers*, 2 (Cambridge, 1975), 362–85.

PUTNAM, H., 'The Nature of Mental States', in *Mind, Language, and Reality: Philosophical Papers*, 2 (Cambridge, 1975), 429–40.

QUINTON, A., 'The Soul', *Journal of Philosophy*, 59 (1962). Reprinted in J. Perry (ed.), *Personal Identity* (Berkeley, 1975), 53–72.

RATKE, H., *Systematisches Handlexicon zu Kants Kritik der reinen Vernunft* (Hamburg, 1965).

REID, T., 'Of Mr. Locke's Account of Our Personal Identity', in *Essays on the Intellectual Powers of Man*. Reprinted in J. Perry (ed.), *Personal Identity* (Berkeley, 1975).

RORTY, R., 'Verificationism and Transcendental Arguments', *Nous*, 5 (1971), 3–14.

—— 'Strawson's Objectivity Argument', *Review of Metaphysics*, 24 (1970), 207–44.

ROSENBERG, J. F., '"I Think": Some Reflections on Kant's Paralogisms', *Midwest Studies in Philosophy*, 10 (1986), 503–30.

—— *Thinking Clearly About Death* (Englewood Cliffs, NJ, 1983).

—— *One World and Our Knowledge of It* (Dordrecht, 1980).

RYLE, G., *The Concept of Mind* (New York, 1949).

SELLARS, W., 'Metaphysics and the Concept of a Person', in Karel Lambert (ed.), *The Logical Way of Doing Things* (New Haven, CT, 1969), 219–52. Reprinted in *Essays in Philosophy and its History* (Dordrecht, 1974), 214–41).

—— '... this I or he or it (the thing) which thinks ...', *Proceedings of the American Philosophical Association*, 44 (1970–1), 5–31. Reprinted in *Essays in Philosophy and its History* (Dordrecht, 1974), 62–90.

—— *Science and Metaphysics: Variations on Kantian Themes* (London, 1967).

—— 'Kant's Views on Sensibility and Understanding', *Monist*, 51 (1967), 463–91.

—— 'Some Remarks on Kant's Theory of Experience', *Journal of Philosophy*, 64 (1967), 633–47. Reprinted in *Essays in Philosophy and its History* (Dordrecht, 1974), 44–61.

SHOEMAKER, S., 'Personal Identity: A Materialist's Account', in S. Shoemaker and R. Swinburne (eds.), *Personal Identity* (Oxford, 1984), 67–132.

—— 'Commentary: Self-Consciousness and Synthesis', in A. W. Wood (ed.), *Self and Nature in Kant's Philosophy* (Ithaca, 1984), 148–55.

—— *Self-Knowledge and Self-Identity* (Ithaca, 1963).

SMYTH, R. A., *Forms of Intuition: An Historical Introduction to the Transcendental Aesthetic* (The Hague, 1978).

SPINOZA, B., *The Chief Works of Spinoza*, trans. R. H. M. Elwes (New York, 1951).

STEVENSON, L., 'Wittgenstein's Transcendental Deduction and Kant's Private Language Argument', *Kant-Studien*, 73 (1982), 321–37.

Van Straaten, Z. (ed.), *Philosophical Subjects: Essays Presented to P. F. Strawson* (Oxford, 1980).

Strawson, P. F., 'Imagination and Perception', in R. C. S. Walker (ed.), *Kant on Pure Reason* (Oxford, 1982), 82–99.

—— 'Reply to Mackie', in Z. van Straaten (ed.), *Philosophical Subjects: Essays Presented to P. F. Strawson* (Oxford, 1980), 266–73.

—— *The Bounds of Sense: An Essay on Kant's Critique of Pure Reason* (London, 1966).

—— *Individuals: an essay in descriptive metaphysics* (London, 1959).

Tetens, J. N., *Philosophische Versuche über die menschliche Natur und ihre Entwicklung* (Berlin, 1911).

Turbayne, C., 'Kant's Refutation of Dogmatic Idealism', *Philosophical Quarterly*, 5 (1955), 225–44.

De Vleeschauwer, H. J., *La Déduction Transcendentale dans l'Œuvre de Kant* (Paris and Antwerp, 1934–7).

Walker, R. C. S. (ed.), *Kant on Pure Reason* (Oxford, 1982).

—— *Kant* (London, 1978).

Walsh, W. H., 'Self-Knowledge', in R. C. S. Walker (ed.), *Kant On Pure Reason* (Oxford, 1982), 150–75.

—— *Kant's Criticism of Metaphysics* (Edinburgh, 1975).

—— *Reason and Experience* (Oxford, 1947).

Wiggins, D., *Sameness and Substance* (Oxford, 1980).

Wilkerson, T., 'Kant On Self-Consciousness', *Philosophical Quarterly*, 30 (1980), 47–60.

Wilson, M. D., *Descartes* (London, 1978).

—— 'Leibniz and Materialism', *Canadian Journal of Philosophy*, 4 (1974), 495–513.

—— 'Kant and the Dogmatic Idealism of Berkeley', *Journal of the History of Philosophy*, 9 (1971), 451–75.

Wittgenstein, L., *Notebooks 1914–1916*, ed. G. H. von Wright and G. E. M. Anscombe, trans. G. E. M. Anscombe (Chicago, 1979).

—— *Tractatus Logico-Philosophicus*, trans. D. F. Pears and B. F. McGuinness (London, 1961).

—— *Philosophical Investigations*, trans. G. E. M. Anscombe (London, 1953).

Wolff, R. P., *Kant's Theory of Mental Activity* (Cambridge, Mass., 1963).

—— 'Kant's Debt to Hume via Beattie', *Journal of the History of Ideas*, 21 (1960), 117–23.

Zweig, A. (ed. and trans.), *Kant: Philosophical Correspondence, 1759–99* (Chicago, 1967).

Index

abortion (and elanguescent persons) 124

'absorption' (Strawson) 45

'Achilles of all dialectical inferences' 91

Allison, Henry 52

Ameriks, Karl
  on Second Paralogism 91 n
  on Third Paralogism 130, 148, 159, 162–3, 173 n.

Analogies, see Kant

Anschauung, see intuition

Anscombe, G. E. M.
  on the first person 208–11, 212–22, 223, 225–6, 228, 234
  'I' not a demonstrative expression 217–21
  'I' not a proper name 208–10, 212–14, 217
  'I' not a referential expression 210–11, 234
  and Kant 212 n.
  and Mackie 224–5
  Strawson on 225–7, 228–9, 231, 235
  and 'unmediated conceptions' 210, 212

Anticipations of Perception, see Kant

'anti-rationalist' argument 92–7, 109

appearances 27, 61, 62, 64, 125

apperception see empirical apperception; transcendental unity of apperception

apperceptionis substantiatae 80–1, 87, 90, 203–4, 211, 222

apprehension 27, 119–20, 128 n.

Aristotle
  on illegitimate employment of categories 89
  on paralogisms 66
  on substance 162

Armstrong, D. M. 205

ass, being a silly 214 n.

association, see interaction

Austin, J. L. 49

Baumgarten, Alexander Gottlieb 65 n.

Begriff, see concept

Belloc, Hilaire 214

Bennett, Jonathan
  A-interpretation of First Paralogism 73–4, 75
  ambiguity of 'subject' 73, 75, 80
  'the Cartesian basis' 70, 71, 75, 142, 206
  definition of substance 69–71
  on Fourth Paralogism 174, 182–4, 189
  'Goethe' interpretation of First Paralogism 74–5, 76
  on inflations of conclusion of First Paralogism 68, 71, 74–6
  interpretations of minor premiss of First Paralogism 72–3, 77
  on intuition and concept 34 n.
  on necessary unity of consciousness 230
  on Second Paralogism 91, 99–100
  S-interpretation of First Paralogism 71–2, 75, 76
  subjectival and adjectival handling of myself 69–71, 73, 75–6
  on Third Paralogism 130 n.
  W-argument and First Paralogism 74, 76, 85, 88

Berkeley, George
  on idealism 53
  on self-knowledge 3–4

Beschaffenheit, see composition

Bewusstsein (consciousness) and Selbstbewusstsein (self-consciousness), confusion of 50

Brave Officer Paradox (Reid) 152, 153–4

Brentano, Franz 113 n.

Broad, C. D.
  on Second Paralogism 91, 93–4, 97, 98 n.
  on Third Paralogism 130 n., 163

Butler, Joseph 145, 148, 162

'the Cartesian basis' see Bennett, Jonathan

Cartesian Ego
'I' as referring to 208, 210–11, 224–5, 227, 228–30, 231, 235
see also experiencing subject; 'I'; transcendental unity of apperception
Categorical Imperative, second formulation of 167–8
category-mistake
and First Paralogism 86, 89–90, 103
and Hobbes 89
and Second Paralogism 103–4
and Third Paralogism 144
causal-connection theory of mental states, *see* Kitcher
central state materialism 99–100
Chisholm, Roderick
on degrees of reality 121–7
no 'speaker's meaning' of 'I' 217
on person as 'natural kind' 122
on personal identity 164–5
on self-presenting mental states 212
Christopher Robin 5
Clemens, Samuel 208, 213
cogito 1–2, 87
as intuitive vs. inferential 4 n.
cognitive psychology 59 n.
communio/commercium see interaction
composition (*Beschaffenheit*) 201–3
concept (*Begriff*)
etymology of 28
and intuition 33–5, 45–6, 60–1, 64
constitution, *see* composition
corporeal soul, possibility of 106 n.
Crowley, Aleister 214–15

Dennett, Daniel C. 203
Descartes, Rene
antinomy between Hume and 212
'Argument from Doubt' (Hooker) 183, 186–8
the *cogito* 1–2, 87
Discourse on Method 183, 186, 188
genie malaign 1
Hume's denial of Cartesian self-knowledge 4–5, 11, 64, 89, 102
and Kant 5, 7–8
as rational psychologist 6
res cogitans 1
Second Meditation 182–3
Sixth Meditation 180, 183
as source of First Paralogism 73

as source of Fourth Paralogism 180–1, 182–8, 189
dualism, *see* mind–body problem

elanguescence 118–27, 128 n., 129
elastic balls case 146, 162
Empfindung, see sensation
empirical apperception 30, 33, 50–1, 55, 56–7, 64, 79, 81, 106–8, 137–9, 194, 204
empirical vs. transcendental 52
Erdmann, Benno 199
Evans, Gareth 221 n.
existence as predicate 122–4, 181, 185–6
experience
conceptualizability of 33–5, 44–6, 47–9, 60–2, 64
manifold of 77
recognitional component in 35, 45–7
self-ascription of 35–49, 50–1, 55
see also concept; intuition; sensation
experiencing subject
aspects of its necessary representation 67, 191
and awareness of experience 50
definitive role in describing experience 23–5, 26–32, 37, 230–1, 233–4, 236
and Mackie 224–5, 229–30, 232
as man or person 51–2
necessary role in synthesis 29–32, 55–7, 133–4
relevance to moral theory 6, 235
relevance to theory of persons 6
and sense-datum theorist 45–6
as tangential point of contact between phenomena and noumena 54
unencounterability of 1, 4–5, 89
see also 'I'; self; transcendental unity of apperception
extensive magnitude 114, 116, 118–20
see also Kant, Anticipations of Perception
external world, existence of 174, 178, 180–1, 183, 184
see also Kant, Fourth Paralogism

'faculties' 58–9
'feats of transference' 225, 227, 228
First Paralogism, *see* Kant, Paralogisms
Ford, Ford Madox 214 n.

Fourth Paralogism, *see* Kant, Paralogisms
freedom 169
functional (vs. compositional) description of mental states 201–2, 203–4, 205–6
functionalism, and Kant 8, 17, 200–6

Gemeinschaft, see interaction
Gesinnung, see moral stance
God 169
  and morality 171 n.
  and purely intelligible objects 54
  unmediated self-concept of 139
Goethe, Johann Wolfgang von 74–5
Goldmann, Lucien 170 n.
Highest Good, the 170, 172
good will, acting from a 166, 170
Gradgrind, Mrs 233 n.
Grice, H. P. 148, 154

Hacker, P. M. S. 75 n.
Hemingway, Ernest 214–15
Hintikka, Jaako 4 n.
Hobbes, Thomas 89
Hooker, Michael 186–8
Howells, William Dean 206
Hume, David
  bundle theory 1, 4–5, 7–8, 11–18, 25, 26–32, 62, 64, 106, 133–4, 137–8, 210, 233
  denial of Cartesian self-knowledge 4–5, 11, 64, 89, 102
  and Descartes 4
  and Kitcher 11–18
  and Leibniz 3
  and personal identity 148
  and Spinoza 4
  thought-experiment 87, 137–8, 232

'I'
  Chisholm and no 'speaker's meaning' of 'I' 217
  and 'I think' as a synthesizing function 57–61, 211
  logical form of 'I think' 60–1, 100 n., 102, 158–9, 200–1, 202, 204, 232–4, 235–6
  Mackie and the 'two-sense' theory of 'I' 222–30, 232, 234–5
  Mackie's meaning-rules governing 'I' 223–4, 229–31

necessarily represented as identical 138
necessarily represented as simple 108–9
necessarily represented as unitary 7–8
  as non-empirical 140
  not an intuition 5, 6, 86–7, 88, 204, 211, 232
  and reference-failure immunity 207–36
Rosenberg on 'I' and reference 232–3
  and sense-switching 226–30, 235–6
Strawson on 'I' and empirical reidentification 209, 217
  and Strawson's 'person' 234–6
  and transcendental unity of apperception 60–1, 76–81, 87, 137, 159, 204
  uses of 'I' 235–6
  see also Cartesian Ego; experiencing subject; self; transcendental unity of apperception
identity, strict vs. relative 162 n.
imagination 27, 61
immortality
  arguments in *Phaedo* 105, 110
  as motivation for moral behaviour 166–73
  necessary belief in 8
  possibility of 8, 104
  see also Kant, Paralogisms; soul
inactivity, perpetual 122
indexicality 1, 222
inner sense 176, 191, 193–4, 196–8
  and empirical apperception 50–1, 106–7
  and 'I think' 55, 137–9, 159
  and synthesis 56
intensive magnitude 118–21, 123, 124–9
  see also Kant, Anticipations of Perception
intentionality of perception (Strawson) 61
interaction (*Gemeinschaft*) 188–200
  ambiguity between 'association' and 'interaction' 189–91
  communio/commercium 190
  see also Kant, Fourth Paralogism; mind–body problem
intuition (*Anschauung*)
  as conceptual 34–5, 60–1, 64

intuition (*cont.*)
  duality of intuition and concept 33–5,
    45–6, 60
  and empirical apperception 50, 139–
    40
  'I' not an intuition 78, 86–7, 88, 144,
    204
  intuition of self/others (Third Para-
    logism) 144–5, 160
  and the logical structure of judgment
    35, 64
  and man 51
  non-sensory 139–40
  of outer objects 196–7, 198
  pure 119, 125, 139
  Rorty on 60
  as a 'seeing-as' 34 n.
  Sellars on intuition and concept 33–5
  and substance 86
  and synthesis 26–8, 61, 77

James, William on unity of conscious-
    ness 95
judgment
  and corrigibility 41–4, 48–9, 61, 64
  and intuition 35, 64
  logical structure of 8, 37
  and objectivity 61–2
  and rule-following 60–1
  and self ascription of experience 37–
    47, 61
  and the unitary subject 95–6

Kant, Immanuel
  *Anthropology from a Pragmatic Point
    of View* 138, 145
  Critique of Practical Reason
    Postulates of Pure Practical
      Reason 169–73
  Critique of Pure Reason
    Analogies of Experience
      First Analogy 84, 125
      Second Analogy 115–16, 177 n.,
        197, 181
      Third Analogy 190
    Anticipations of Perception 114–
      15, 118, 120, 124–7, 128–9
    Antinomies 51, 172 n.
    Canon of Pure Reason 166
    Paralogisms of Pure Reason 5, 6, 7,
      8, 9, 50, 63, 64, 174, 179, 185,
      195, 204, 212, 224, 231, 232
    and Aristotle 66 n.

  etymology of 'paralogism' 66 n.
  general strategy 65, 81, 85–6,
    89–90, 131–3, 136–7, 142, 145
  Kemp Smith on form of Para-
    logisms 67
  logical structure 65–8
  as patchwork 9
  and possible complexity of 'the
    thing which thinks' 97–8
  and rational psychology 54
  as syllogisms 9, 64
  and synthesis of representations
    31
  and Table of Categories 9
  and Transcendental Deduction
    11
  Walsh on 65 n.
  Wolff on 65 n.
First Paralogism 65–90, 143
  Bennett and the ambiguity of
    'subject' 73, 75, 80
  Bennett on inflations of con-
    clusion of First Paralogism 68,
    71, 74–6
  Bennett's A-interpretation 73–4,
    75
  Bennett's 'Goethe' interpretation
    of First Paralogism 74–5, 76
  Bennett's interpretations of
    minor premiss of First
    Paralogism 72–3, 77
  Bennett's S-interpretation of
    First Paralogism 71–2, 75, 76
  Bennett's W-argument 74, 76,
    85, 88
  category-mistake 86, 89–90, 103
  compared to Second Paralogism
    91, 92, 101–4, 105
  fallacy of 131, 136
  formal presentation 69
  inflations of conclusion 83–90,
    109
  interpretation of premises 79–
    80
  moral 80–1
  and Schematism 84–9
  substance in 69, 75, 80–1, 83
  and transcendental illusion 80–
    3, 87
Second Paralogism 29–30, 67, 78,
  91, 139, 161
  'Achilles of all dialectical
    inferences' 91

Ameriks on 91 n.
'anti-rationalist' argument 92–7,
   98
Bennett on Second Paralogism
   91, 99–100
Broad on Second Paralogism
   91, 93–4, 97, 98 n.
and the Categories 103
category-mistake 103–4
Descartes as source 73
and dismissal of interaction
   problem 195, 196, 198–9, 202
elanguescence 118–27, 128 n.,
   129
first two inflations of conclusion
   102–8
formal presentation 92
Kant's first argument 96–7
Kant's second argument 97
Kant's third argument 101–4
Kant's fourth argument 104–9
Kemp Smith on 91
and Moses Mendelssohn 65,
   86 n., 110–21, 124, 129
and other minds 98–101
and phenomenalism 72
Strawson on 102
third inflation of conclusion (and
   Mendelssohn's argument)
   109–29
Third Paralogism 67, 184
Ameriks on 130, 148, 159, 162–
   3, 173 n.
Bennett on 130 n.
Broad on 130 n., 163
category-mistake 144
as conforming to other Paralogisms 136–42
elastic balls case 146, 162
formal presentation 130
and immortality 141, 142–4,
   160–1, 166–73
intuition of self/others 144–5,
   160
and Locke 154, 157–62
and moral/practical employment
   of personal identity 165–73
and other minds 131
outside observer case 144–7,
   159–60
and Sellars 146–7
and time as form of inner sense
   133–5

transcendental ground of minor
   premiss 131–5
and transcendental illusion 167–
   72
Walker on 170 n.
Fourth Paralogism 67, 142, 174
B version 185–7
Bennett on Fourth Paralogism
   174, 182–4, 189
and the Categories 175, 185,
   189
formal presentation 175
and functionalism 204–5
and *Gemeinschaft* 188–200
and Kant's *ignorabimus* 174,
   189, 196–200, 201–2
Kant's solution to interaction
   problem 193–200
Kitcher on 174
and 'outer objects' 175–82, 187–
   8, 193–5, 196
and the Prolegomena 199
as response to Cartesian dualism
   182–8
as response to Cartesian scepticism 180–1
Sellars on 174
Walker on 175
Postulates of Empirical Thought
   177 n.
and interaction of substances
   191
Refutation of Idealism 87, 174,
   188, 199
Schematism 189
and First Paralogism 84–9
reality and negation 125
Table of Categories 189
and Fourth Paralogism 175,
   185, 189
as modes of representing 200–1
and Second Paralogism 103
Transcendental Aesthetic
and appearances of outer sense
   105
and time as form of inner sense
   134–5
Transcendental Deduction of the
   Categories 6–8, 11–63, 138,
   197, 212, 231
Subjective Deduction 7, 11–33,
   77–8, 206; and necessary
   representation of unitary self

Kant, Immanuel (*cont.*)
   100; as phenomenology 58–9;
   role in Transcendental
   Deduction 63; strategy of
   Subjective Deduction 26–33;
   and synthesis 95–6; and 'tran-
   scendental psychology' 58–9;
   and transcendental unity of
   apperception 15–16, 58–9
   Objective Deduction 33–64;
   Kant's objectivity argument
   60–2
   Transcendental Dialectic 172
   Critique of Judgment 170
   Dreams of Spirit-Seer 192, 206, 236
   Inaugural Dissertation 192
   *Prolegomena to Any Future Meta-
   physics*
   and Fourth Paralogism 199
   and permanence of soul 160–1
   and Transcendental Deduction 60
   *Metaphysical Foundations of Natural
   Science* 63 n.
Kemp Smith
   on form of Paralogisms 67
   on Second Paralogism 91
Kenny, Anthony 186–7
Kitcher, Patricia
   causal-connection theory as no-
   ownership theory 25
   on existential dependence of mental
   states 12–15
   on Fourth Paralogism 174
   and Hume 11–18
   on Kant as functionalist 205 n., 206
   interpretation of Kant's argument
   against Hume 12–18, 32–3
   and psychological continuity condition of personal identity 148
   on purpose of Subjective Deduction
   11–12
   Shoemaker on 25 n.
   on synthesis of mental states 13–18
   transcendental synthesis 15–18
   two senses of synthesis 15
Kripke, Saul 11 n.

Leibniz, Gottfried
   and Hume 3
   and Kant 5
   as rational psychologist 6
   'Reflective Acts' 2

on self-knowledge 2–3, 89
   'wholly bare monads' 3
Leibniz's Law 185, 186–7
Lewis, David 148
Locke, John
   definition of 'person' 152
   equivalence of 'person' and 'self' 155
   'forensic' account of personal identity
   155–7, 166, 173 n.
   and memory condition of personal
   identity 148, 151–7
   prince and cobbler 149–50, 160, 161
   and psychological continuity condition of personal identity 155–7
   and Reid 152–7
   self-ascription of co-conscious
   experiences (Mackie) 223, 230
   and Third Paralogism 157–62, 166–
   73

Mackie, J. L.
   and Anscome 224–5
   and the experiencing subject 224–5,
   229–30, 232
   and Locke 223, 230
   meaning-rules governing 'I' 223–4,
   229–31
   on self-ascription of co-conscious
   experiences 36–8, 46, 223, 230,
   231 n.
   Strawson on 225–7, 228–9, 231, 235
   on Strawson's objectivity argument
   36–47
   'two-sense' theory of 'I' 222–30, 232,
   234–5
materialism 99–100, 146
matter 184
   conflated with the composite 105
   interaction with mind 191, 193–5,
   203
   possible simplicity of 107–10
   and substance 84–5
Matthews, H. E. 53
memory 28, 56
   see also Locke; personal identity
Mendelssohn, Moses
   argument for immortality 110–13
   and Brentano 113 n.
   as interlocutor in Second Paralogism
   65
   Kant's refutation of 86 n., 117–21,
   124, 129

Kant's version of 114–17
Phaedo 111–13
mental counting 28
methodological solipsism 15 n., 88, 142
and functionalism 205–6
mind–body problem 8, 51–2, 106–8,
174, 182–8
dualism 184
heterogeneity in representations of
mind and body 191–6
and Kant's *Traume* 236
and panpsychism 192
pre-determined harmony 184, 192
and problem of interaction 188–200,
203
Putnam's dismissal of interaction
problem 204
and 'supernatural intervention' 192
and transcendental idealism 189,
193, 194–5, 198–9, 200
see also interaction; Kant, Fourth
Paralogism; reciprocity
moral law 170
moral stance (*Gesinnung*) 166 n.

Nagel, Thomas
and bat experience 99–100
subjective/objective points of view
99–100
necessary unity of consciousness
definition of 62
and self-ascription of experience
47–9
Stevenson on 47–9, 55
and synthesis of representations 7–8,
55–7, 59–60, 62–4, 76–7, 95–6,
98
see also synthesis; transcendental
unity of apperception
Nietzsche, Friedrich 9–10
no-ownership theories of self 24–5,
148
'noble lie', possibility of Kant committing 167–8
noumenal objects/things in themselves
54, 176–82, 198–9, 205
see also transcendental idealism
noumenal self 52–4, 56, 67, 78, 81, 87,
96–8, 107, 163, 195
Nozick, Robert 165
numerical identity (of person) 130,
134–5, 136–43

'object', Kant's use of 78, 83
see also intuition; Kant, Fourth Paralogism
Objective Deduction, *see* Kant, Transcendental Deduction
objectivity argument (Strawson) 33, 35–
63
Ontological Argument 124
other minds
and Second Paralogism 98–101
and Third Paralogism 131
see also outside observer case
outer sense 106 n., 191, 193–4, 196–8,
203–4
outside observer case (Third Paralogism) 144–7

panpsychism 192
Paralogisms, *see* Kant, Immanuel
Parfit, Derek 148
Pascal's Wager 166 n.
permanence of soul 141–4
vs. immortality 171–2
Perry, John
and psychological continuity condition of personal identity 148
on criteria for ascriptions of personal
identity 149
person
Kant's definition of 157
or man 51–2
as 'natural kind' (Chisholm) 122
practical employment of concept of
'personality' 165–73
person-stages 164–5
personal identity
bodily condition of 140, 147, 149–51,
159–61
brain condition of 148, 150–1
and Brain State Transfer cases 150
Butler on 145, 148, 162
consciousness of 141
criteria in first- and third-person
cases 144–7, 148–9, 157–62
criterion vs. ground/constitution
148–9, 165
embodiment and consciousness 148,
161
and 'fission'-cases 152–3
as illusory 147
Kant's scepticism regarding knowledge of 145–6, 162, 165, 173

personal identity (*cont.*)
  Kant's view of moral implications of
    130 *passim.*, 141 *passim.*, 166–73
  knowable empirically 138–41
  Locke on 148, 151–62, 166–73
  memory condition of 147–8
  psychological continuity condition of
    147, 151, 160, 165, 172–3
  Reid on 145, 148, 152–7, 158
  'strict and philosophical' 162–5
  theories of 147–51
  as unanalysable concept 147
phenomenalism Kant's (putative) 72 n.,
    174
  and First Paralogism 72
  and 'standard picture' (Allison) 52
phenomenology (in Subjective Deduc-
    tion) 58–9
Plato
  affinity argument (*Phaedo*) 110
  on immortality (*Phaedo*) 105, 110
  road to Larisa (*Meno*) 38, 43
Powell, C. T. 208
Properties, reducible vs. emergent
    93–4
punishment, related to personal identity
    166, 173
Putnam, Hilary
  dismissal of interaction problem 204
  on functional descriptions of mental
    states 201

Quinton, Anthony 148, 154, 156

rational psychology 6, 52 n., 54, 65, 66,
    68, 71, 74, 75, 79, 85–6, 88, 90, 91,
    92, 93, 96, 98, 103, 104, 105, 106,
    108–10, 128, 130, 138, 140, 141,
    142, 143, 144, 146, 169, 174, 178,
    179, 182, 183, 184–5, 188, 189, 211
'the real'
  and 'degrees of reality' 118–20,
    121–9
  and substance 84–5
reciprocity (*Wechselwirkung*) between
    mind and body 189–90
reference
  demonstrative 217–22
  hearer's vs. speaker's reference-
    failure 215–16
  Kant and reference-failure immunity
    of 'I' 230–6

reference-failure immunity and 'I'
    207–36
  reidentification of referent 209–17,
    221
  types of reference-failure 206–10,
    214–30, 231, 234
regulative (vs. constitutive) ideas 168–
    9, 171–3
Reid, Thomas
  Brave Officer Paradox 152, 153–4
  on Locke 152–7, 158
  on personal identity 145, 148
representation
  of sequence 26–8
  and temporality 29
  see also synthesis
representations, obscure 121, 128
Rorty, Richard
  no intuitions 60
  on Strawson's objectivity argument
    33, 47 n.
  on transcendental arguments 17
Rosenberg, Jay 9, 10, 31 n., 32, 34 n.,
    150 n., 204
  'I' and reference 232–3
rule-following and judging 60–1
Russellian denoting expressions 213,
    232
Russell's chicken 142
Ryle, Gilbert 5

Schlick, Moritz 148
Second Paralogism, *see* Kant, Para-
    logisms
self
  as moral agent 8
  necessarily represented as continuing
    subject 63, 102
  no-ownership theories 24–5, 148
  Ryle on systematically elusive self 5
  as sequence of impressions 5
  as simple 2, 7–8
  as substantial 2, 7
  as unitary 2, 7–8
  see also experiencing subject
self-presenting mental states (Chisholm)
    212
Sellars, Wilfrid
  on intuition and concept 33–5
  on Kant's categories and logical
    form 200–1, 202, 206
  on Kant's *ignorabimus* 174

on outside observer case 146–7
interpretation of Kant 10
sensation (*Empfindung*) 34, 118–19,
123, 125–9, 176
sense-datum theory and Strawson's
objectivity argument 44–7
'sense-switching' 226–30, 235–6
Shoemaker, Sydney
and body condition of personal
identity 148
on brain identity as ground of
personal identity 150–1
and Kitcher 25 n.
and psychological continuity condition of personal identity 151
simplicity
as schematized/unschematized 103–4
see also Kant, Second Paralogism;
soul
Socrates 105, 108
soul
'animality' of 141–2
as composite 92–110
as immaterial 141–2
immortality of 74, 83, 86, 141
incorruptibility of 141–2
'personality' of 141–2
represented as imperishable 74
represented as substantial 69–71, 74,
75, 78–83, 129, 143, 146
simplicity of 78, 91–110
'spirituality' of 141
Spinoza, Benedictus
as example of morality without
immortality (Kant) 170–1
and Hume 4
on persons 52
on self-knowledge 3
Stevenson, Leslie
on ambiguity of 'corrigibility' 38–9,
42–3
on necessary unity of consciousness
and transcendental unity of apperception 47–9, 55
on Strawson's objectivity argument
36–49
Strawson, P. F.
and 'absorption' 45
and body condition of personal
identity 148
and 'the Cartesian illusion' 102–3
on first-person criteria of personal
identity 158

formal structure of objectivity argument 35–6
on 'I' and empirical reidentification
209, 217
'I' and (Strawson's) 'person' 234–6
intentionality of perception 61
on Mackie and Anscombe 225–7,
228–9, 231, 235
Mackie on objectivity argument 36–
47
on no-ownership theories 24–5
objectivity argument 33, 35–63
Rorty on objectivity argument 33,
47 n.
and Second Paralogism 102
on sense-datum theory 44–7
Stevenson on objectivity argument
36–49
on synthesis and 'transcendental
psychology' 58–9
theory of persons 3, 51–2, 107 n.,
226, 234, 236
on the Transcendental Deduction 7
on 'transcendental self-consciousness' 49, 58
Subjective Deduction, *see* Kant, Transcendental Deduction
substance
Bennett's definition 69–71
and empirical intuition 86
in First Paralogism 69, 75, 80–1, 83
and intensive magnitude 128 n.
interaction of 197–9
Kant's definition 69, 83–5
and matter 84–5
and permanence 84–5, 139
and 'the real' 84–5
schematized vs. unschematized 84–9,
104
'sempiternity' of 74, 76, 83, 85–90
substantives, grammatical 69
synthetic *a priori* judgments
as conclusions of Paralogisms 67
and noumenal unity of the subject 98
and Paralogisms 67, 101, 132–3, 135,
136, 140, 184
synthesis 27–33, 59 n., 190
in accordance with rule 27–8
and inner sense 56
and intuition 26–8, 61, 77
Kitcher on synthesis of mental states
13–18
Kitcher's vs. Kant's 15 n.

synthesis (*cont.*)
  reproductive 28–9, 133–4
  synthesis and attribution of mental
    states 14–15, 18–22, 23–6, 31–2
  and 'transcendental psychology'
    58–9
  transcendental synthesis 15–18, 30–
    2, 62–3, 76–7
  see also intuition; necessary unity of
    consciousness; synthesis; tran-
    scendental unity of apperception;
  synthetic unity of apperception 31–2,
    55–7, 58–9, 64
  see also synthesis; transcendental
    unity of apperception

Tetens, Johann Nicolaus 59
theoretical entities 182
Third Paralogism, *see* Kant, Paralogisms
time and alteration 115–17
transcendent vs. transcendental 198
transcendental arguments 16, 17–18,
  70
Transcendental Deduction of the
  Categories, *see* Kant, Immanuel
transcendental idealism
  and functionalism 205–6
  and mind–body problem 189, 193,
    194–5, 198–9, 200
  and phenomena/noumena 52–3
transcendental illusion 7, 227, 231, 235
  and First Paralogism 80–3, 87
  and Third Paralogism 167–72
transcendental object 203
'transcendental psychology' and synthesis (Strawson) 58–9
transcendental realism/empirical
  idealism 178–9, 180–1, 182, 188
'transcendental self-consciousness'
  (Strawson) 49, 58
transcendental unity of apperception
  12, 55, 106, 194
  and empirical apperception 30, 33

and 'I think' 60–1, 76–81, 87, 137,
  159, 204
as necessary representation of continuing subject 63–4, 134, 163,
  165, 169
and objectivity argument 62–3
Stevenson on 47–9, 55
and transcendental synthesis 15–18,
  30–2, 62–3, 76–7
and Wittgenstein 75 n.
see also Cartesian Ego; experiencing
  subject, 'I', necessary unity of consciousness; synthesis

unicorns 122–3
'unmediated conceptions' (Anscombe)
  210, 212

Varcoe, Rick 166 n.
verificationism and empirical employment of concepts 89

Walker, R. C. S.
  on faculty psychology 59
  on Fourth Paralogism 175
  on event-ordered regularities and
    corrigibility 63 n.
  and 'tangential point of contact' 54 n.
  on Third Paralogism 170 n.
Walsh, W. H.
  on Paralogisms 65 n.
  on transcendental and empirical
    apperception 30
Wechselwirkung, see reciprocity
Whitehead, Alfred North 112
Wiggins, David 148
Wilson, Margaret D. 4 n.
Wittgenstein, Ludwig 211
  on ostensive definition 218, 221
  and transcendental unity of apper-
    ception 75 n.
Wolff, Christian 65 n.

Ziff, Paul 99 n.